D1568979

LUTHERAN WORSHIP

Agenda

LUTHERAN WORSHIP

Agenda

Prepared by
The Commission on Worship
of
The Lutheran Church—Missouri Synod

Copyright © 1984
Concordia Publishing House

ISBN 0-570-01024-1

4 5 6 7 8 9 10 11 12 13   03 02 01 00 99 98 97 96 95 94

CONTENTS

Introduction 9

The Church Year 11
    Sundays and Major Festivals 11
    Minor Festivals 12
    Occasions 12
    Movable Festivals and Holy Days 13
    Date of Easter 13
    Table of Movable Festivals According to the Date of Easter 14

Ash Wednesday 15
The Passion of Our Lord Jesus Christ Drawn from the Four Gospels ... 20
Palm Sunday Procession with Palms 35
Maundy Thursday, Stripping of the Altar 39
Good Friday at Noonday 45
Good Friday I 48
Good Friday II 58
Vigil of Easter 73

Holy Baptism 91
Holy Baptism Short Form 100
Recognition by the Church of an Emergency Baptism 105
Confirmation 110
Receiving of Members 115
Announcement of Excommunication and of Reinstatement 118

Marriage 120
Blessing of a Civil Marriage 129
Anniversary of a Marriage 134
Service of Corporate Confession and Absolution 137
Individual Confession and Absolution 141
Ministry to the Sick and Infirm 145
Communion of the Sick and Homebound 154
Commendation of the Dying 162
Burial of the Dead 169
    At the Home or the Mortuary 169
    At the Church 173
    The Committal 193
Burial of the Stillborn 197
    At the Home 197
    The Committal 200

Farewell and Godspeed to a Candidate for Ordination 202
Ordination 205
    Installation of a Pastor at Ordination 214
    Installation of a Missionary or Chaplain at Ordination 216
Installation of a Pastor 222
Installation of a Missionary or Chaplain 228
Anniversary of an Ordination 238
Farewell and Godspeed to a Pastor 241

Farewell and Godspeed to a Candidate for Commissioning 244
Installation of a Professor or Instructor at a College or Seminary ... 247
Commissioning and Installation of One Called to the Teaching Ministry 254
Installation of One Called to the Teaching Ministry 260
Anniversary of a Commissioning 265
Farewell and Godspeed to a Teacher 268

Consecration and Installation of a Certified Lay Church Worker ... 271
Installation of a Certified Lay Church Worker 276

Placing in Office of the Church Council 281
Placing of Sunday and Other Church School Officers and Teachers 284
Placing of Servants of the Congregation 286
Recognition of Officers of Congregational Auxiliaries 290

Ground Breaking 292
Laying of a Cornerstone 298
Dedication of a Church Building 304
Dedication of Sacramental Vessels, Furnishings, and Ornaments 311
    Longer Rite of Dedication 314
Dedication of an Organ 316

Dedication of a School, Parish Hall, Hospital, Home for the Aged, or Other Facility 321
Dedication of a Cemetery 327
    Rite of Dedication 327
    Service of Dedication 328
Dedication of a Parsonage or Teacherage 334
    Rite of Dedication 334
    Service of Dedication 335
Dedication of a Dwelling 338
Thanksgiving at the Retirement of a Debt 341
Disposition of a Church Building 343

Opening of the Conventions of the Synod and Its Districts 346
Closing of the Conventions of the Synod and Its Districts 348
Installation of the President of the Synod or of a District 351
Installation of Vice-Presidents, Other Officers and Members of the Board of Directors, and Members of Boards and Commissions of the Synod or of a District 356
Installation of an Executive of the Synod or of a District 362

Collects and Prayers 366

Acknowledgments 378

Indexes 379
    Comprehensive Index of Collects and Prayers 379
    Index to Psalms and Readings 401

INTRODUCTION

The rites and services in this book were prepared by the Commission on Worship of The Lutheran Church—Missouri Synod in response to the directive of that Church assembled in convention at St. Louis in July 1981. In November 1982 the first drafts were distributed to pastors, teachers, professors, missionaries, and deaconesses of the Church for reactions and comments. This process resulted in a number of significant emendations. Subsequently the 1983 convention of the Synod approved and accepted the drafts as revised, declaring them to constitute an official service book entitled *Lutheran Worship Agenda.*

This book is a successor to *The Lutheran Agenda* (1948), authorized by the Synods then constituting the Evangelical Lutheran Synodical Conference. It is a companion volume to *Lutheran Worship* ("Pew Edition"), *Lutheran Worship Accompaniment for the Liturgy, Lutheran Worship Accompaniment for the Hymns,* all of which appeared early in 1982, and *Lutheran Worship Altar Book,* which appeared in July 1982. In using the *Agenda,* it is recommended and urged that *Lutheran Worship Altar Book,* especially the Notes on the Liturgy (pages 11—37), be consulted.

As in *Lutheran Worship* ("Pew Edition") and *Lutheran Worship Altar Book,* symbols are used to designate those participating in the rites or services. But whereas in the aforementioned books the parts of the service reserved for pastors, or ordained ministers, are designated with P=presiding minister, denoting the one who presides over the entire service, in this agenda the symbol P has a wider usage.

Rites of a congregational nature use the symbol P to designate the one who presides, with the rubrics referring to him as "pastor." Rites that may be or are of a District or synodical nature use the symbol P to designate the one who presides, with the rubrics referring to him as "the presiding minister" or "the minister." While it may be desirable that one person preside over the entire service (including the rite), there may be situations where it would be considered more appropriate for the pastor, or other ordained minister, to preside over the service itself (whether this be the Divine Service or a service of another type) with another pastor, or ordained minister, doing only the rite.

Portions appropriate for an assisting minister, ordained or unordained, are marked A. Assisting ministers should not be confused with assistant or associate pastors. In the Divine Service, for instance, the pastor of a congregation might be an assisting minister and the assistant pastor might be the presiding minister. Portions for the entire congregation are marked C. The responses of individuals or specific groups are marked R. The symbol All is used to designate an assembly regardless of size.

A red line around certain portions of the services or rites indicates optional material. An *OR* is placed between optional sections.

In the rubrics and notes, the numbers printed in parentheses ( ) refer to rubric numbers in *Lutheran Worship* ("Pew Edition"); the numbers printed in angle brackets ⟨ ⟩ are references to *Lutheran Worship Agenda.*

Bracketed words in Scripture readings indicate insertions or substitutions to clarify what are otherwise verbatim texts; they should be spoken. Brackets are elsewhere used to set off conditional material that may or may not be spoken, depending on the circumstances (e.g., "We present for dedication this item for your praise and glory [and in memory of _____name_____]").

The directives "Stand" and "Sit," printed in bold italic type, refer to the congregation, not necessarily to those involved in a given service or rite.

All Scripture references and all verse divisions reflect the versification in The Holy Bible: *New International Version* (NIV). If another version is used, it is important to check its versification against the NIV.

For ease of reference, prayers exclusively in this book are identified by numbers in angle brackets beginning with number 250, thus continuing the number sequence in *Lutheran Worship Altar Book.* Numbers in parentheses indicate prayers from either the "Pew Edition" or the *Altar Book.* Identical prayers occurring at two or more places will have the same number.

A "Comprehensive Index of Collects and Prayers" is included for ease of reference. It outlines the topic(s) and number of each prayer throughout the *Lutheran Worship* series, as well as designating the page(s) on which the prayer is located in the "Pew Edition," *Altar Book,* or *Agenda.* Also included is an "Index to Psalms and Readings."

Lex orandi, lex credendi (the rule or praying [i.e., worshiping] is the rule of believing), first enunciated by Celestine I (fifth century), constituted an important principle in the early Church. Simply stated, the liturgy is a way in which the Christian Church confesses its faith.

This places a heavy responsibility on those who would formulate liturgies and rites. In carrying out its assignment, the Commission on Worship took this maxim seriously. It was concerned that the various rites and liturgies be in conformity with Holy Scripture and the Lutheran Confessions, or Symbols, and that, first and foremost, these formulations proclaim the great truths of God in Jesus Christ for the salvation of lost and condemned mankind. It bent every effort to turn the formal theology into the practical, living, public theology of the Church.

The liturgy may also be considered as a uniquely effective vehicle by which both the Church's historical identity and its theology can be preserved. Unfortunately, liturgy has often suffered at the hands of those who would stray from the biblical moorings, as well as by those who would pursue ill-conceived liturgical experimentation.

Moreover, as pastors serve at the baptismal font and the graveside, at dedications, and on other festivals and occasions, the use of the Church's rites and liturgies helps to avoid subjective forms and arbitrary procedures. The liturgy is not the voice of so many disparate individuals but the voice of the Church at prayer. It would be well occasionally to remind ourselves of the apostolic dictum about worship, "God is not a God of disorder but of peace" (1 Corinthians 14:33), and that the official pastoral ministrations as well as public corporate worship come under this principle.

It is the prayer of the Commission on Worship that this book be well received by the Church and that the almighty and merciful God accompany with his blessing its use in ministering to his people, for the sake of his Son Jesus Christ, our Lord and Savior.

The Annunciation of our Lord, 1984

The Commission on Worship

THE CHURCH YEAR

SUNDAYS AND MAJOR FESTIVALS

The Time of Christmas

Advent Season
First Sunday in Advent P/B*
Second Sunday in Advent P/B
Third Sunday in Advent P/B
Fourth Sunday in Advent P/B

Christmas Season
THE NATIVITY OF OUR LORD W
   Christmas Eve
   Christmas Dawn
   Christmas Day
First Sunday after Christmas W
Second Sunday after Christmas W

Epiphany Season
The Epiphany of Our Lord W
The Baptism of Our Lord W
   First Sunday after the Epiphany
Second Sunday after the Epiphany G
Third Sunday after the Epiphany G
Fourth Sunday after the Epiphany G
Fifth Sunday after the Epiphany G
Sixth Sunday after the Epiphany G
Seventh Sunday after the Epiphany G
Eighth Sunday after the Epiphany G
The Transfiguration of Our Lord W
   Last Sunday after the Epiphany

The Time of Easter

Lenten Season
Ash Wednesday BK/P
First Sunday in Lent P
Second Sunday in Lent P
Third Sunday in Lent P
Fourth Sunday in Lent P
Fifth Sunday in Lent P

Holy Week
PALM SUNDAY S/P
   Sunday of the Passion
Monday in Holy Week S/P
Tuesday in Holy Week S/P
Wednesday in Holy Week S/P
Maundy Thursday S/W
GOOD FRIDAY BK

Easter Season
THE RESURRECTION OF OUR LORD
   Easter Eve W
   Easter Day W/GO
   Easter Evening W/GO
Second Sunday of Easter W
Third Sunday of Easter W
Fourth Sunday of Easter W
Fifth Sunday of Easter W
Sixth Sunday of Easter W
The Ascension of Our Lord W
Seventh Sunday of Easter W

---

* *The letters indicate the suggested colors: P=purple, B=blue, W=white, G=green, BK=black, S=scarlet, GO=gold, R=red*

PENTECOST R
> *Pentecost Eve*
> *The Day of Pentecost*
> *Pentecost Evening*

The Time of the Church

The Season after Pentecost
The Holy Trinity W
> *First Sunday after Pentecost*

Second through Twenty-seventh
> Sunday after Pentecost G

Sunday of the Fulfillment G
> *Last Sunday after Pentecost*

MINOR FESTIVALS

November
30 St. Andrew, Apostle* R

December
21 St. Thomas, Apostle R
26 St. Stephen, The First Martyr R
27 St. John, Apostle and Evangelist W
28 The Holy Innocents, Martyrs R
31 New Year's Eve W
> *Eve of the Name of Jesus*

January
 1 New Year's Day W
> *The Circumcision of Our Lord*

18 The Confession of St. Peter W
24 St. Timothy, Pastor and
> Confessor W

25 The Conversion of St. Paul W
26 St. Titus, Pastor and Confessor W

February
 2 The Presentation of Our Lord W
18 Martin Luther, Doctor and
> Confessor W

24 St. Matthias, Apostle R

March
25 The Annunciation of Our Lord W

April
25 St. Mark, Evangelist R

May
 1 St. Philip and St. James,
> Apostles R

 7 C.F.W. Walther, Doctor W
31 The Visitation W

June
11 St. Barnabas, Apostle R
24 The Nativity of St. John
> the Baptist W

25 Presentation of the Augsburg
> Confession W

29 St. Peter and St. Paul, Apostles R

July
22 St. Mary Magdalene W
25 St. James the Elder, Apostle R

August
10 St. Laurence, Martyr R
15 St. Mary, Mother of Our Lord W
24 St. Bartholomew, Apostle R

September
14 Holy Cross Day R
21 St. Matthew, Apostle and
> Evangelist R

29 St. Michael and All Angels W

October
18 St. Luke, Evangelist R
28 St. Simon and St. Jude, Apostles R
31 Reformation Day R

November
 1 All Saints' Day W
 2 Commemoration of the Faithful
> Departed W

OCCASIONS

Dedication of a Church R
Anniversary of a Congregation R
Mission Festival W
Harvest Festival Color of Season
Day of Supplication and Prayer P
Day of Special or National
> Thanksgiving W

---

* *St. Andrew's Day determines the First Sunday in Advent and therefore
begins the enumeration of the minor festivals.*

MOVABLE FESTIVALS AND HOLY DAYS

The First Sunday in Advent is always the Sunday nearest November 30, St. Andrew's Day, whether before or after.

Ash Wednesday, the first day of Lent, falls in the seventh week before Easter.

Holy Week, the week before Easter Day, includes Palm Sunday (Sunday of the Passion), Maundy Thursday, Good Friday, and Easter Eve.

Easter Day is always the Sunday after the full moon that occurs on or after the spring equinox on March 21. This full moon may happen on any date between March 21 and April 18 inclusive. If the full moon falls on a Sunday, Easter Day is the Sunday following. Easter Day cannot be earlier than March 22 or later than April 25.

The Ascension of Our Lord occurs on a Thursday, forty days after Easter Day.

The Day of Pentecost is seven weeks, or the fiftieth day, after Easter Day.

The Sunday of the Holy Trinity (First Sunday after Pentecost) is eight weeks after Easter Day.

For additional information on the Church Year, consult the Notes on the Liturgy in Lutheran Worship Altar Book, *pages 11—12.*

DATE OF EASTER

1984	April 22	2010	April 4
1985	April 7	2011	April 24
1986	March 30	2012	April 8
1987	April 19	2013	March 31
1988	April 3	2014	April 20
1989	March 26	2015	April 5
1990	April 15	2016	March 27
1991	March 31	2017	April 16
1992	April 19	2018	April 1
1993	April 11	2019	April 21
1994	April 3	2020	April 12
1995	April 16	2021	April 4
1996	April 7	2022	April 17
1997	March 30	2023	April 9
1998	April 12	2024	March 31
1999	April 4	2025	April 20
2000	April 23	2026	April 5
2001	April 15	2027	March 28
2002	March 31	2028	April 16
2003	April 20	2029	April 1
2004	April 11	2030	April 21
2005	March 27	2031	April 13
2006	April 16	2032	March 28
2007	April 8	2033	April 17
2008	March 23	2034	April 9
2009	April 12	2035	March 25

TABLE OF MOVABLE FESTIVALS ACCORDING TO THE DATE OF EASTER

Sundays after Christmas (/leap year)	Sundays after the Epiphany (/leap year)	Ash Wednesday (/leap year)	Easter	Ascension	Pentecost	Sundays after Pentecost	First Sunday in Advent
2/2	4/4	Feb. 4/5	Mar. 22	Apr. 30	May 10	28	Nov.29
2/1	4/4	5/6	23	May 1	11	28	30
1/1	4/5	6/7	24	2	12	28	Dec. 1
1/1	5/5	7/8	25	3	13	28	2
1/2	5/5	8/9	26	4	14	28	3
2/2	5/5	9/10	27	5	15	27	Nov.27
2/2	5/5	10/11	28	6	16	27	28
2/2	5/5	11/12	29	7	17	27	29
2/1	5/5	12/13	30	8	18	27	30
1/1	5/6	13/14	31	9	19	27	Dec. 1
1/1	6/6	14/15	Apr. 1	10	20	27	2
1/2	6/6	15/16	2	11	21	27	3
2/2	6/6	16/17	3	12	22	26	Nov.27
2/2	6/6	17/18	4	13	23	26	28
2/2	6/6	18/19	5	14	24	26	29
2/1	6/6	19/20	6	15	25	26	30
1/1	6/7	20/21	7	16	26	26	Dec. 1
1/1	7/7	21/22	8	17	27	26	2
1/2	7/7	22/23	9	18	28	26	3
2/2	7/7	23/24	10	19	29	25	Nov.27
2/2	7/7	24/25	11	20	30	25	28
2/2	7/7	25/26	12	21	31	25	29
2/1	7/7	26/27	13	22	June 1	25	30
1/1	7/8	27/28	14	23	2	25	Dec. 1
1/1	8/8	28/29	15	24	3	25	2
1/2	8/8	Mar. 1/1	16	25	4	25	3
2/2	8/8	2/2	17	26	5	24	Nov.27
2/2	8/8	3/3	18	27	6	24	28
2/2	8/8	4/4	19	28	7	24	29
2/1	8/8	5/5	20	29	8	24	30
1/1	8/9	6/6	21	30	9	24	Dec. 1
1/1	9/9	7/7	22	31	10	24	2
1/2	9/9	8/8	23	June 1	11	24	3
2/2	9/9	9/9	24	2	12	23	Nov.27
2/2	9/9	10/10	25	3	13	23	28

ASH WEDNESDAY

1. The ministers enter and go to their places as a hymn is sung.

Stand

2. The Divine Service begins with the INTROIT OF THE DAY.

3. The pastor addresses the congregation with these or similar words:

℗ **Dear brothers and sisters of our Lord Jesus Christ, on this day the Church begins a holy season of prayerful and penitential reflection. Our attention is especially directed to the holy sufferings and death of our Lord Jesus Christ.**

From ancient times the season of Lent has been kept as a time of special devotion, self-denial, and humble repentance born of a faithful heart that dwells confidently on his Word and draws from it life and hope.

Let us pray that our dear Father in heaven, for the sake of his beloved Son and in the power of his Holy Spirit, might richly bless this Lententide for us that we may come to Easter with glad hearts and keep the feast in sincerity and truth.

Silence for reflection

Kneel/Stand

4. The pastor continues:

℗ **God the Father, in heaven,**

℃ have mercy.

15

P **God the Son, Redeemer of the world,**

C have mercy.

P **God the Holy Spirit,**

C have mercy.

P **Be gracious to us.**

C Spare us, good Lord.

P **Be gracious to us.**

C Help us, good Lord.

P **By the mystery of your holy incarnation;**
by your holy nativity;
by your baptism, fasting, and temptation;
by your agony and bloody sweat;
by your cross and Passion;
by your precious death and burial;
by your glorious resurrection and ascension;
and by the coming of the Holy Spirit, the Comforter:

C Help us, good Lord.

P **In all time of our tribulation;**
in all time of our prosperity;
in the hour of death; and in the day of judgment:

C Help us, good Lord.

P **We poor sinners implore you**

C to hear us, O Lord.

P **To prosper the preaching of your Word;**
to bless our prayer and meditation;
to strengthen and preserve us in the true faith;
to give heart to our sorrow and strength to our repentance:

C We implore you to hear us, good Lord.

℘ **To draw all to yourself;**
to bless those who are instructed in the faith;
to watch over and console the poor, the sick, the distressed, the lonely, the
forsaken, the abandoned, and all who stand in need of our prayers;
to give abundant blessing to all works of mercy;
and to have mercy on us all:

℅ We implore you to hear us, good Lord.

℘ **To turn our hearts to you;**
to turn the hearts of our enemies, persecutors, and slanderers; and graciously to
hear our prayers:

℅ We implore you to hear us, good Lord.

℘ **Lord Jesus Christ, Son of God,**

℅ we implore you to hear us.

℘ **Christ, the Lamb of God, who takes away the sin of the world,**

℅ have mercy.

℘ **Christ, the Lamb of God, who takes away the sin of the world,**

℅ have mercy.

℘ **Christ, the Lamb of God, who takes away the sin of the world,**

℅ grant us your peace.

℘ **O Christ,**

℅ hear us.

℘ **O Lord,**

℅ have mercy.

℗ **O Christ,**

ⓒ have mercy.

ⓒ O Lord, have mercy. Amen

| ℗ **The Lord be with you.** | OR | ℗ **The Lord be with you.** |
| ⓒ And with your spirit. | | ⓒ And also with you. |

℗ **Let us pray.**

Almighty and everlasting God, because you hate nothing you have made and forgive the sins of all who are penitent, create in us new and contrite hearts that we, worthily repenting our sins and acknowledging our wretchedness, may obtain from you, the God of all mercy, perfect remission and forgiveness; through Jesus Christ, your Son, our Lord, who lives and reigns with you and the Holy Spirit, one God, now and forever. (20)

ⓒ Amen

Sit

5. The Divine Service continues with the OLD TESTAMENT READING.

NOTES

General

▶ *The services for Lent and Holy Week link together events in the life of Christ as preparation for and as celebration of the mighty acts of God for our redemption.*

▶ *The mood of the Ash Wednesday service is one of penitence and reflection upon the quality of one's faith and life, with the goal of strengthening that faith by Word and Sacrament. The character of the Divine Service will be restrained. The Gloria in Excelsis ("Glory to God in the highest"), "This is the feast . . . ," and alleluias are appropriately omitted. The liturgy is in simple form.*

▶ *For midweek services during Lent, Matins or Morning Prayer, Vespers or Evening Prayer, and Prayer at the Close of the Day are appropriate.*

THE PASSION OF
OUR LORD JESUS CHRIST
DRAWN FROM
THE FOUR GOSPELS

I. THE LORD'S SUPPER

■ "You know that after two days is the Feast of the Passover, and the Son of Man will be given over to be crucified."

■ Now the Feast of Unleavened Bread, also called the Passover, drew near, and the chief priests and scribes sought how they might kill him. They assembled with the elders of the people in the palace of the high priest, who was called Caiaphas, and consulted how they might take Jesus craftily and put him to death. But they said, "Not on the feast day, lest there be an uproar among the people."

■ Then Satan entered into Judas, surnamed Iscariot, one of the Twelve. He went his way to the chief priests and captains and spoke together with them how he might betray Jesus to them. They were glad to hear him. He said to them, "What will you give me to betray him to you?"
   They promised to give him money and agreed with him for thirty pieces of silver. He accepted, and from that time he sought opportunity to betray him in the absence of the multitude.

■ Then came the first day of Unleavened Bread when they sacrificed the Passover lamb. Jesus sent Peter and John, saying, "Go and prepare the Passover, that we may eat it."
   They said to him, "Where do you want us to prepare it?"

■ He said to them, "Go into the city and, when you have entered the city, watch for a man bearing a pitcher of water. When he meets you, follow him into

20

the house where he enters. You shall say to the man who lives there, 'The Master says to you, "My time is at hand; I will keep the Passover at your house. Where is the guest chamber where I shall eat the Passover with my disciples?"' And he will show you a large upper room, furnished and prepared; there make ready for us."

The disciples did as Jesus had directed them. They came into the city and found it as he had told them; and they made ready the Passover.

■ When the hour was come, Jesus sat down and the apostles with him. As they were eating, he said, "I have longed to eat this Passover with you before I suffer, for I say to you I shall not eat of it until it is fulfilled in the kingdom of God."

As they were eating, Jesus took bread, and when he had given thanks, he broke it and gave it to his disciples, saying, "Take, eat; this is my body which is given for you. This do in remembrance of me."

■ In the same way also he took the cup, and when he had given thanks, he gave it to them, saying, "Drink of it, all of you; this is my blood of the new testament, which is shed for you and for many for the forgiveness of sins. This do, as often as you drink it, in remembrance of me.

"Truly I say to you, I will not drink henceforth of this fruit of the vine until that day when I drink it new with you in the kingdom of my Father."

■ There was also a strife among them as to which of them should be accounted the greatest. He said to them, "The kings of the Gentiles exercise lordship over them; and they that exercise authority over them are called 'benefactors.' It shall not be so among you. He that is greatest among you, let him be as the younger; and he that is chief, as he that serves. For who is greater, he that sits at the table or he that serves? Is it not he that sits at the table? But I am among you as a servant. You are they who have continued with me in my temptations. I appoint you to a kingdom, as my Father has appointed me. You shall eat and drink at my table in my kingdom and sit on thrones, judging the twelve tribes of Israel."

■ Jesus knew that his hour was come to depart from the world and go to the Father. Having loved his own who are in the world, he loved them to the finish. Already Satan had put into the heart of Judas Iscariot, Simon's son, to betray him. Jesus knew that the Father had given all things into his hands and that he had come from God and was going to God. He rose from supper, laid aside his garments, and girded himself with a towel. He poured water into a basin and began to wash the disciples' feet and to wipe them with the towel with which he was girded.

■ When he came to Simon Peter, Peter said to him, "Lord, do you wash my feet?"

Jesus answered and said to him, "What I am doing you do not know now, but after these things you will understand."

Peter said to him, "You shall never wash my feet."

Jesus answered him, "If I do not wash you, you have no part with me."

Simon Peter said to him, "Lord, not my feet only, but also my hands and my head."

Jesus said to him, "He who has been bathed does not need to wash more than his feet, for he is clean altogether. You are clean, but not all of you." He knew who was to betray him; that was why he said not every one was clean.

■ So after he had washed their feet and taken his garments and sat down again, he said to them, "Do you know what I have done to you? You call me the Master and the Lord, and it is good that you say this, for so I am. If I, then, your Lord and Master, have washed your feet, you also ought to wash one another's feet. I have done this to show you the way to do as I have done to you. Truly, truly, I say to you, a servant is not greater than his lord; neither is he that is sent greater than he that sent him. If you know these things, happy are you if you do them.

"I do not speak of you all; I know whom I have chosen. The Scripture must be fulfilled, 'He that eats bread with me has lifted up his heel against me.' Already now I tell you of this, before it happens, so that when it does happen you may believe that I am he.

"Truly, truly, I say to you, whoever receives anyone whom I shall send, receives me; and whoever receives me, receives him who sent me."

■ When Jesus had said these things, his spirit was in turmoil. He bore witness and said, "Truly, truly, I say to you that one of you will betray me."

The disciples looked at one another dumbfounded about whom he spoke. One of his disciples, whom Jesus loved, was leaning on Jesus' bosom. Simon Peter said to him, "Ask who it is of whom he is speaking."

That disciple who was reclining on Jesus' chest said to him, "Lord, who is it?"

■ Jesus then answered, "It is the one to whom I shall give the piece of bread after I have dipped it."

He dipped the piece of bread he had in his hand and gave it to Judas, son of Simon Iscariot. After the piece of bread had been dipped, Satan entered into that one. Jesus said to him, "What you are doing, do quickly."

■ No one at the table knew what the purpose was of what Jesus had said to him. Because Judas kept the money bag, some thought Jesus had told him to buy what was needed for the feast or to give something to the poor. When that man had received the piece of bread, he went out immediately, and it was night.

■ When he had gone out, Jesus said, "Now is the Son of Man glorified, and in him God is glorified. If God is glorified in him, God will glorify him in himself, and straightway he will glorify him.

■ "Little children, yet a little while I am with you. You will seek me; and as I said to the Jews so now I say to you, 'Where I am going you cannot come.' A new commandment I give to you, that you love one another as I have loved you. For this I have loved you, that you also love one another. By this all men will know that you are my disciples, if you have love for one another."

■ Simon Peter said to him, "Lord, where are you going?"
Jesus answered him, "Where I am going you cannot follow me now, but afterwards you will follow me."

II. GETHSEMANE

■ When they had sung a hymn, he went out, as was his custom, to the Mount of Olives, and the disciples followed him. Then Jesus said to them, "You will all be offended because of me this night; for it is written, 'I will smite the shepherd, and the sheep of the flock will be scattered.' But after I am risen again, I will go before you into Galilee."

■ Peter answered and said to him, "Though all be offended because of you, yet will I never be offended."
Jesus said to him, "Truly, I say to you that this night, before the cock crows twice, you will deny me three times."
But Peter said more vehemently, "If I have to die with you, I will never deny you." And all the others said likewise.

■ They went over the brook Kedron and came to a place which was called Gethsemane. There was a garden there, and he went into it with his disciples. Judas, who betrayed him, knew the place, for Jesus often met there with his disciples. And when he was at the place, he said to them, "Sit down here, while I go on ahead and pray. Pray that you do not enter into temptation."

■ He took with him Peter and James and John and began to be full of sorrow and turmoil. Then he said to them, "My soul is exceedingly sorrowful, even to death. Wait here, and watch with me." He went on a little from them, about a stone's throw. He fell on his face and prayed that, if it were possible, the hour might pass from him. He said, "Abba, Father, all things are possible to you. Take this cup from me; nevertheless, not what I will, but what you will."

■ An angel appeared to him from heaven, strengthening him; and he prayed, saying, "O my Father, if it is possible, let this cup pass from me; nevertheless,

23

not as I will, but as you will." In agony, he prayed more earnestly, "Father, if you are willing, remove this cup from me; nevertheless, not my will, but yours be done." His sweat fell on the ground like great drops of blood.

■ When he got up from prayer, he came to his disciples and found them sleeping. He said to Peter, "Simon, are you asleep? Could you not watch with me one hour? Watch and pray, lest you enter into temptation; the spirit indeed is willing, but the flesh is weak."

■ He went away again the second time and prayed, saying, "O my Father, if this cup may not pass away from me, except I drink it, your will be done." When he returned, he found them asleep again; for their eyes were heavy, and they did not know what to answer him. He left them, and went away again, and prayed the third time, saying the same words.

■ Then he came to his disciples and said to them, "Are you still sleeping and taking your rest? It is enough; the hour is come; behold, the Son of Man is betrayed into the hands of sinners. Rise, let us be going. Look, he is at hand who betrays me."

■ Even while he was saying this, Judas, one of the Twelve, came with a detachment and officers from the chief priests and Pharisees. They came to the place with lanterns and torches and weapons. Jesus therefore, knowing all things that would come upon him, went out to them and said, "Whom do you seek?"

They answered him, "Jesus of Nazareth."

Jesus said to them, "I am he."

■ Judas, who betrayed him, had taken his stand with them. When Jesus said to them, "I am he," they drew back and fell to the ground. Again he asked them, "Whom do you seek?"

They said, "Jesus of Nazareth."

Jesus replied, "I told you that I am he. If I am the one you seek then let these go away." This was to fulfill the word he had spoken, "Of those you gave me I have lost none."

■ Now he that was betraying Jesus had given them a sign, saying, "The one whom I shall kiss, that is he; seize him and be sure to take him away securely." He went straight up to Jesus and said, "Hail, Master," and kissed him.

Jesus said to him, "Friend, why have you come? Judas, do you betray the Son of Man with a kiss?"

■ They came then and laid their hands on Jesus and took him. When those who were about him saw what would happen, they said to him, "Lord, shall we

24

strike with the sword?" Then Simon Peter, having a sword, drew it and struck the high priest's servant and cut off his right ear. The servant's name was Malchus.

■ Jesus answered and said, "Let it be." And he touched his ear and healed him. Then Jesus said to Peter, "Put your sword into its sheath. All they that take the sword shall perish with the sword. Do you imagine that I cannot now pray to my Father, and he will presently give me more than twelve legions of angels? But how then shall the Scriptures be fulfilled that thus it must be? The cup which my Father has given me, shall I not drink of it?"

■ Then Jesus said to the chief priests, and the captains of the temple, and the elders who had come out against him, "Have you come out as against a thief, with swords and clubs to take me? When I was with you day after day teaching in the temple, you did not lay your hands on me; but this is your hour and the hour of the power of darkness. All this has happened that the Scriptures of the prophets might be fulfilled." Then all the disciples forsook him and fled.

■ There was a certain young man who followed along. He had only a linen cloth about his naked body. They laid hold on him, but he slipped out of the linen cloth and fled away naked.

■ Then the detachment and its captain and the officers of the Jews seized Jesus, and bound him, and led him away to Annas first; for he was the father-in-law to Caiaphas, who was the high priest that year. Now Caiaphas was the one who gave counsel to the Jews that it was good that one man should die for the people.

III. THE PALACE OF THE HIGH PRIEST

■ Those who had arrested Jesus brought him to the high priest's house, where the scribes and elders were assembled. Peter followed him afar off, and so did another disciple. That disciple was known to the high priest and went in with Jesus into the palace of the high priest, but Peter stood outside at the door. So that other disciple, who was known to the high priest, went out and spoke to the doorkeeper and brought Peter in. He went in and sat with the servants to see the end. He was warming himself at the fire they had kindled in the middle of the courtyard.

■ Meanwhile, the chief priests and the whole council were seeking evidence that might make the case for a death sentence, but they could not find any. Many bore false witness against him, but their statements did not agree. Two stepped forward and said, "We heard him say, 'I shall destroy this temple made with hands and after the beginning of the third day I shall build another, not made with hands.' " But even on this point their evidence did not agree.

■ Then the High Priest stood up, moved to the center, and put this question to Jesus, "Do you have no answer? What is this evidence they have given against you?" But he was silent and gave no answer.

Again the High Priest put a question to him and said, "Are you the Christ, the Son of the Blessed?"

Jesus said, "I am. You will see the Son of Man seated at the right hand of God's power and coming with the clouds of heaven."

The High Priest tore his garments and said, "Do we still need any witnesses? You have heard this blasphemy. What is your opinion?" They all declared that he was liable for death.

■ Then some of them began to spit on him; they blindfolded him, struck him, and said to him, "Prophesy to us, O Christ, who is he that struck you?" The guards beat him as they took him away.

■ Meanwhile Peter was sitting outside in the courtyard. One of the maidservants of the High Priest came and saw Peter warming himself. She looked at him closely as he sat in the light of the fire, and said, "You also were along with the man from Nazareth, that Jesus."

■ Peter denied it and said, "I do not know what you mean." He went out to the forecourt.

Another maidservant saw him there and said to those who were standing around, "This man was with Jesus of Nazareth."

Peter denied it again with an oath, "I do not know the man."

A little later those standing around said to Peter, "Surely you are one of them. You are a Galilean. Your accent gives you away."

Peter took an oath calling down a curse upon himself, "I do not know the man."

■ And immediately while he was still speaking, the cock crowed a second time, and the Lord turned and looked on Peter. Then Peter remembered that Jesus had said to him, "Before the cock crows twice, you will deny me three times." Peter broke down, and went out, and wept bitterly.

■ As soon as it was morning the chief priests with the elders and the scribes held the court session with all the Sanhedrin. Then they bound him, led him away, and turned him over to Pilate. Then Judas, who had betrayed him, when he saw that he was condemned, was sorry and brought back the thirty pieces of silver to the chief priests and elders, saying, "I have sinned. I have betrayed innocent blood."

■ They said, "What is that to us? That is your affair." Judas threw down the pieces of silver in the temple and departed. He went and hanged himself.

■ The chief priests took the silver pieces and said, "It is not lawful to put them into the treasury, because it is the price of blood." They took counsel and bought with them the potter's field to bury strangers in. That is why to this day that field has been called "the field of blood."

■ In this way was fulfilled what was spoken by Jeremiah the prophet, saying, "They took the thirty pieces of silver, the price of him on whom a price had been set by the children of Israel, and gave them for the potter's field."

IV. THE PRAETORIUM

■ When they had bound Jesus, they led him from Caiaphas to the hall of judgment and gave him over to Pontius Pilate, the governor. It was early. They themselves did not go into the judgment hall, so that they might not be defiled, but might eat the Passover.

■ Pilate then went out to them, and said, "What charge do you bring against this man?"
They answered and said to him, "If he were not a criminal, we would not have handed him over to you."
Then Pilate said to them, "Take him, then, and judge him according to your law."
The Jews said to him, "It is not lawful for us to put any man to death." So the word of Jesus was fulfilled, signifying by what death he should die.

■ The charges they brought against him were: "We found this fellow perverting the nation, and forbidding us to pay taxes to Caesar, and saying that he himself is Christ, a king."

■ Then Pilate entered into the judgment hall again, and called Jesus, and said to him, "Are you the King of the Jews?"
Jesus answered him, "Do you say this for yourself, or did others say it to you about me?"
Pilate answered, "Do you take me for a Jew? Your own nation and the chief priests have given you over to me. What have you done?"

■ Jesus answered, "My kingdom is not of this world; if my kingdom were of this world, then my servants would have fought that I should not be given over to the Jews; but now my kingdom is not in the ways of this place."
Pilate therefore said to him, "Are you a king then?"
Jesus answered, "You say rightly that I am a king. I was born and I came

into the world that I should bear witness to the truth. Everyone that is of the truth hears my voice."

Pilate said to him, "What is truth?"

After he had said this, he went out again to the Jews and said to them, "I find no fault in this man."

■ The chief priests kept laying one charge after another against him, but he answered not a word. Pilate questioned him again, saying, "Do you answer nothing? See how many charges they lay against you." Jesus answered him not a word. Pilate was utterly amazed. He said to the chief priests and the crowd, "I find no case against this man."

■ They pressed their charges more vehemently: "He stirs up the people, teaching throughout all Judaea, beginning from Galilee to this place."

When Pilate heard of Galilee, he asked whether the man was a Galilean. When he learned that he belonged in Herod's jurisdiction, he sent him on to Herod, who was also in Jerusalem for those days.

■ When Herod saw Jesus, he was delighted, for he had long wished to see him because of what he had heard of him, and he hoped to see him do a miracle. He questioned Jesus repeatedly, but he gave him no answer. The chief priests and scribes stood there and vehemently accused him. Herod and his soldiers mocked him. They put on him a splendid robe and sent him back to Pilate.

Herod and Pilate became friends with each other that same day, for before this they had been at enmity with each other.

■ Pilate then called together the chief priests and the rulers and the people, and said to them, "You have brought this man before me as one subverting the people. See now, I have examined him before you and have found nothing in this man guilty of any of your charges against him, and neither did Herod, for he sent him back to us. Mark this, he has done nothing worthy of death. I will have him punished and release him."

■ Now at the feast it was the governor's custom to release to the crowd any one prisoner whom they asked for. They had then a notorious prisoner named Barabbas. He was in prison with the rebels who had committed murder in the uprising in the city. Pilate knew that it was out of malice that the chief priests handed Jesus over. Therefore he said to them, "Do you want me to release for you Barabbas or Jesus who is called Christ?"

■ The chief priests and elders persuaded the crowd to ask for Barabbas and destroy Jesus.

Pilate asked them again, "Which of the two do you want me to release for you?"

28

And they cried out all together, saying, "Away with this man, and release for us Barabbas."

■ While Pilate was sitting in the judgment seat, his wife sent him a message: "Do not have anything to do with that man; I have suffered much over him today in a dream."

■ Again Pilate addressed them, for he wished to release Jesus. He said to them, "What shall I do then with Jesus who is called Christ? What shall I do with him whom you call the King of the Jews?"

They all cried out, "Crucify him!"

Pilate said to them, "Why, what evil has he done? I have found no guilt worthy of death in him; I will therefore punish him and let him go."

They cried out all the louder, "Crucify him! Crucify him!"

■ Then Pilate took Jesus and had him flogged. The soldiers of the governor led him away into the praetorium. They gathered the whole band of soldiers around him. They stripped him and put on him a purple robe. When they had woven a crown of thorns, they put it on his head and a reed in his right hand, and they knelt before him and mocked him, saying, "Hail, King of the Jews!" They spat on him and took the reed and struck him on the head. They knelt down and did him homage.

■ Pilate went out again and said to them, "See, I bring him out to you that you may know I find him not guilty." So Jesus came out wearing the crown of thorns and the purple robe. Pilate said to them, "Behold the man!"

■ When the chief priests and officers saw him, they cried, "Crucify him! Cruficy him!"

Pilate said to them, "Take him yourselves and crucify him, for I do not find him guilty."

The Jews answered him, "We have a law, and by that law he ought to die, because he made himself the Son of God."

■ When Pilate heard this, he was more afraid and went again into the judgment hall and said to Jesus, "Where are you from?" Jesus gave him no answer. Then Pilate said to him, "Do you refuse to speak to me? Do you not know that I have power to crucify you, and I have power to release you?"

Jesus answered, "You would not have any power at all over me, unless it had been given to you from above. For that reason he who handed me over to you has the greater sin."

29

■ This prompted Pilate to go on trying to release him, but the Jews cried out, "If you let this man go, you are no friend of Caesar. Everyone who makes himself a king sets himself against Caesar."

When Pilate heard these words, he brought Jesus out and sat down in the judgment seat in a place that is called the Pavement or, in Hebrew, Gabbatha. It was the Preparation of the Passover, about the sixth hour. He said to the Jews, "Behold your king!"

They cried out, "Away with him, away with him, crucify him!"

Pilate said unto them, "Shall I crucify your king?"

The chief priest answered, "We have no king but Caesar."

■ When Pilate saw that he was getting nowhere, but rather a riot was under way, he took water and washed his hands before the crowd, saying, "I am innocent of the blood of this man; see to it yourselves."

Then all the people responded, "His blood be on us and on our children."

■ Then Pilate, wishing to satisfy the crowd, gave sentence that it should be as they demanded. He released to them Barabbas for whom they asked, the man who had been thrown into prison for insurrection and murder. He had Jesus flogged and then gave him over to their will to be crucified. The soldiers mocked him, stripped him of the purple robe, put his own clothes on him, and led him out to crucify him.

V. CALVARY

■ The soldiers now had charge of Jesus. Carrying his own cross, he went out of the city to a place called Skull Hill, in Hebrew, Golgotha. As they led him away, they laid hold of Simon of Cyrene, the father of Alexander and Rufus, who was coming in from the country. On him they laid the cross that he might bear it after Jesus. Following him was a great company of people and of women who bewailed and lamented him. Jesus turned to them and said,

■ "Daughters of Jerusalem, do not weep for me, but weep for yourselves and for your children. The days are surely coming when they will say, 'Blessed are the barren and the wombs that never bore, and the breasts that never gave suck.' Then they will begin to say to the mountains, 'Fall on us,' and to the hills, 'Cover us.' For if they do these things with a green tree, what will happen with a dry one?"

■ There were also two others, criminals whom they led along to be put to death with him. When they came to the place called Golgotha, they gave him wine mingled with gall to drink, but when he tasted it, he would not drink it.

■ It was the third hour, and there they crucified him.

Jesus said, "Father, forgive them, for they know not what they do."

The two criminals they crucified with him—one on his right, the other on his left, with Jesus in the middle. The Scripture was then fulfilled which says, "And he was numbered with the transgressors."

■ When the soldiers had crucified Jesus, they cast lots to divide his clothes and decide what each should take. They made four parts, one for each soldier. There remained his tunic. This was without seam, woven in one piece from the top to the bottom. They said to one another, "Let us not tear it, but cast lots for it to decide who shall have it." The Scripture was thus fulfilled which says, "They divided my garments among them and cast lots for my clothing." These things the soldiers did and, sitting down, they kept watch over him there.

■ Over his head was put the charge against him. Pilate wrote the notice to be put on the cross. It read, JESUS OF NAZARETH, KING OF THE JEWS. This title was read by many of the Jews, for the place where Jesus was crucified was near to the city, and it was written in Hebrew, Greek, and Latin. The chief priests of the Jews then said to Pilate, "You should not write 'The King of the Jews,' but 'This man said, I am the King of the Jews.'"

Pilate answered, "What I have written, I have written."

■ People stood by, watching. Those who passed by derided him, wagging their heads, and saying, "Aha! You who would destroy the temple and build it in three days, save yourself. If you are the Son of God, come down from the cross."

■ So also the chief priests, with the scribes and elders, mocked him to one another saying, "He saved others; he cannot save himself. Let the Christ, the King of Israel, now come down from the cross that we may see and believe. He trusts in God; let God deliver him now, if he wants him, for he said, 'I am the Son of God.'"

■ The soldiers also mocked him, coming to him and offering him wine, and saying, "If you are the King of the Jews, save yourself." The thieves also who were crucified with him cast the same in his teeth. And one of the criminals who hung there with him mocked him.

"Are you not the Christ? Save yourself and us."

■ But the other rebuked him, saying, "Do you not fear God since you are under the same condemnation? And we indeed justly, for we are getting what we deserve for what we have done; but this man has done nothing wrong." Then he said, "Jesus, remember me when you come into your kingdom."

31

Jesus said to him, "Truly, I say to you, today you will be with me in paradise."

■   Near to the cross of Jesus stood his mother, his mother's sister, Mary the wife of Clopas, and Mary Magdalene. When Jesus saw his mother and the disciple whom he loved standing near, he said to his mother, "Woman, behold your son!" Then he said to the disciple, "Behold your mother!" And from that hour the disciple took her into his own home.

■   About the ninth hour Jesus cried out with a loud voice, *"Eli, Eli, lama sabachthani?"* which means, "My God, my God, why have you forsaken me?"
    When some of them that were standing there heard it, they said, "He is calling for Elijah."

■   After this, Jesus knew that all things were accomplished. Fulfilling the Scripture he said, "I thirst." There was a jar of wine standing there. One of them ran immediately to get a sponge. He filled it with wine, put it on a reed, held it up to his mouth, and gave it to him to drink.
    Others said, "Wait and see if Elijah will come and save him."

■   When Jesus had received the wine, he cried with a loud voice, "It is finished!" Then he said, "Father, into your hands I commend my spirit." Having said this, he bowed his head and gave up his spirit.

■   At that moment the curtain of the temple was torn in two from top to bottom. The earth shook and the rocks split. The tombs broke open and the bodies of many holy people who had died were raised to life. They came out of the tombs, and after Jesus' resurrection they went into the holy city and appeared to many people.
    When the centurion who stood facing him saw how he died, he said, "Truly, this man was the Son of God."

■   All the people who had gathered to see the sight, when they saw what had happened, turned away beating their breasts. Those who had known him stood at a distance, as also the women who had followed him from Galilee. Among them was Mary Magdalene, Mary the mother of James the younger and of Joses, and Salome the mother of the sons of Zebedee.

■   It was the day of Preparation before the Sabbath, and this was Passover Sabbath. Therefore, so that the bodies should not remain on the crosses during the Sabbath, the Jews asked Pilate to have the legs broken and the bodies removed. So the soldiers came and broke the legs of the first and of the other who was crucified with him. But when they came to Jesus and saw that he was dead already, they did not break his legs, but one of the soldiers pierced his side with a spear, and at once there came out blood and water. One who saw it is our witness, and his testimony is true. He knows that he tells the truth that you also may believe. These things were done that the Scripture should be fulfilled, "Not one of his bones shall be broken." And again, another Scripture says, "They shall look on him whom they pierced."

■ By this time evening had come. A respected member of the council, Joseph of Arimathea, was one who was looking for the kingdom of God, a good and righteous man who had not consented to their purpose and deed. He was a disciple of Jesus secretly, for he feared the Jews. Now he took courage and went to Pilate and asked for the body of Jesus.

■ Pilate was astonished that he could be dead already. He called for the centurion and asked him whether Jesus was already dead. When he was assured by the centurion that it was so, Pilate granted Joseph the corpse and commanded that it be given over to him.

■ Joseph bought fine linen and came and took the body of Jesus. Nicodemus came also, bringing a mixture of myrrh and aloes, about a hundred pound weight. It was he who had first come to Jesus by night. They then took the body of Jesus and wrapped it in linen cloths with the spices, as is the burial custom of the Jews.

■ Now in the place where he was crucified there was a garden; and in the garden a new tomb, where no one had ever been buried. Joseph laid the body in his own new tomb, which he had hewn out in the rock, and rolled a great stone to the door of the tomb, and departed.

Mary Magdalene and Mary the mother of Joses were sitting there opposite the sepulcher and saw where he was laid. Then they returned and prepared spices and ointments. On the sabbath day they rested according to the commandment.

■ On the next day, the day after the Preparation, the chief priests and Pharisees went together to Pilate and said, "Sir, we remember that that imposter said, while he was still alive, 'After three days I will rise again.' Therefore command that the sepulcher be made secure until the third day to stop his disciples from coming and stealing him and saying to the people, 'He has risen from the dead,' making the final deception worse than the first."

■ Pilate said to them, "You have a guard. Go and make it as secure as you know how." They went and made the sepulcher secure. They sealed the stone and set a watch.

NOTES

General

▶ *This harmony of the Gospel accounts of the Passion is divided in order to facilitate presentation by a number of readers. At each symbol ■, another reader may begin.*

PALM SUNDAY
PROCESSION WITH PALMS

1. Before the Divine Service the congregation gathers in some convenient place, the branches or fronds of palm are distributed, and the pastor says:

℗ **The grace of our Lord Jesus Christ and the love of God and the communion of the Holy Spirit ✛ be with you all.**

℃ And with your spirit.

℗ **Blessed is he who comes in the name of the Lord.**

℃ Hosanna to the Son of David.

℗ **Let us pray.**

Most merciful God, as the people of Jerusalem, with palms in their hands, gathered to greet your dearly beloved Son when he came into his Holy City, grant that we may ever hail him as our King and, when he comes again, may go forth to meet him with trusting and steadfast hearts and follow him in the way that leads to eternal life; who lives and reigns with you and the Holy Spirit, one God, now and forever. ⟨250⟩

℃ Amen

2. The HOLY GOSPEL is announced and read.

℗ **The Holy Gospel according to St. John, the twelfth chapter.**

℃ Glory to you, O Lord.

Ⓐ **The next day the great crowd that had come for the Feast heard that Jesus was on his way to Jerusalem. They took palm branches and went out to meet him, shouting, "Hosanna! Blessed is he who comes in the name of the Lord! Blessed is** the King of Israel!" Jesus found a young donkey and sat upon it, as it is written, "Do not be afraid, O Daughter of Zion; see, your king is coming, seated on a donkey's colt." At first his disciples did not understand all this. Only after Jesus was glorified did they realize that these things had been written about him and that they had done these things to him. Now the crowd that was with him had continued to spread the word that he had called Lazarus from the tomb, raising him from the dead. Many people, because they had heard that he had given this miraculous sign, went out to meet him. So the Pharisees said to one another, "See, this is getting us nowhere. Look how the whole world has gone after him!" (John 12:12-19)

Ⓐ **This is the Gospel of the Lord.**

Ⓒ Praise to you, O Christ.

Ⓟ **Let us go forth in peace**

Ⓒ in the name of the Lord.

3. The PROCESSION into the church begins with the congregation, branches raised, following the pastor and assisting minister(s) and singing "All Glory, Laud, and Honor," Hymn 102. "Lift Up Your Heads, You Mighty Gates," Hymn 23 or 24, may be sung instead.

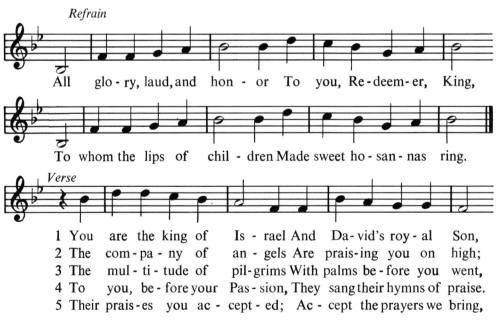

Refrain

All glo - ry, laud, and hon - or To you, Re - deem - er, King,

To whom the lips of chil - dren Made sweet ho - san - nas ring.

Verse

1 You are the king of Is - rael And Da - vid's roy - al Son,
2 The com - pa - ny of an - gels Are prais - ing you on high;
3 The mul - ti - tude of pil - grims With palms be - fore you went,
4 To you, be - fore your Pas - sion, They sang their hymns of praise.
5 Their prais - es you ac - cept - ed; Ac - cept the prayers we bring,

Refrain

Now in the Lord's name com - ing, Our King and Bless-ed One.
Cre - a - tion and all mor - tals In cho - rus make re - ply.
Our praise and prayer and an - thems Be - fore you we pre - sent.
To you, now high ex - alt - ed, Our mel - o - dy we raise.
Great au - thor of all good-ness, O good and gra-cious King.

*4. When all have entered the church and gone to their places, the pastor,
standing before the altar steps, chants or says:*

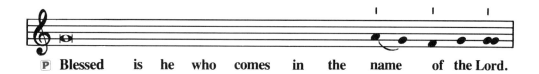

P Blessed is he who comes in the name of the Lord.

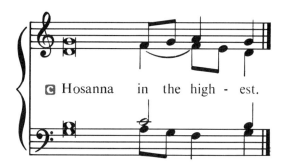

C Hosanna in the high - est.

5. The Divine Service continues with the COLLECT OF THE DAY.

NOTES

The Service in Detail

2. ▶ Instead of John 12:12-19, the processional Gospels as here appointed may be read:

A. Matthew 21:1-11   B. Mark 11:1-10   C. Luke 19:28-40

MAUNDY THURSDAY
STRIPPING OF THE ALTAR

1. Immediately after the Benediction in the Divine Service, the Communion vessels are reverently removed from the altar, the altar is stripped, and the chancel is cleared in preparation for the solemn services of Good Friday.

2. While this is done, one of the following psalms is sung antiphonally by the choir and congregation or by two groups within the congregation. The Gloria Patri is omitted.

PSALM 22

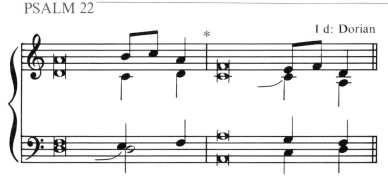

¹ My God, my God, why have you forsaken me?*
    Why are you so far from saving me, so far from the words of my groaning?

² O my God, I cry out by day, but you do not answer,*
    by night, and am not silent.

³ Yet you are enthroned as the Holy One;*
    you are the praise of Israel.

⁴ In you our fathers put their trust;*
    they trusted and you delivered them.

⁵ They cried to you and were saved;*
    in you they trusted and were not disappointed.

IX a: Aeolian

⁶ But I am a worm and not a man,*
  scorned by men
  and despised by the people.

⁷ All who see me mock me;*
  they hurl insults, shaking their
  heads:

⁸ "He trusts in the Lord;
  let the Lord rescue him.*
  Let him deliver him,
  since he delights in him."

⁹ Yet you brought me out of the womb;*
  you made me trust in you
  even at my mother's breast.

¹⁰ From birth I was cast upon you;*
  from my mother's womb
  you have been my God.

¹¹ Do not be far from me,*
  for trouble is near
  and there is no one to help.

I d: Dorian

¹² Many bulls surround me;*
  strong bulls of Bashan encircle me.

¹³ Roaring lions tearing their prey*
  open their mouths wide against me.

¹⁴ I am poured out like water,
  and all my bones are out of joint.*
  My heart has turned to wax;
  it has melted away within me.

¹⁵ My strength is dried up like a
  potsherd, and my tongue sticks to the

roof of my mouth;*
  you lay me in the dust of death.

¹⁶ Dogs have surrounded me;
  a band of evil men has encircled me,*
  they have pierced
  my hands and my feet.

¹⁷ I can count all my bones;*
  people stare and gloat over me.

¹⁸ They divide my garments
  among them *
  and cast lots for my clothing.

IX a³ : Aeolian

¹⁹ But you, O Lord, be not far off;*
  O my Strength, come quickly to
  help me.

²⁰ Deliver my life from the sword,*
  my precious life from the power
  of the dogs.

²¹ Rescue me from the mouth of the
  lions;*
    save me from the horns
    of the wild oxen.

²² I will declare your name to my
  brothers;*

in the congregation
I will praise you.

²³ You who fear the Lord, praise him!*
  All you descendants of Jacob,
  honor him! Revere him, all you
  descendants of Israel!

²⁴ For he has not despised or disdained
  the suffering of the afflicted one;*
    he has not hidden his face
    from him but has listened
    to his cry for help.

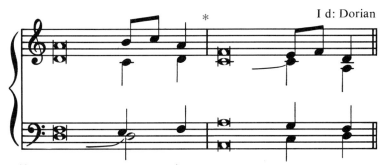

I d: Dorian

²⁵ From you comes my praise
  in the great assembly;*
    before those who fear you will I
    fulfill my vows.

²⁶ The poor will eat and be satisfied;
  they who seek the Lord
  will praise him—*
    may your hearts live forever!

²⁷ All the ends of the earth
  will remember and turn to the Lord,*
    and all the families of the nations
    will bow down before him,

²⁸ for dominion belongs to the Lord*

and he rules over the nations.

²⁹ All the rich of the earth
  will feast and worship;*
    all who go down to the dust will
    kneel before him—those who
    cannot keep themselves alive.

³⁰ Posterity will serve him;*
    future generations will
    be told about the Lord.

³¹ They will proclaim his righteousness
  to a people yet unborn—*
    for he has done it.

OR

PSALM 51

IX a: Aeolian

¹ Have mercy on me, O God,
    according to your unfailing love;*
        according to your great compassion
        blot out my transgressions.

² Wash away all my iniquity*
    and cleanse me from my sin.

³ For I know my transgressions,*
    and my sin is always before me.

⁴ Against you, you only, have I sinned
    and done what is evil in your sight,*

so that you are proved right when
you speak and justified when you
judge.

⁵ Surely I have been a sinner from
birth,*
    sinful from the time my mother
    conceived me.

⁶ Surely you desire truth in the inner
parts;*
    you teach me wisdom in the inmost
    place.

IX a² : Aeolian

⁷ Cleanse me with hyssop, and I will
be clean;*
    wash me, and I will be whiter than
    snow.

⁸ Let me hear joy and gladness;*
    let the bones you have crushed
    rejoice.

⁹ Hide your face from my sins*
    and blot out all my iniquity.

¹⁰ Create in me a pure heart, O God,*
    and renew a steadfast spirit
    within me.

¹¹ Do not cast me from your presence*
    or take your Holy Spirit from me.

¹² Restore to me the joy of your
salvation*
    and grant me a willing spirit, to
    sustain me.

IX a: Aeolian

13 Then I will teach transgressors your ways,*
    and sinners will turn back to you.

14 Save me from bloodguilt, O God, the God who saves me,*
    and my tongue will sing of your righteousness.

15 O Lord, open my lips,*
    and my mouth will declare your praise.

16 You do not delight in sacrifice, or I would bring it;*
    you do not take pleasure in burnt offerings.

17 The sacrifices of God are a broken spirit;*
    a broken and contrite heart, O God, you will not despise.

18 In your good pleasure make Zion prosper;*
    build up the walls of Jerusalem.

19 Then there will be righteous sacrifices, whole burnt offerings to delight you;*
    then bulls will be offered on your altar.

3. The Psalm ended, all leave the church silently.

43

NOTES

General

▶ *The candles are extinguished before the altar is stripped.*

▶ *The stripping should proceed in a deliberate and orderly manner, with several persons carrying the items to the sacristy—the ornaments and candles first, thereafter the linens and paraments.*

▶ *The stripping of the altar (and washing) is an ancient feature of Maundy Thursday, symbolic of the humiliation of Jesus at the soldiers' hands. Psalm 22 rehearses that and other themes of the Passion. In addition to Psalm 51, Psalm 88 may be considered another option.*

GOOD FRIDAY
AT NOONDAY

1. The ministers enter in silence and go to their places.

Stand

SENTENCES AND COLLECTS

Ⓐ **He was wounded for our transgressions, he was bruised for our iniquities; the chastisement of our peace was upon him,**

Ⓒ and with his stripes we are healed.

Ⓐ **Almighty God, graciously behold this your family, for whom our Lord Jesus Christ was willing to be betrayed, to be given into the hands of sinners, and to suffer death on the cross; who now lives and reigns with you and the Holy Spirit, one God, now and forever.** (31)

Ⓒ Amen

Ⓐ **We all, like sheep, have gone astray;**

Ⓒ and the Lord has laid on him the iniquity of us all.

Ⓐ **Almighty and most merciful God, give us grace so to contemplate the Passion of our Lord that we may find in it the forgiveness of our sins; through Jesus Christ, your Son, our Lord.** ⟨251⟩

Ⓒ Amen

2. The HYMN, "Jesus, I Will Ponder Now," Hymn 109, is sung, stanzas 1 and 5.

45

Sit

SCRIPTURE READINGS

HYMN

SERMON

3. An OFFERING may be received.

HYMN

Kneel/Stand

PRAYERS

P **O Savior of the world, by your cross and precious blood you redeemed the world.**

C Save us and help us, we humbly implore you, O Lord.

P **We adore you, Lord Jesus, in your cross and Passion, through which you have brought life and joy into the world.**

C Be gracious to us according to your mercy and bless us and lift up the light of your countenance upon us and give us your peace.

P **Gracious Jesus, our Lord and our God, at this hour you bore our sins in your own body on the tree so that we, being dead to sin, might live unto righteousness. Have mercy upon us now and at the hour of our death and grant to us, your servants, with all others who devoutly remember your blessed Passion, a holy and peaceful life in this world and through your grace eternal glory in the life to come, where, with the Father and the Holy Spirit, you live and reign, God forever.** (188)

C Amen

P **Lamb of God, you take away the sin of the world;**

C have mercy on us.

46

P **Lamb of God, you take away the sin of the world;**

C have mercy on us.

P **Lamb of God, you take away the sin of the world;**

C grant us peace.

Stand

BLESSING

P Christ crucified draw you to himself, to find in him a sure ground of faith, a firm support for hope, and the assurance of sins forgiven; and the blessing of almighty God, the Father, the ✠Son, and the Holy Spirit, be with you now and forever.

C Amen

4. The ministers and worshipers leave in silence.

NOTES

General

▶ *This brief service is designed for congregations in larger cities that invite the public for worship during the lunch period.*

GOOD FRIDAY I

1. The reflective and intercessory character of this service suggests that instrumental music be used only to support the singing.

2. The ministers enter in silence and go to their places.

Stand

3. The COLLECT OF THE DAY is said.

Ⓟ **Almighty God, graciously behold this your family, for whom our Lord Jesus Christ was willing to be betrayed, to be given into the hands of sinners, and to suffer death on the cross; who now lives and reigns with you and the Holy Spirit, one God, now and forever.** (31)

Ⓒ Amen

Sit

4. The OLD TESTAMENT READING is announced and read.

Ⓐ **The Old Testament Reading for Good Friday is from the _____ chapter of _____ .**

5. The HYMN, "Jesus, I Will Ponder Now," Hymn 109, is sung. Another appropriate hymn may be sung instead.

6. The HOLY GOSPEL is announced and read. It may be presented by several readers, or the choir may sing a setting appropriate to liturgical use. The congregation may remain seated during all or part of the reading.

P **The Holy Gospel according to St. _____ , the _____ chapter.**

7. A Sermon may follow.

Kneel/Stand

8. The BIDDING PRAYER is said.

A **Let us pray for the whole Church, that our Lord God would defend her against all the assaults and temptations of the adversary and keep her perpetually on the true foundation, Jesus Christ:**

P **Almighty and everlasting God, since you have revealed your glory to all nations in Jesus Christ and in the Word of his truth, keep, we ask you, in safety the works of your mercy so that your Church, spread throughout all nations, may be defended against the adversary and may serve you in true faith and persevere in the confession of your name; through Jesus Christ, our Lord.** (192)

C Amen

A **Let us pray for all the ministers of the Word and for all the people of God:**

P **Almighty and everlasting God, by whose Spirit the whole body of the Church is governed and sanctified, receive the supplications and prayers which we offer before you for all your servants in your holy Church that every member of the same may truly serve you; through Jesus Christ, our Lord.** (193)

C Amen

A **Let us pray for our catechumens, that our Lord God would open their hearts and the door of his mercy that, having received the remission of all their sins by the washing of regeneration, they may be mindful of their Baptism and throughout their lives remain faithful to Christ Jesus, our Lord:**

P **Almighty God and Father, because you always grant growth to your Church, increase the faith and understanding of our catechumens that, recalling the new birth by the water of Holy Baptism, they may forever continue in the family of those whom you adopt as your sons and daughters; through Jesus Christ, our Lord.** (194)

C Amen

A **Let us pray for all in authority that we may lead a quiet and peaceable life in all godliness and honesty:**

[P] O merciful Father in heaven, because you hold in your hand all the might of man and because you have ordained, for the punishment of evildoers and for the praise of those who do well, all the powers that exist in all the nations of the world, we humbly pray you graciously to regard your servants,

(USA) especially the President and Congress of the United States, the Governor of this State (Commonwealth), and all those who make, administer, and judge our laws

(Canada) especially Her (His) Gracious Majesty, the Queen (King); the Governor General; the Prime Minister and the Parliament; the Governments of this Province and all who have authority over us

that all who receive the sword as your ministers may bear it according to your Word; through Jesus Christ, our Lord. (195)

[C] Amen

[A] Let us pray our Lord God Almighty that he would deliver the world from disease, ward off famine, set free those in bondage, grant health to the sick and a safe journey to all who travel:

[P] Almighty and everlasting God, the consolation of the sorrowful and the strength of those who labor, may the prayers of those who in any tribulation or distress cry to you graciously come before you, so that in all their necessities they may rejoice in your manifold help and comfort; through Jesus Christ, our Lord. (196)

[C] Amen

[A] Let us pray for all who are outside the Church, that our Lord God would be pleased to deliver them from their error, call them to faith in the true and living God and his only Son, Jesus Christ, our Lord, and gather them into his family, the Church:

[P] Almighty and everlasting God, because you seek not the death but the life of all, hear our prayers for all who have no right knowledge of you, free them from their error, and for the glory of your name bring them into the fellowship of your holy Church; through Jesus Christ, our Lord. (197)

[C] Amen

[A] Let us pray for our enemies, that God would remember them in mercy and graciously grant them such things as are both needful for them and profitable to their salvation:

[P] O almighty, everlasting God, through your only Son, our blessed Lord, you have commanded us to love our enemies, to do good to those who hate us, and to

50

pray for those who persecute us. We therefore earnestly implore you that by your gracious visitation all our enemies may be led to true repentance and may have the same love and be of one accord and one mind and heart with us and with your whole Church; through Jesus Christ, our Lord. (198)

C Amen

A Let us pray for the fruits of the earth, that God would send down his blessing upon them and graciously dispose our hearts to enjoy them according to his own goodwill:

P O Lord, Father Almighty, by your Word you created and you still continue to bless and uphold all things. We pray you so to reveal to us your Word, our Lord Jesus Christ, that he may dwell in our hearts and we may by your grace be made ready to receive your blessing on all the fruits of the earth and those things that pertain to our bodily need; through Jesus Christ, our Lord. (199)

C Amen

A Finally let us pray for all those things for which our Lord would have us ask, saying:

C Our Father who art in heaven,	OR	**C** Our Father in heaven,
hallowed be thy name,		hallowed be your name,
thy kingdom come,		your kingdom come,
thy will be done		your will be done
on earth as it is in heaven.		on earth as in heaven.
Give us this day our daily bread;		Give us today our daily bread.
and forgive us our trespasses		Forgive us our sins
as we forgive those		as we forgive those
who trespass against us;		who sin against us.
and lead us not into temptation,		Lead us not into temptation,
but deliver us from evil.		but deliver us from evil.
For thine is the kingdom		For the kingdom, the power,
and the power and the glory		and the glory are yours
forever and ever. Amen		now and forever. Amen

Stand

9. If it was not placed before the service began, a roughhewn cross may be carried in procession through the church and placed in front of the altar.

10. If the cross is carried in procession, the following SENTENCE and RESPONSE is sung or said three times, the first time as the procession begins, the second time as the procession is halfway to the altar, the third time as the procession ends at the altar. When there is no procession, the sentence and response is simply sung or said three times in sequence.

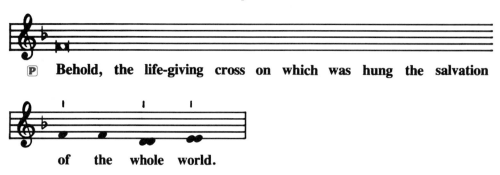

℗ Behold, the life-giving cross on which was hung the salvation of the whole world.

℃ Oh, come, let us wor - ship him.

Sit/Kneel

11. The following REPROACHES (Improperia) are chanted or said by the presiding minister or cantor, the congregation responding with the appointed hymn stanza. Instead of the hymn stanza, the VERSE appointed for Good Friday (Lutheran Worship, *page 45*) *may be sung by the choir.*

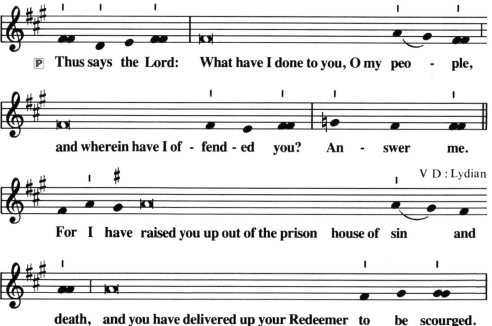

℗ Thus says the Lord: What have I done to you, O my peo - ple, and wherein have I of - fend - ed you? An - swer me.

V D : Lydian

For I have raised you up out of the prison house of sin and death, and you have delivered up your Redeemer to be scourged.

For I have redeemed you from the house of bond-age, and you have nailed your Sav - ior to the cross. O my peo - ple.

Choir or cantor

VI D : Hypolydian

Ho - ly Lord God, holy and might - y God, holy and most merciful Re-deem - er; God eternal, leave us not to bit - ter death. O Lord, have mer - cy.

🄲 "Lamb of God, Pure and Sinless," Hymn 208, st. 1.

P Thus says the Lord: What have I done to you, O my peo - ple,

and wherein have I of - fend - ed you? An - swer me.

For I have conquered all your foes, and you have given me over and

delivered me to those who per - se - cute me. For I have fed you with

my Word and refreshed you with living wa - ter, and you have given

me gall and vin - e - gar to drink. O my peo - ple.

Choir or cantor

Ho - ly Lord God, holy and might - y God, holy and most merciful Re-

deem - er; God eternal, allow us not to lose hope in the face of

death and hell. O Lord, have mer - cy.

C "Lamb of God, Pure and Sinless," Hymn 208, st. 2.

P Thus says the Lord: What have I done to you, O my peo - ple,

and wherein have I of - fend - ed you? An - swer me.

What more could have been done for my vine - yard than I have done

for it? When I looked for good grapes, why did it yield on - ly bad?

My people, is this how you thank your God? O my peo - ple.

Choir or cantor

Ho - ly Lord God, holy and might - y God, holy and most merciful Re-

deem - er; God eternal, keep us steadfast in the

true faith. O Lord, have mer - cy.

C "Sing, My Tongue," Hymn 117, st. 4.

Kneel

12. Silence is kept for meditation on the crucified Savior and redemption.

13. The HYMN, "O Dearest Jesus, What Law Have You Broken," Hymn 119, may be sung to conclude the meditation.

Stand

14. The Hymn, "The Royal Banners Forward Go," Hymn 103 or 104, is sung, either singly or combined in alternation. If the latter, the congregation may sing stanzas 1, 3, and 5 to the chorale melody (Hymn 103); and the choir, stanzas 2 and 4 to the plainsong melody (Hymn 104).

Kneel

P **We adore you, O Christ, and we bless you.**

C By your holy cross you have redeemed the world.

15. The ministers and worshipers leave in silence.

NOTES

General

▶ *The older and more primitive custom is that Holy Communion not be celebrated on Good Friday.*

▶ *This solemn service incorporates material drawn from the older services of this day, notably the Bidding Prayer, the Reproaches, and the adoration of Christ on the cross.*

▶ *It is most appropriate that this service be held in the afternoon near 3:00, the traditional hour of Jesus' death. Local circumstances, however, may dictate another hour.*

▶ *It is preferable that the altar, previously stripped of its ornaments and paraments, not be used in this service. Rather, one or more reading desks, or lecterns, may provide the focal point. If paraments are used, they should be black or scarlet.*

▶ *If offerings are brought, they are received at the entrance to the nave of the church.*

▶ *The ministers are vested simply in albs or cassocks with surplices.*

The Service in Detail

6. ▶ Appropriate settings of the St. John's Passion history—by William Byrd, Heinrich Schütz, Thomas Luis de Vittoria, Richard Hillert, and other composers—are readily available.

8. ▶ The assisting minister leads the congregation in the Bidding Prayer from a reading desk. The presiding minister may say the actual prayers either from where he is standing or from a second reading desk.

   ▶ The Bidding Prayer is in *Lutheran Worship* ("Pew Edition"), page 276.

9. ▶ A large, roughhewn wooden cross is provided. If it is to be carried in the procession ⟨10⟩, it may be placed ready in the narthex or some other convenient place. Instead of being carried in the procession, it may be placed in front of the altar before the service begins, either upright in a stand or leaning against the top of the altar. Tall, lighted candles may be placed in stands on either side of the cross.

10. ▶ The presiding minister carries the cross in the procession. The cross may be accompanied by two torchbearers.

    ▶ If feasible, the cross may be raised each time the sentence "Behold, the life-giving cross . . ." is sung or said.

15. ▶ No blessing or benediction is given to conclude the service.

GOOD FRIDAY II

1. The Divine Service on Good Friday follows a simple form. The Invocation is omitted, as well as the invitations to pray, salutations, responses, and acclamations.

2. When there is Communion, the altar is vested only with a fair linen, upon which the corporal is to be placed. The altar candles are lighted, and the cross or crucifix is covered with a plain cloth. When there is no Communion, the altar is bare of paraments, linens, and ornaments.

3. After the opening hymn the minister(s) and congregation join in the confession of sins.

Kneel/Stand

C O almighty God, merciful Father, I, a poor, miserable sinner, confess to you all my sins and iniquities with which I have ever offended you and justly deserved your punishment now and forever. But I am heartily sorry for them and sincerely repent of them, and I pray you of your boundless mercy and for the sake of the holy, innocent, bitter sufferings and death of your beloved Son, Jesus Christ, to be gracious and merciful to me, a poor sinful being.

The minister stands and pronounces the absolution.

OR **P** **Almighty God, our Maker and Redeemer, we poor sinners confess to you that we are by nature sinful and unclean and that we have sinned against you by thought, word, and deed; therefore we flee for refuge to your boundless mercy, seeking and imploring your grace for the sake of our Lord Jesus Christ.**

P & **C** O most merciful God, since you have given your only-begotten Son to die for us, have mercy on us and for his sake grant us forgiveness of all our sins; and by your Holy Spirit increase in us true knowledge

P Upon this your confession, I, as a called and ordained servant of the Word, announce the grace of God to all of you, and in the stead and by the command of my Lord Jesus Christ I forgive you all your sins in the name of the Father and of the ☩ Son and of the Holy Spirit.

of your will and true obedience to your Word, to the end that by your grace we may come to everlasting life; through Jesus Christ, our Lord. Amen

The minister stands and pronounces the declaration of grace.

P Almighty God, our heavenly Father, has had mercy on us and has given his only Son to die for us and for his sake forgives us all our sins. To those who believe on his name he gives power to become the children of God and has promised them his Holy Spirit. He that believes and is baptized shall be saved. Grant this, Lord, to us all.

C Amen

Stand

4. The INTROIT OF THE DAY is sung.

5. The KYRIE is sung. Hymn 209, "Kyrie, God Father," may be used as an alternate.

6. The COLLECT OF THE DAY is chanted or said.

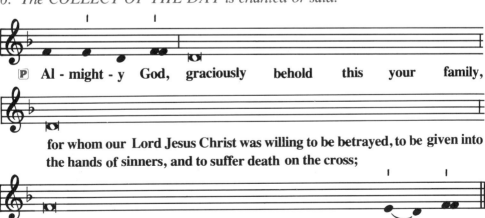

P Al - might - y God, graciously behold this your family,

for whom our Lord Jesus Christ was willing to be betrayed, to be given into the hands of sinners, and to suffer death on the cross;

who now lives and reigns with you and the Holy Spirit, one God, now and for - ev - er. (31)

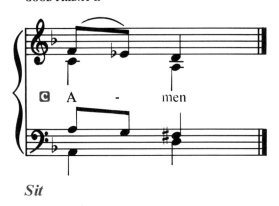

C A - men

Sit

7. The OLD TESTAMENT READING is announced and read.

Ⓐ **The Old Testament Reading for Good Friday is from the** _____
chapter of _____ **.**

8. The GRADUAL FOR THE SEASON or the appointed PSALM is sung or said.

9. The EPISTLE is announced and read.

Ⓐ **The Epistle is from the** _____ **chapter of** _____ **.**

10. The following REPROACHES (Improperia) are chanted or said by the pastor or cantor, the congregation responding with the appointed hymn stanza. Instead of the hymn stanza, the VERSE appointed for Good Friday (Lutheran Worship, *page 45*) *may be sung by the choir.*

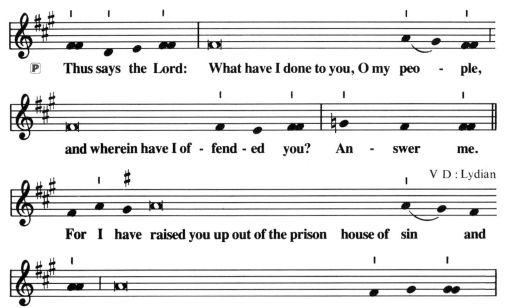

Ⓟ **Thus says the Lord: What have I done to you, O my peo - ple,**

and wherein have I of - fend - ed you? An - swer me.

V D : Lydian

For I have raised you up out of the prison house of sin and

death, and you have delivered up your Redeemer to be scourged.

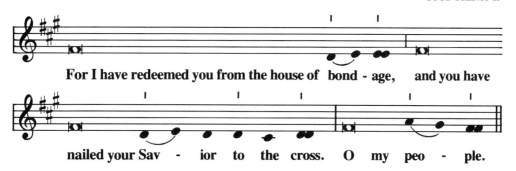

For I have redeemed you from the house of bond - age, and you have nailed your Sav - ior to the cross. O my peo - ple.

Choir or cantor

VI D : Hypolydian

Ho - ly Lord God, holy and might - y God, holy and most merciful Re- deem - er; God eternal, leave us not to bit - ter death. O Lord, have mer - cy.

Ⓒ "Lamb of God, Pure and Sinless," Hymn 208, st. 1.

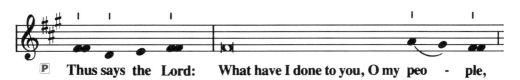

Ⓟ Thus says the Lord: What have I done to you, O my peo - ple,

and wherein have I of - fend - ed you? An - swer me.

For I have conquered all your foes, and you have given me over and

delivered me to those who per - se - cute me. For I have fed you with

my Word and refreshed you with living wa - ter, and you have given

me gall and vin - e - gar to drink. O my peo - ple.

Choir or cantor

Ho - ly Lord God, holy and might - y God, holy and most merciful Re-

deem - er; God eternal, allow us not to lose hope in the face of

death and hell. O Lord, have mer - cy.

C "Lamb of God, Pure and Sinless," Hymn 208, st. 2.

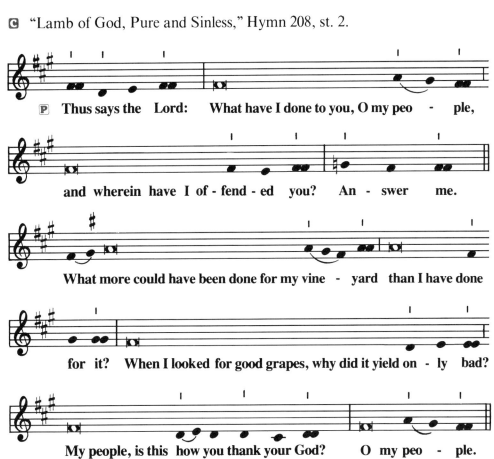

P Thus says the Lord: What have I done to you, O my peo - ple,

and wherein have I of - fend - ed you? An - swer me.

What more could have been done for my vine - yard than I have done

for it? When I looked for good grapes, why did it yield on - ly bad?

My people, is this how you thank your God? O my peo - ple.

Choir or cantor

Ho - ly Lord God, holy and might - y God, holy and most merciful Re-

deem - er; God eternal, keep us steadfast in the

true faith. O Lord, have mer - cy.

🄲 "Lamb of God, Pure and Sinless," Hymn 208, st. 3.

11. The HOLY GOSPEL is announced.

🄿 **The Passion of Our Lord Jesus Christ according to St. John, the eighteenth and nineteenth chapters.**

12. The HOLY GOSPEL is read. The congregation intersperses sections of the reading with the appointed hymn stanzas.

🄿 **John 18:1-11**

🄲 "Jesus, I Will Ponder Now," Hymn 109, st. 1.

🄿 **John 18:12-27**

🄲 "O Sacred Head, Now Wounded," Hymn 113, st. 1.

🄿 **John 18:28-40**

🄲 "O Sacred Head, Now Wounded," Hymn 113, st. 2.

🄿 **John 19:1-15**

🄲 "O Sacred Head, Now Wounded," Hymn 113, st. 3.

P John 19:16-24

C "O Sacred Head, Now Wounded," Hymn 113, st. 4.

P John 19:25-30

C "O Sacred Head, Now Wounded," Hymn 113, st. 5.

P John 19:31-37

C "O Sacred Head, Now Wounded," Hymn 113, st. 6.

OR

P **The Passion of Our Lord Jesus Christ Drawn from the Four Gospels, Part V: Calvary.**

13. The HOLY GOSPEL is read (pages 30-33). It may be presented by several readers.

14. The SERMON

15. The OFFERING is received. When there is Communion, the Lord's Table is prepared.

Stand/Kneel

16. The BIDDING PRAYER is said.

A Let us pray for the whole Church, that our Lord God would defend her against all the assaults and temptations of the adversary and keep her perpetually on the true foundation, Jesus Christ:

P Almighty and everlasting God, since you have revealed your glory to all nations in Jesus Christ and in the Word of his truth, keep, we ask you, in safety the works of your mercy so that your Church, spread throughout all nations, may be defended against the adversary and may serve you in true faith and persevere in the confession of your name; through Jesus Christ, our Lord. (192)

C Amen

65

Ⓐ Let us pray for all the ministers of the Word and for all the people of God:

Ⓟ Almighty and everlasting God, by whose Spirit the whole body of the Church is governed and sanctified, receive the supplications and prayers which we offer before you for all your servants in your holy Church that every member of the same may truly serve you; through Jesus Christ, our Lord. (193)

Ⓒ Amen

Ⓐ Let us pray for our catechumens, that our Lord God would open their hearts and the door of his mercy that, having received the remission of all their sins by the washing of regeneration, they may be mindful of their Baptism and throughout their lives remain faithful to Christ Jesus, our Lord:

Ⓟ Almighty God and Father, because you always grant growth to your Church, increase the faith and understanding of our catechumens that, recalling the new birth by the water of Holy Baptism, they may forever continue in the family of those whom you adopt as your sons and daughters; through Jesus Christ, our Lord. (194)

Ⓒ Amen

Ⓐ Let us pray for all in authority that we may lead a quiet and peaceable life in all godliness and honesty:

Ⓟ O merciful Father in heaven, because you hold in your hand all the might of man and because you have ordained, for the punishment of evildoers and for the praise of those who do well, all the powers that exist in all the nations of the world, we humbly pray you graciously to regard your servants,

(USA) especially the President and Congress of the United States, the Governor of this State (Commonwealth), and all those who make, administer, and judge our laws

(Canada) especially Her (His) Gracious Majesty, the Queen (King); the Governor General; the Prime Minister and the Parliament; the Governments of this Province and all who have authority over us

that all who receive the sword as your ministers may bear it according to your Word; through Jesus Christ, our Lord. (195)

Ⓒ Amen

Ⓐ Let us pray our Lord God Almighty that he would deliver the world from disease, ward off famine, set free those in bondage, grant health to the sick and a safe journey to all who travel:

℗ Almighty and everlasting God, the consolation of the sorrowful and the strength of those who labor, may the prayers of those who in any tribulation or distress cry to you graciously come before you, so that in all their necessities they may rejoice in your manifold help and comfort; through Jesus Christ, our Lord. (196)

🄲 Amen

🄰 Let us pray for all who are outside the Church, that our Lord God would be pleased to deliver them from their error, call them to faith in the true and living God and his only Son, Jesus Christ, our Lord, and gather them into his family, the Church:

℗ Almighty and everlasting God, because you seek not the death but the life of all, hear our prayers for all who have no right knowledge of you, free them from their error, and for the glory of your name bring them into the fellowship of your holy Church; through Jesus Christ, our Lord. (197)

🄲 Amen

🄰 Let us pray for our enemies, that God would remember them in mercy and graciously grant them such things as are both needful for them and profitable to their salvation:

℗ O almighty, everlasting God, through your only Son, our blessed Lord, you have commanded us to love our enemies, to do good to those who hate us, and to pray for those who persecute us. We therefore earnestly implore you that by your gracious visitation all our enemies may be led to true repentance and may have the same love and be of one accord and one mind and heart with us and with your whole Church; through Jesus Christ, our Lord. (198)

🄲 Amen

🄰 Let us pray for the fruits of the earth, that God would send down his blessing upon them and graciously dispose our hearts to enjoy them according to his own goodwill:

℗ O Lord, Father Almighty, by your Word you created and you still continue to bless and uphold all things. We pray you so to reveal to us your Word, our Lord Jesus Christ, that he may dwell in our hearts and we may by your grace be made ready to receive your blessing on all the fruits of the earth and those things that pertain to our bodily need; through Jesus Christ, our Lord. (199)

C Amen

A Finally let us pray for all those things for which our Lord would have us ask, saying:

C Our Father who art in heaven,	OR	C Our Father in heaven,
hallowed be thy name,		hallowed be your name,
thy kingdom come,		your kingdom come,
thy will be done		your will be done
on earth as it is in heaven.		on earth as in heaven.
Give us this day our daily bread:		Give us today our daily bread.
and forgive us our trespasses		Forgive us our sins
as we forgive those		as we forgive those
who trespass against us;		who sin against us.
and lead us not into temptation.		Lead us not into temptation,
but deliver us from evil.		but deliver us from evil.
For thine is the kingdom		For the kingdom, the power,
and the power and the glory		and the glory are yours
forever and ever. Amen		now and forever. Amen

Stand

17. When there is no Communion, the service concludes with the Benediction ⟨22⟩. ▶

18. The WORDS OF INSTITUTION are chanted or said.

P **Our Lord Je - sus Christ, on the night when he was be - trayed, took**

bread, and when he had giv - en thanks, he broke it and gave it to the dis -

68

ci - ples and said: Take, eat; this is my ✠ bod - y, which is giv - en

for you. This do in re - mem-brance of me. In the same way al -

so he took the cup after sup - per, and when he had giv - en thanks,

he gave it to them, say - ing: Drink of it, all of you; this is my ✠ blood of the

new tes - ta - ment, which is shed for you for the for-give-ness of sins.

This do, as often as you drink it, in re - mem - brance of me.

19. The presiding minister, holding the Communion vessels in his hands and facing the congregation, says:

P **Come and receive the body and blood of the Lamb of God, who takes away the sin of the world.**

Sit

20. During the DISTRIBUTION the congregation sings "Upon the Cross Extended," Hymn 120 or 121, singly or in alternation with the choir. Other appropriate hymns may be sung instead.

Stand

21. One of the following POST-COMMUNION COLLECTS is chanted or said.

Ⓐ Let us pray to the Lord.

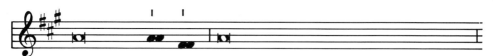

Ⓐ O God, the Fa - ther,   the fountain and source of all goodness,
who in loving-kindness sent your only-
begotten Son into the flesh, we thank
you that for his sake you have given
us pardon and peace in this sacrament,

and we ask you not to forsake your children but always to rule our
hearts and minds by your Holy Spirit that we may be enabled to serve
you constantly;

through Jesus Christ, your Son, our Lord, who lives and
reigns with you and the Holy Spirit, one God, now and for - ev - er. (164)

OR

Ⓐ We give thanks to you, al - might - y God,   that you have refreshed us
through this salutary gift,

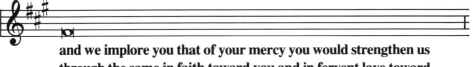

and we implore you that of your mercy you would strengthen us
through the same in faith toward you and in fervent love toward
one another;

through Jesus Christ, your Son, our Lord, who lives and
reigns with you and the Holy Spirit, one God, now and for - ev - er. (163)

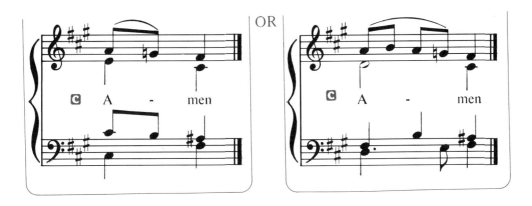

OR

22. ▶ *The BENEDICTION is chanted or said.*

P The Lord bless you and keep you. The Lord make his face shine on you and be gra-cious to you. The Lord lift up his countenance on you and ☩ give you peace.

C A-men, a-men, a-men

NOTES

General

▶ *This service, essentially the Divine Service, incorporates some material from the early services of Good Friday. It is used with or without Holy Communion.*

▶ *Consult the notes on Good Friday I, page 57.*

The Service in Detail

11. ▶ Instead of announcing and reading ⟨12⟩ the Holy Gospel, the choir may sing one of the numerous appropriate settings of St. John's Passion history available by William Byrd, Heinrich Schütz, Thomas Luis de Vittoria, Richard Hillert, and other composers.

VIGIL OF EASTER

CELEBRATION OF THE RESURRECTION OF OUR LORD AND OUR BAPTISM

Service of Light

1. The congregation gathers in some convenient place outside the nave of the church. All are given candles, later to be lighted from the paschal candle.

Stand

2. In the semidarkness a fire is kindled. The pastor says:

P **In the name of the Father and of the ☩ Son and of the Holy Spirit.**

C Amen

3. The pastor continues with these or similar words:

P **Beloved in the Lord, on this most holy night, in which our Lord Jesus passed over from death to life, we are gathered here in vigil and prayer. This is the Passover of the Lord in which, by hearing his Word and celebrating his sacraments, we share in his victory over death.**

P **Let us pray.**

O God, you are like a refiner's fire, and your Spirit enkindles the hearts of your faithful people with the fire of your love. Bless, we implore you, this new flame and those who keep this joyful Easter festival that, burning with desire for life with you, we may be found rightly prepared to share in the Feast of Light which has no end;

through Jesus Christ, your Son, our Lord, who lives and reigns with you and the Holy Spirit, one God, now and forever. ⟨252⟩

🅲 Amen

4. An assisting minister, holding the paschal candle, steps forward. The pastor traces the cross and the Greek letters Alpha and Omega upon it, saying:

🅿 **Christ Jesus, the same yesterday, today, and forever, the beginning and the ending, the Alpha and Omega.**

5. He traces the year upon the candle, saying:

🅿 **His are time and eternity; his are the glory and dominion, now and forever.**

6. He puts the five wax nails into the candle, saying:

🅿 **By his wounds we have healing both now and forever. Amen**

7. Then, lighting the candle from the newly kindled fire, he says:

🅿 **May the light of Christ, who is risen in glory from the dead, scatter all the darkness of our hearts and minds.**

🅿 **Let us pray.**

Almighty and most merciful God, pour out on us your abundant blessing that all who in true faith share this night in joyful celebration of the resurrection of our Lord Jesus Christ from the dead may be filled with your heavenly benediction. Once we were in darkness, but now we are in the Light, even Jesus Christ, our Lord. ⟨253⟩

🅲 Amen

8. All light their candles from the paschal candle. Then, the paschal candle held aloft by the assisting minister, all follow the candle bearer in procession into the darkened church.

9. As the procession is begun, the bearer of the paschal candle stops and chants:

🅰 The light of Christ.

C   Thanks be   to   God.

10. As the procession is halfway to the altar, the candle bearer chants for the second time:

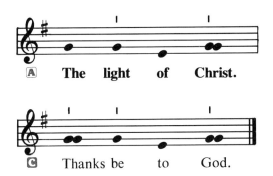

A   **The   light   of   Christ.**

C   Thanks be   to   God.

11. When the candle bearer arrives before the altar, he turns to face the congregation. The pastor and other assisting ministers proceed to the baptismal font. When all have reached their places, the candle bearer lifts the candle high and chants the third time:

A   **The   light   of   Christ.**

C   Thanks be   to   God.

12. After placing the paschal candle in its stand, the assisting minister moves to the baptismal font, turns to face the people, and begins to chant the EASTER PROCLAMATION (Exsultet).

III d: Phrygian

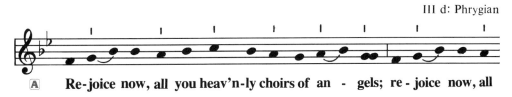

A   **Re-joice now, all you heav'n-ly choirs of an - gels; re-joice now, all**

75

cre-a - tion; sound forth, trum-pet of sal-va - tion, and pro-claim

the tri - umph of our King. Re - joice too, all the earth,

in the radiance of the light now poured up - on you

and made brilliant by the brightness of the ev - er-last-ing King;

know that the an - cient dark - ness has been for-ev -

er ban - ished. Re - joice, O Church of Christ, clothed in the

bright ness of this light; let all this house of God ring out with re -

joic ing, with the prais-es of all God's faith-ful peo - ple.

13. The pastor, standing before the font, continues the Easter Proclamation by chanting or saying:

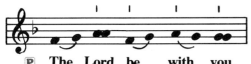

77

It is truly good, right, and sal - u - tar - y that we

should at all times and in all plac - es, with all our heart and mind and

voice, praise you, O Lord, Holy Father, almighty ev - er -

last - ing God, and your only - be - got - ten Son, Je -

sus Christ. For he is the very Pas - chal Lamb who offered

himself for the sin of the world, who has cleansed us by the

shed - ding of his pre - cious blood. This is the

night when you brought our fathers, the chil - dren of Is - ra - el,

out of bondage in Egypt and led them through the Red Sea on

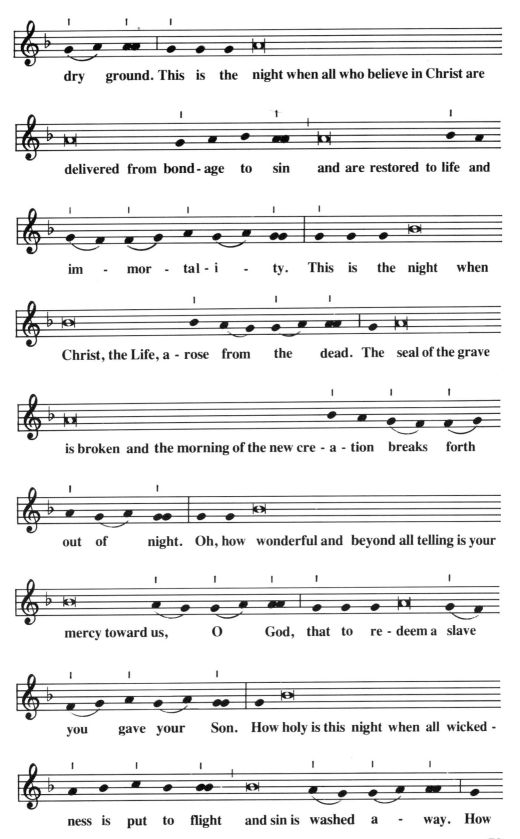

dry ground. This is the night when all who believe in Christ are

delivered from bond - age to sin and are restored to life and

im - mor - tal - i - ty. This is the night when

Christ, the Life, a - rose from the dead. The seal of the grave

is broken and the morning of the new cre - a - tion breaks forth

out of night. Oh, how wonderful and beyond all telling is your

mercy toward us, O God, that to re - deem a slave

you gave your Son. How holy is this night when all wicked -

ness is put to flight and sin is washed a - way. How

holy is this night when innocence is re - stored to the fall - en

and joy is giv - en to those down - cast. How blessed

is this night when man is reconciled to God in Christ. Ho - ly

Father, accept now the evening sacrifices of our thanks - giv - ing

and praise. Let Christ, the true light and morning star, shine in

our hearts, he who gives light to all cre - a - tion, who

lives and reigns with you and the Ho - ly Spir - it, one God,

now and for - ev - er.

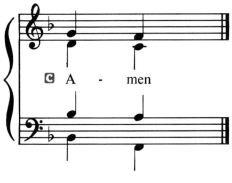

Sit

Service of Readings

14. The members of the congregation extinguish their candles. A few lights in the nave may be turned on.

15. The assisting minister goes to a lectern, while the pastor says:

P **In this most holy night our Savior, Christ, the Lord, broke the power of death and by his resurrection brought life and salvation to all creation. Let us praise the Lord, for he truly keeps his Word. The sun of righteousness has dawned upon us who have sat in darkness and in the shadow of death.**

16. The assisting minister reads one or more of the following portions of Holy Scripture; Exodus 14:10—15:1 is always read. Each reading may be followed by a brief silence for reflection on God's Word. The pastor reads the appointed Collect. The congregation may sit throughout or may stand or kneel for each collect.

The Creation
Genesis 1:1—2:2

P **Let us pray.**

Almighty God, you most wonderfully created human nature and yet more wonderfully redeemed it. Grant that in your mercy we may be conformed to the image of him who came to share our humanity, your Son Jesus Christ, our Lord. ‹254›

C Amen

The Flood
Genesis 7:1-5, 11-18; 8:6-18; 9:8-13

P Let us pray.

O Lord, whose wrath burned for the evil of men, you kill and bring again to life according to your own purpose; you brought the flood on a wicked and perverse generation yet saved faithful Noah and his family. Open your eyes to behold in mercy your Church that in it your work of mercy may come to its fullness and that the ends of the earth may know your salvation; through Jesus Christ, our Lord.⟨255⟩

C Amen

Abraham's Sacrifice of Isaac
Genesis 22:1-18

P Let us pray.

O God, you promised to faithful Abraham that he would be the father of many peoples, and in the Easter Sacrament of Holy Baptism you raised up for yourself one people. Grant to your Church a hearty trust in all your promises; through Jesus Christ, our Lord. ⟨256⟩

C Amen

Israel's Deliverance at the Red Sea
Exodus 14:10—15:1

P Let us pray.

O God, you once delivered your people Israel from bondage under Pharaoh and led them in safety through the Red Sea, thereby giving us a picture of our Baptism. Grant that we may ever be faithful to your baptismal promise, live in its grace, and show forth to all people your desire that all should be made the children of Abraham; through Jesus Christ, our Lord. ⟨257⟩

C Amen

Salvation Offered Freely to All
Isaiah 55:1-11

P Let us pray.

Almighty God, by the power of your Word all things were created and are sustained; you send forth your Spirit to renew your creation. Grant now the water of life to all who thirst for you that they may bring forth abundant fruit in your glorious kingdom; through Jesus Christ, our Lord. ⟨258⟩

C Amen

A New Heart and a New Spirit
Ezekiel 36:24-28

P Let us pray.

Almighty and everlasting God, in the miracle of Easter you raised your Son for our justification. Grant that all who are brought to new birth and newness of life in the fellowship of the body of Christ may show forth in their lives what they confess with their lips; through Jesus Christ, our Lord. ⟨259⟩

C Amen

Faith Strained but Victorious
Job 19:20-27

P Let us pray.

Almighty God, who in the Passover of your Son brought us out of sin into righteousness and out of death to life, grant to all whom you have sealed by the Holy Spirit with the sign of Christ's sacrifice both the will and the strength to speak your Word in all the world; through Jesus Christ, our Lord. ⟨260⟩

C Amen

The Gathering of God's People
Zephaniah 3:12-20

P Let us pray.

Look in mercy, O Lord, upon your faithful people, and by Word and Spirit bring to completion that good work which you have begun in them. Let all the world see and know that what has been cast down is raised up, what has grown old is made new, and that the work you have begun in us is being brought to its joyful fulfillment in the day of our Lord Jesus Christ; who lives and reigns with you and the Holy Spirit, one God, now and forever. ⟨261⟩

C Amen

17. The BENEDICITE OMNIA OPERA (Lutheran Worship, *Canticles and Chants, No. 9) may be sung.*

18. The assisting minister carries the paschal candle to the font and places it in its stand.

Service of Holy Baptism

Sit

19. The pastor addresses the congregation:

℗ On this holiest of nights the whole Church of our Lord Jesus Christ recalls his death and burial, rejoicing with great joy in the Gospel of his glorious and mighty resurrection from the dead. The apostle Paul says: "[Do you not know] that all of us who were baptized into Christ Jesus were baptized into his death? We were therefore buried with him through baptism into death in order that, just as Christ was raised from the dead through the glory of the Father, we too may live a new life. If we have been united with him in his death, we will certainly also be united with him in his resurrection. For we know that our old self was crucified with him so that the body of sin might be rendered powerless, that we should no longer be slaves to sin—because anyone who has died has been freed from sin. Now if we died with Christ, we believe that we will also live with him. For we know that since Christ was raised from the dead, he cannot die again; death no longer has mastery over him. The death he died, he died to sin once for all; but the life he lives, he lives to God. In the same way, count yourselves dead to sin but alive to God in Christ Jesus." (Rom. 6:3-11)

20. The congregation sings "All Who Believe and Are Baptized," Hymn 225.

21. If there are candidates for Holy Baptism, they gather at the font with their sponsors and families and are baptized according to the Church's usual order.

Stand

22. The members of the congregation join in the renunciation and in the profession of faith as a remembrance of their Baptism.

℗ In Holy Baptism we are forgiven our sins and granted a new life in Christ, our Lord. We solemnly renounce the devil and all his works and all his ways; we confess the gift of faith in God the Father, the Son, and the Holy Spirit.

84

I ask you anew: Do you renounce the devil and all his works and all his ways?

C I do renounce them.

P **Do you believe in God, the Father Almighty?**

C Yes, I believe in God, the Father Almighty,
      maker of heaven and earth.

P **Do you believe in Jesus Christ, his only Son?**

C Yes, I believe in Jesus Christ, his only Son, our Lord,
      who was conceived by the Holy Spirit,
      born of the virgin Mary,
      suffered under Pontius Pilate,
      was crucified, died and was buried.
      He descended into hell.
      The third day he rose again from the dead.
      He ascended into heaven
         and sits at the right hand of God
         the Father Almighty.
      From thence he will come to judge the living and the dead.

P **Do you believe in the Holy Spirit?**

C Yes, I believe in the Holy Spirit,
      the holy Christian Church,*
      the communion of saints,
      the forgiveness of sins,
      the resurrection of the body,
      and the life everlasting.

* The ancient text: the holy catholic Church

P **Is it your earnest purpose to continue steadfast in this faith and in the promise of your Baptism and, as a member of the Church, to be diligent in the use of the means of grace and prayer?**

C Yes, with the help of God.

23. The pastor blesses the congregation.

P **Almighty God, the Father of our Lord Jesus Christ, who has given you the new birth of water and of the Spirit and has forgiven you all your sins, strengthen you with his grace to life everlasting.**

C Amen

Service of Holy Communion

24. When there is no Communion, the service continues at rubric 28. ▶

Stand

25. The altar candles may now be lighted from the paschal candle. The lights in the church are turned on, the bells may be rung, and the pastor says:

P **Alleluia. Christ is risen.**

C The Lord is risen indeed. Alleluia.

26. "Glory to God in the highest" is intoned by the assisting minister, the congregation continuing the Hymn of Praise (Gloria in Excelsis).

27. The Holy Communion continues with the Collect of the Day in the Divine Service. The Old Testament Reading and the Creed may be omitted.

28. ▶When there is no Communion, the Vigil concludes as follows.

29. The EASTER GOSPEL is announced and read.

P **The Holy Gospel according to St. Mark, the 16th chapter.**

C Glo-ry to you, O Lord.

P **When the Sabbath was over, Mary Magdalene, Mary the mother of James, and Salome bought spices so that they might go to anoint Jesus' body. Very early on the first day of the week, just after sunrise, they were on their way to the tomb and they asked each other, "Who will roll the stone** away from the entrance of the tomb?" But when they looked up, they saw that the stone, which was very large, had been rolled away. As they entered the tomb, they saw a young man dressed in a white robe sitting on the right side, and they were alarmed. "Don't be alarmed," he said. "You are looking for Jesus the Nazarene, who was crucified. He has risen! He is not here. See the place where they laid him. But go, tell his disciples and Peter, 'He is going ahead of you into Galilee. There you will see him, just as he told you.' " Trembling and bewildered, the women went out and fled from the tomb. They said nothing to anyone, because they were afraid. (Mark 16:1-8)

30. After the reading the pastor says:

Ⓟ This is the Gospel of the Lord.

Ⓒ Praise to you, O Christ.

31. The pastor continues:

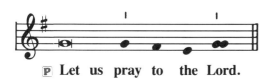

Ⓟ Let us pray to the Lord.

Ⓟ O God, who made this most holy night to shine with the glory of the resurrection of our Lord,

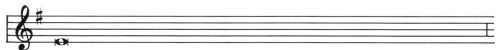

preserve in all your people the spirit of adoption which you have given that, made alive in body and soul, they may serve you purely;

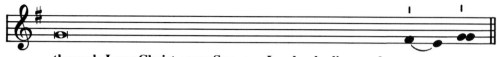

through Jesus Christ, your Son, our Lord, who lives and
reigns with you and the Holy Spirit, one God, now and for - ev - er. (32)

A - men

32. *The BENEDICAMUS and the BLESSING conclude the Vigil.*

Bless we the Lord.

Thanks be to God.

The almighty and mer - ci - ful Lord, the Fa - ther, the Son,

and the Ho - ly Spir - it, bless and pre - serve you.

A - men

NOTES

General

▶ *What early began simply as a lengthy vigil consisting of prayers, supplications, and reading of the prophets, of the Gospel, and of psalms gradually developed into the Vigil of Easter, a service of four parts: the Service of Light, the Service of Readings, the Service of Holy Baptism, and the Service of Holy Communion.*

▶ *This vigil—the Great Vigil, "the mother of all vigils"—may be variously used: it may constitute the first service of Easter Day, just before dawn; the first three parts may be celebrated early Easter Eve, reserving the Service of Holy Communion for Easter morning; the first part may be celebrated prior to the (first) Divine Service on Easter morning. In this instance "Christ Is Arisen," Hymn 124, or another appropriate hymn may replace the Easter Proclamation ⟨12⟩ and ⟨13⟩.*

▶ *It is customary that, from Easter Day on, the paschal candle be positioned near the altar and lighted at all services until the Ascension of Our Lord or the Day of Pentecost.*

Preparation for the Service

▶ *The church is made ready for Easter with white or gold paraments and flowers. Ornaments are returned to the altar and elsewhere. Lighting in the church for the first three parts may be so managed that the paraments, flowers, and ornaments are not too obvious.*

▶ *For the Holy Communion, the usual preparations are made. If there are candidates for Holy Baptism, the font is filled for the third part of the vigil.*

▶ *The stand for the paschal candle may be centrally placed in the approach to the altar.*

The Service in Detail

2. ▶ A large fire may be built on the ground or in a large brazier. If this is not feasible, fire may be struck with flint and steel or in some other convenient manner.

8. ▶ The procession is in the following order: paschal candle carried by the assisting minister, congregation, choir, and the ministers.

   ▶ The route of the procession may be around the outside of the church building, around the interior of the church, or directly down the center aisle of the nave.

12. ▶ The biblical gesture of hands uplifted and outstretched is appropriate for the assisting minister and the pastor during the chanting of the Easter Proclamation ⟨12⟩ and ⟨13⟩. To convey the spirit of exultation, it is preferable that the entire Easter Proclamation be chanted.

14. ▶ The Service of Readings should continue in semidarkness, but sufficient light from candles or other sources must be provided at the lectern, or reading desk, and for the pastor.

16. ▶ Several assisting ministers may share in the reading of portions of Holy Scripture.

23. ▶ If the Service of Holy Baptism concludes the vigil, the people leave the church in silence after this blessing.

25. ▶ The sentence "Alleluia. Christ is risen" and its response marks the dramatic transition from darkness to light.

26. ▶ Trumpets and other instruments may augment the organ in the Gloria in Excelsis.

27. ▶ The vigil Communion should remain relatively simple in form and style. The more solemn celebration of Holy Communion is reserved for the Divine Service later on Easter morning.

   ▶ It is appropriate to sing Easter hymns during the distribution.

HOLY BAPTISM

---

1. A hymn may be sung. The candidate/candidates and sponsors (and family/families) gather with the pastor in the nave.

P **In the name of the Father and of the ✠ Son and of the Holy Spirit.**

C Amen

2. The pastor addresses the baptismal group and the congregation:

P **Our Lord commanded Baptism, saying to his disciples in the last chapter of Matthew: "All authority in heaven and on earth has been given to me. Therefore go and make disciples of all nations, baptizing them in the name of the Father and of the Son and of the Holy Spirit and teaching them to obey everything I have commanded you. And surely I will be with you always, to the very end of the age." The holy apostles of the Lord have written: "The promise is for you and your children," and: "Baptism now saves you."**

We also learn from the Word of God that we all are conceived and born sinful and are in need of forgiveness. We would be lost forever unless delivered from sin, death, and everlasting condemnation. But the Father of all mercy and grace has sent his Son Jesus Christ, who atoned for the sin of the whole world that whoever believes in him shall not perish but have eternal life.

3. The pastor turns to the candidate/candidates to be baptized.

P **Receive the sign of the holy cross both upon your forehead ✠ and upon your heart ✠ to mark you as one redeemed by Christ the crucified.**

4. For the baptism of infants and young children the pastor says:

P Hear how our Lord Jesus Christ has opened the kingdom of God to little children.

People were bringing little children to Jesus to have him touch them, but the disciples rebuked them. When Jesus saw this, he was indignant. He said to them, "Let the little children come to me, and do not hinder them, for the kingdom of God belongs to such as these. I tell you the truth, anyone who will not receive the kingdom of God like a little child will never enter it."

P This is the Gospel of the Lord.

C Praise to you, O Christ.

OR

5. For the baptism of older children and adults the pastor says:

P Hear the word of our Savior Jesus Christ telling of the new birth by water and the Spirit.
"I tell you the truth, unless a man is born of water and the Spirit, he cannot enter the kingdom of God. Flesh gives birth to flesh, but the Spirit gives birth to spirit."

P This is the Gospel of the Lord.

C Praise to you, O Christ.

6. For the baptism of infants and young children the pastor addresses the sponsors:

P It is your task as sponsors to confess with the whole Church the faith in our God, Father, Son, and Holy Spirit, in whose name this child is to be baptized.

After this child has been baptized you are at all times to remember ___him/her___ in your prayers, put ___him/her___ in mind of ___his/her___ Baptism, and, as much as in you lies, give your counsel and aid, especially if ___he/she___ should lose ___his/her___ parents, that ___he/she___ be brought up in the true knowledge and worship of God and be taught the Ten Commandments, the Creed, and the Lord's Prayer; and that, as ___he/she___ grows in years, you place in ___his/her___ hands the Holy

Scriptures, bring ___him/her___ to the services of God's house, and provide for ___his/her___ further instruction in the Christian faith, that ___he/she___ come to the Sacrament of Christ's Body and Blood and thus, abiding in ___his/her___ baptismal grace and in communion with the Church, ___he/she___ may grow up to lead a godly life to the praise and honor of Jesus Christ.

This, then, you intend gladly and willingly to do?

℟ Yes.

℘ God enable you both to will and to do this faithful and loving work and with his grace fulfill what we are unable to do.

℘ In order to implore the blessing of our Lord Jesus Christ upon the gathering of this child into the family of our Father, let us with all the family pray the prayer he gave us.

7. The pastor lays his hand upon the head of the child. The congregation joins in praying:

ℭ Our Father who art in heaven,
    hallowed be thy name,
    thy kingdom come,
    thy will be done
        on earth as it is in heaven.
Give us this day our daily bread;
and forgive us our trespasses
    as we forgive those
        who trespass against us;
and lead us not into temptation,
    but deliver us from evil.
For thine is the kingdom
    and the power and the glory
    forever and ever. Amen
	OR	ℭ Our Father in heaven,
		    hallowed be your name,
		    your kingdom come,
		    your will be done
		        on earth as in heaven.
		Give us today our daily bread.
		Forgive us our sins
		    as we forgive those
		        who sin against us.
		Lead us not into temptation,
		    but deliver us from evil.
		For the kingdom, the power,
		    and the glory are yours
		    now and forever. Amen

℘ The Lord preserve your coming in and your going out from this time forth and even forevermore.

ℭ Amen

8. The baptismal group gathers at the font.

9. For the baptism of infants and young children the pastor says:

P **Because this child cannot answer for __himself/herself__ , we shall all, together with sponsors and parents, faithfully speak on __his/her__ behalf in testimony of the forgiveness of sin and the birth of the life of faith which God our Father bestows in and through Baptism.**

OR

10. For the baptism of older children and adults the pastor says:

P **Because you have been called by the Gospel and instructed in the faith, it is right and good that you should now confess with the Church what God works in and through Baptism.**

P **Do you renounce the devil and all his works and all his ways?**

C I do renounce them.

P **Do you believe in God, the Father Almighty?**

C Yes, I believe in God, the Father Almighty,
maker of heaven and earth.

P **Do you believe in Jesus Christ, his only Son?**

C Yes, I believe in Jesus Christ, his only Son, our Lord,
who was conceived by the Holy Spirit,
born of the virgin Mary,
suffered under Pontius Pilate,
was crucified, died and was buried.
He descended into hell.
The third day he rose again from the dead.
He ascended into heaven
and sits at the right hand of God
the Father Almighty.
From thence he will come to judge the living and the dead.

P **Do you believe in the Holy Spirit?**

C Yes, I believe in the Holy Spirit,
    the holy Christian Church,*
    the communion of saints,
    the forgiveness of sins,
    the resurrection of the body,
    and the life everlasting.

* The ancient text: the holy catholic Church

11. For the baptism of infants and young children the pastor may address the parents:

P **Who brings this child to be baptized?**

R We do.

P **How is this child to be named?**

R _____name_____

OR

12. For the baptism of older children and adults the pastor may address the candidate:

P **Do you wish to be baptized into this Christian faith?**

R I do.

P **How are you named?**

R _____name_____

13. The pastor pours water three times on the head of the candidate, saying:

P _____name_____ , **I baptize you in the name of the Father and of the Son and of the Holy Spirit ✠.**

C Amen

14. The pastor lays his hand upon the one baptized and gives this blessing:

P **Almighty God, the Father of our Lord Jesus Christ, who has given you the new birth of water and of the Spirit and has forgiven you all your sins, strengthen you with his grace to life everlasting. Peace be with you.**

C Amen

15. A white garment may be put upon the one baptized.

P **Receive this white garment to show that Christ has taken away and borne your sin and put upon you his perfect righteousness. So shall you in faith ever stand before him.**

16. A baptismal candle may be lighted from the paschal or altar candle. In giving the candle, the pastor says:

P **Receive this burning light. Live always by the light of Christ, and be ever watchful for his coming that you may meet him with joy and enter with him to the marriage feast of the Lamb in his kingdom, which shall have no end.**

17. The baptismal group gathers before the altar.

P **Let us pray.**

Almighty and merciful God and Father, we thank and praise you that you graciously preserve and enlarge your family and have granted _____name_____ the new birth in Holy Baptism and made __him/her__ a member of your Son, our Lord Jesus Christ, and an heir of your heavenly kingdom. We humbly implore you that, as __he/she__ has now become your child, you would keep __him/her__ in __his/her__ baptismal grace that according to all your good pleasure __he/she__ may faithfully grow to lead a godly life to the praise and honor of your holy name and finally with all your saints obtain the promised inheritance in heaven; through Jesus Christ, our Lord. (169)

C Amen

18. When infants and young children are baptized, this prayer may also be said.

P **Lord and giver of life, look with kindness upon the father(s) and mother(s) of __this child/these children__ and upon all our parents. Let them ever rejoice in the gift you have given them. Enable them to be teachers and examples of righteousness for their children. Strengthen them in their own Baptism so that they may share**

eternally with their children the salvation you have given them; through Jesus Christ, our Lord. (170)

🅲 Amen

19. The baptismal group may turn toward the congregation; a representative of the congregation may say:

Through Baptism God has added _____name(s)_____ to his own people to declare the wonderful deeds of our Savior, who has called us out of darkness into his marvelous light.

🅲 We welcome you into the Lord's family. We receive you as (a) fellow member(s) of the body of Christ, (a) child(ren) of the same heavenly Father, to work with us in his kingdom.

🅿 **And you, _____name(s)_____ , the Lord bless you in all your ways from this time forth and even forevermore.**

🅲 Amen

20. All return to their places. The service continues with the Introit, Psalm, or Entrance Hymn.

NOTES

General

▶ *This rite for the Sacrament of Holy Baptism is for use with candidates of all ages.*

▶ *Candidates for Holy Baptism are infants born to members of the congregation or those for whom members assume the responsibility of nurture and older persons who, after adequate preparation and instruction in the Christian faith, declare their faith in Jesus Christ and their desire for Baptism.*

▶ *Parents will, as a matter of course, assume responsibility for the spiritual nurture of their children baptized in infancy or as young children. It is appropriate for others to sponsor the children and share that responsibility. Sponsors (God-parents), parents, and their families accompany the infant and participate in the rite of Baptism. Sponsors should be chosen with great care. They should be practicing Christians and members of the Evangelical Lutheran Church.*

▶ *The congregation should participate in the rite as indicated in the rubrics.*

▶ *Holy Baptism should be celebrated within the chief service of the congregation. When extraordinary circumstances require Baptism at other times, a public announcement should be made at the service the Sunday following. (See also Recognition by the Church of an Emergency Baptism, page 105.)*

Preparation for the Rite

▶ *It is desirable that the baptismal font be given a prominent place within the church to symbolize the entrance into the community of faith. There should be ample space around it for the participants.*

▶ *The font should be filled with water from an ewer immediately before or after the opening hymn.*

▶ *Appropriate napkins or small towels should be laid ready.*

▶ *A baptismal shell may be used for pouring water over the candidate's head.*

▶ *After The Ascension of Our Lord, it is appropriate to move the paschal candle from its original place on the Gospel side of the altar to a place near the font. It should be lighted for all baptisms as a reminder of the relationship between the death and resurrection of our Lord and Baptism.*

The Rite in Detail

1. ▶ This rite envisions celebrating Holy Baptism within the Divine Service immediately after the opening hymn, thus supplanting, if necessary, the preparatory part of the Divine Service with its confession of sins and absolution or declaration of grace. It is therefore preferable that the opening hymn be a hymn on Holy Baptism.

   ▶ Following the Collect of the Day in the Divine Service, one of the collects for Holy Baptism, page 366, may be chanted or said.

3. ▶ Signing each candidate with the cross is a significant part of this rite, traceable to the early Church. Other uses of the sign of the cross in worship services become acknowledgments and affirmations of Baptism.

11. ▶ For the baptism of infants and young children the parents say the responses ⟨11⟩. For the baptism of children and adults they themselves say the responses ⟨12⟩. Both Christian name and surname may be used. At other places in the rite, only Christian names are used.

15. ▶ The white garment calls attention to a significant biblical image of Baptism (Galatians 3:27).

    ▶ For an infant the white garment may consist of a rectangular cloth with an opening in the center for the child's head. For older persons a simple garment in the style of a poncho may be provided.

16. ▶ When a candle is given, it may be lighted from the paschal or altar candle. It should be extinguished immediately after the final Amen in this rite.

17. ▶ The congregation may stand for this prayer and the one following ⟨18⟩.

20. ▶ The service continues with the Introit of the Day, the appointed Psalm, or an Entrance Hymn.

    ▶ Limitations of time may dictate continuing the service with the Salutation and the Collect of the Day.

HOLY BAPTISM
SHORT FORM

Sit

1. The candidate(s) and sponsors (and family/families) gather at the font. The pastor says:

P **In the name of the Father and of the ✠ Son and of the Holy Spirit.**

C Amen

2. The pastor addresses the baptismal group and the congregation:

P **Dearly beloved, we learn from the Word of God that from the fall of Adam we all are conceived and born sinful, are under the wrath of God, and thus are in need of forgiveness. We would be lost forever unless delivered from sin, death, and everlasting condemnation. But the Father of all mercy and grace has sent his Son Jesus Christ, who atoned for the sin of the whole world, that whoever believes in him shall not perish but have eternal life.**

To this end our Lord commanded Baptism, saying: "All authority in heaven and on earth has been given to me. Therefore go and make disciples of all nations, baptizing them in the name of the Father and of the Son and of the Holy Spirit and teaching them to obey everything I have commanded you. And surely I will be with you always, to the very end of the age." He says furthermore: "I tell you the truth, unless a man is born of water and the Spirit, he cannot enter the kingdom of God. Flesh gives birth to flesh, but the Spirit gives birth to spirit." The holy apostles of the Lord have written: "The promise is for you and your children," and: "Baptism now saves you."

3. The pastor turns to the candidate(s) to be baptized.

℗   **Receive the sign of the holy cross both upon your forehead ✝ and upon your heart ✝ to mark you as one redeemed by Christ the crucified.**

4. For the baptism of infants and young children the pastor addresses the parents and sponsors:

℗   **After this child has been baptized, it is your duty and privilege as parents and sponsors to remember __him/her__ in your prayers, put __him/her__ in mind of __his/her__ Baptism, give your counsel and aid that __he/she__ be brought up in the true knowledge and worship of God and be taught the Ten Commandments, the Creed, and the Lord's Prayer; and that, as __he/she__ grows in years, you place in __his/her__ hands the Holy Scriptures, bring __him/her__ to the services of God's house, and provide for __his/her__ further instruction in the Christian faith, that __he/she__ come to the Sacrament of Christ's Body and Blood and thus, abiding in __his/her__ baptismal grace and in communion with the Church, __he/she__ may grow up to lead a godly life to the praise and honor of Jesus Christ.**

Do you promise to fulfill these obligations?

℞   **Yes.**

℗   **God enable you both to will and to do this faithful and loving work and with his grace fulfill what we are unable to do.**

5. The pastor addresses the congregation:

℗   **In order to implore the blessing of our Lord Jesus Christ upon the gathering of this (these) person(s) into the family of our Father, let us rise and pray the prayer he gave us.**

Stand

6. The pastor lays his hand upon the head of the candidate(s). The congregation joins in praying:

ℂ Our Father who art in heaven,	OR	ℂ Our Father in heaven,
hallowed be thy name,		hallowed be your name,
thy kingdom come,		your kingdom come,
thy will be done		your will be done
on earth as it is in heaven.		on earth as it is in heaven.
Give us this day our daily bread;		Give us today our daily bread.

| and forgive us our trespasses
   as we forgive those
     who trespass against us;
and lead us not into temptation,
   but deliver us from evil.
For thine is the kingdom
   and the power and the glory
   forever and ever. Amen | Forgive us our sins
   as we forgive those
     who sin against us.
Lead us not into temptation,
   but deliver us from evil.
For the kingdom, the power,
   and the glory are yours
   now and forever. Amen |

P **The Lord preserve your coming in and your going out from this time forth and even forevermore.**

C Amen

7. The pastor asks the parents and sponsors, who speak on behalf of the infants and young children, and the older children and adults, who can speak for themselves:

P **Do you renounce the devil and all his works and all his ways?**

R I do renounce them.

8. The pastor addresses the baptismal group and the congregation:

P **I ask you to profess your faith in Christ Jesus and to confess the faith of the Church, the faith into which we baptize.**

C I believe in God, the Father Almighty,
   maker of heaven and earth.

And in Jesus Christ, his only Son, our Lord,
   who was conceived by the Holy Spirit,
   born of the virgin Mary,
   suffered under Pontius Pilate,
   was crucified, died and was buried.
   He descended into hell.
   The third day he rose again from the dead.
   He ascended into heaven
     and sits at the right hand of God
     the Father Almighty.
   From thence he will come to judge the living and the dead.

102

I believe in the Holy Spirit,
    the holy Christian Church,*
    the communion of saints,
    the forgiveness of sins,
    the resurrection of the body,
    and the life everlasting. Amen

* The ancient text: the holy catholic Church

Sit

9. When an (older child or) adult is baptized, he/she need not be confirmed in a separate rite, but the pastor may ask him/her the following additional question:

℗ **Will you continue steadfast in the true Christian faith as confessed by the Evangelical Lutheran Church, be diligent in the use of God's Word and sacraments, and lead a godly life, even to death?**

℟ I do so intend with the help of God.

10. The pastor pours water three times upon the head of the candidate(s), saying:

℗ **_____name_____ , I baptize you in the name of the Father and of the Son and of the Holy Spirit ✛.**

C Amen

11. The pastor lays his hand upon the newly baptized and gives this blessing:

℗ **Almighty God, the Father of our Lord Jesus Christ, who has given you the new birth of water and of the Spirit and has forgiven you all your sins, strengthen you with his grace to life everlasting. Peace be with you.**

C Amen

12. All return to their places.

Stand

13. The service continues with the Introit, Psalm, or Entrance Hymn.

NOTES

General

▶ *For notes on Holy Baptism, see page 98.*

RECOGNITION
BY THE CHURCH
OF AN EMERGENCY
BAPTISM

1. This rite is intended to be set within the Divine Service immediately after the opening hymn.

Sit

2. The baptized and sponsors (and family/families) gather at the font.

3. The pastor addresses the congregation with these or similiar words:

P It is with joy and gratitude that we welcome _____name(s)_____ and this (their) child _____name_____ who, because of extreme illness, was given emergency Baptism. The Lord, however, in his mercy spared this child's life. For this we join them in praise and thanksgiving to the Lord.

4. The pastor addresses the baptismal group and the congregation:

P Our Lord commanded Baptism, saying to his disciples in the last chapter of Matthew: "All authority in heaven and on earth has been given to me. Therefore go and make disciples of all nations, baptizing them in the name of the Father and of the Son and of the Holy Spirit and teaching them to obey everything I have commanded you. And surely I will be with you always, to the very end of the age." The holy apostles of the Lord have written: "The promise is for you and your children," and: "Baptism now saves you."

We also learn from the Word of God that we all are conceived and born sinful and are in need of forgiveness. We would be lost forever unless delivered from sin, death, and everlasting condemnation. But the Father of all mercy and grace has sent his

Son Jesus Christ, who atoned for the sin of the whole world that whoever believes in him shall not perish but have eternal life.

In Baptism God puts his name on us with the water and his word, and there is then no doubt that we are surely his with all that Christ achieved for us by his saving death and resurrection.

5. *The pastor addresses the baptismal group:*

P That we may have this certainty for _____name_____ , you have come to attest that you did baptize _____him/her_____ in the name of the Father and of the Son and of the Holy Spirit when it appeared that there might not be time for _____him/her_____ to be brought here and be baptized in the presence of the Church.

Before the Lord and his Church I therefore ask you, did you baptize _____name_____ in the name of the Father and of the Son and of the Holy Spirit?

6. *The one who did the baptizing answers:*

R I did.

OR

7. *An authorized proxy testifies:*

R _____name_____ was thus baptized by _____name_____ .

P When was this done?

R On the ____ day of _____ in this year of our Lord _____ .

8. *The pastor marks the cross upon the forehead and the heart of the baptized and, laying his right hand upon the head, he says:*

P The Lord has put his name upon you with the water and the word of Baptism. You are his. Almighty God, the Father of our Lord Jesus Christ, who has given you the new birth of water and of the Spirit and has forgiven you all your sins, strengthen you with his grace to life everlasting. Peace be with you.

C Amen

9. The pastor addresses the parents and sponsors:

Ⓟ In Christian love you had this child baptized. It is, therefore, your duty and privilege as parents and sponsors to remember _____him/her_____ in your prayers, put _____him/her_____ in mind of _____his/her_____ Baptism, give your counsel and aid that _____he/she_____ be brought up in the true knowledge and worship of God and be taught the Ten Commandments, the Creed, and the Lord's Prayer; and that, as _____he/she_____ grows in years, you place in _____his/her_____ hands the Holy Scriptures, bring _____him/her_____ to the services of God's house, and provide for _____his/her_____ further instruction in the Christian faith, that _____he/she_____ come to the Sacrament of Christ's Body and Blood and thus, abiding in _____his/her_____ baptismal grace and in communion with the Church, _____he/she_____ may grow up to lead a godly life to the praise and honor of Jesus Christ.

Do you promise to fulfill these obligations?

Ⓡ Yes.

Ⓟ God enable you both to will and to do this faithful and loving work and with his grace fulfill what we are unable to do.

10. A white garment may be put upon the baptized.

Ⓟ Receive this white garment to show that Christ has taken away and borne your sin and put upon you his perfect righteousness. So shall you in faith ever stand before him.

11. A baptismal candle may be lighted from the paschal or altar candle. In giving the candle, the pastor says:

Ⓟ Receive this burning light. Live always by the light of Christ, and be ever watchful for his coming that you may meet him with joy and enter with him to the marriage feast of the Lamb in his kingdom, which shall have no end.

12. The pastor and the baptismal group go before the altar.

Stand

Ⓟ Let us pray.

Almighty and merciful God and Father, we thank and praise you that you graciously preserve and enlarge your family and have granted _____name_____ the new birth in Holy Baptism and made _____him/her_____ a member of your Son, our Lord Jesus Christ, and an heir of your heavenly kingdom. We humbly implore you that, as _____he/she_____ has now become your child, you would keep _____him/her_____ in _____his/her_____ baptismal grace that according to all your good pleasure ___he/she___ may faithfully grow to lead a godly life to the praise and honor of your holy name and finally with all your saints obtain the promised inheritance in heaven; through Jesus Christ, our Lord. (169)

C Amen

13. The following Prayer may also be said.

P **Lord and Giver of life, look with kindness upon the father and mother of this child, and upon all our parents. Let them ever rejoice in the gift you have given them. Enable them to be teachers and examples of righteousness for their children. Strengthen them in their own Baptism so that they may share eternally with their children the salvation you have given them; through Jesus Christ, our Lord.** (170)

C Amen

14. The baptismal group may turn toward the congregation; a representative of the congregation may say:

Through Baptism God has added ___name___ to his own people to declare the wonderful deeds of our Savior, who has called us out of darkness into his marvelous light.

C We welcome you into the Lord's family. We receive you as a fellow member of the body of Christ, a child of the same heavenly Father, to work with us in his kingdom.

P ___name___ , the Lord bless you in all your ways from this time forth and even forevermore.

C Amen

15. The pastor says:

P **And now with all the baptized we call upon God, our Abba, Father.**

C Our Father who art in heaven,	OR	**C** Our Father in heaven,
hallowed be thy name,		hallowed be your name,
thy kingdom come,		your kingdom come,

thy will be done
    on earth as it is in heaven.
Give us this day our daily bread;
and forgive us our trespasses
    as we forgive those
        who trespass against us;
and lead us not into temptation,
    but deliver us from evil.
For thine is the kingdom
    and the power and the glory
    forever and ever. Amen

your will be done
    on earth as in heaven.
Give us today our daily bread.
Forgive us our sins
    as we forgive those
        who sin against us.
Lead us not into temptation,
    but deliver us from evil.
For the kingdom, the power,
    and the glory are yours
    now and forever. Amen

16. All return to their places. The service continues with the Introit, Psalm, or Entrance Hymn.

NOTES

General

▶ *Although sponsors may not have been involved in an emergency baptism, it is appropriate that they be selected to share responsibility for the spiritual nurture and welfare of the child.*

▶ *For notes on Holy Baptism, see page* 98.

CONFIRMATION

---

1. After a hymn of invocation of the Holy Spirit has been sung, the catechumens gather before the altar, and the pastor addresses them:

℗ Beloved in the Lord, our Lord Jesus Christ said: "All authority in heaven and on earth has been given to me. Therefore go and make disciples of all nations, baptizing them in the name of the Father and of the Son and of the Holy Spirit and teaching them to obey everything I have commanded you. And surely I will be with you always, to the very end of the age."

You have been baptized and you have been taught the faith according to our Lord's bidding. The fulfillment of his bidding we now celebrate with thankful hearts, rejoicing to confess the faith into which you were baptized and which you yourselves will now confess before the Church.

Jesus said: "Whoever confesses me before men, I will also confess him before my Father in heaven. But he that denies me before men, I will deny him before my Father in heaven."

Lift up your hearts therefore to the God of all grace and joyfully give answer to what, in the name of the Lord, as a minister of his Church, I now shall ask you.

℗ Do you this day in the presence of God and of this congregation acknowledge the gifts which God gave you in your Baptism?

℟ I do.

℗ Do you renounce the devil and all his works and all his ways?

℟ I do.

110

P **Do you believe in God, the Father Almighty?**

R Yes, I believe in God, the Father Almighty,
   maker of heaven and earth.

P **Do you believe in Jesus Christ, his only Son?**

R Yes, I believe in Jesus Christ, his only Son, our Lord,
   who was conceived by the Holy Spirit,
   born of the virgin Mary,
   suffered under Pontius Pilate,
   was crucified, died and was buried.
   He descended into hell.
   The third day he rose again from the dead.
   He ascended into heaven
     and sits at the right hand of God
     the Father Almighty.
   From thence he will come to judge the living and the dead.

P **Do you believe in the Holy Spirit?**

R Yes, I believe in the Holy Spirit,
   the holy Christian Church,*
   the communion of saints,
   the forgiveness of sins,
   the resurrection of the body,
   and the life everlasting.

* The ancient text: the holy catholic Church

P **Do you intend to continue steadfast in this confession and Church and to suffer all, even death, rather than fall away from it?**

R I do so intend with the help of God.

P **Do you hold all the prophetic and apostolic Scriptures to be the inspired Word of God and confess the doctrine of the Evangelical Lutheran Church, drawn from them, as you have learned to know it from the Small Catechism, to be faithful and true?**

R I do.

111

P Do you desire to be a member of the Evangelical Lutheran Church and of this congregation?

R I do.

P Do you intend faithfully to conform all your life to the divine Word, to be faithful in the use of God's Word and sacraments, which are his means of grace, and in faith, word, and action to remain true to God, Father, Son, and Holy Spirit, even to death?

R I do so intend by the grace of God.

P Give then your hand as pledge of your promise, and kneel to receive the blessing.

2. The catechumens, in turn, give their right hand and kneel. The pastor lays his hands upon the head of each one and gives the following blessing. A confirmation text is then given to each.

P _____name_____ , God, the Father of our Lord Jesus Christ, give you his Holy Spirit, the Spirit of wisdom and knowledge, of grace and prayer, of power and strength, of sanctification and the fear of God.

3. After all catechumens have received the blessing and text of Holy Scripture, the pastor says:

P Upon this your profession and promise I invite and welcome you, as members of the Evangelical Lutheran Church and of this congregation, to share with us in all the gifts our Lord has for his Church and to live them out continually in his worship and service.

4. The pastor invites the congregation to pray for the newly confirmed.

P Let us pray for the newly confirmed.

Lord God, heavenly Father, we thank and praise you for your great goodness in bringing these your sons and daughters to the knowledge of your Son, our Savior, Jesus Christ, and enabling them both with the heart to believe and with the mouth to confess his saving name. Grant that, bringing forth the fruits of faith, they may continue steadfast and victorious to the day when all who have fought the good fight of faith shall receive the crown of righteousness; through Jesus Christ, your Son, our Lord, who lives and reigns with you and the Holy Spirit, one God, now and forever. (171)

C Amen

5. The pastor dismisses the newly confirmed, saying:

P **The almighty and most merciful God, Father,✠ Son, and Holy Spirit, bless and keep you.**

C Amen

6. The service continues with the Offering (19) in Divine Service I, the Prayers (18) in Divine Service II.

NOTES

General

▶ *Confirmation is a public rite of the Church that is preceded by a period of instruction designed to help baptized Christians identify with the life and mission of the Christian community.*

▶ *Having been instructed in the Christian faith prior to admission to the Lord's Supper (1 Corinthians 11:28), the rite of Confirmation provides an opportunity for the individual Christian, relying on God's promise given in Holy Baptism, to make a personal public confession of the faith and a lifelong pledge of fidelity to Christ.*

▶ *This rite may follow the sermon in the Divine Service.*

The Rite in Detail

1. ▶ Since the Apostles' Creed has been said by the catechumens, it is appropriate to omit the Creed in the Divine Service itself.
4. ▶ The congregation may be invited to stand for this prayer for the newly confirmed.

RECEIVING OF MEMBERS

1. This rite may serve for receiving Christians as communicant members by confirmation, transfer, or profession of faith.

2. The rite immediately follows the Offertory in Divine Service I, the Creed in Divine Service II, or the Canticle in Matins or Morning Prayer, Vespers or Evening Prayer.

Sit

3. The candidates present themselves before the altar, and the pastor addresses them:

℗ Dear friends in Christ, the members of our congregation are happy that you are to become part of our Christian fellowship. Our Lord Jesus Christ bids us to confess him before men, with the promise that he will then confess us before his Father in heaven. That we may rejoice in your confession, I now ask you in the presence of God and of this congregation: Do you accept and confess that the teachings of the Evangelical Lutheran Church, as you have learned to know them [from the Small Catechism], are faithful and true to the Word of God? If so, answer: I do.

℞ I do.

℗ As a member of this Church, do you intend to continue in the confession of this Church, attend corporate worship, make diligent use of the means of grace, and lead a righteous and godly life? If so, answer: I do so intend with the help of God.

℟ I do so intend with the help of God.

℘ **Will you support the work our gracious Lord has given this congregation with your prayers, time, treasure, and talent? If so, answer: I will with the help of God.**

℟ I will with the help of God.

℘ **Upon this your promise, I, in the name of this congregation, extend to you the right hand of fellowship and love, acknowledging you as a member of the Evangelical Lutheran Church and inviting you to receive the Lord's Supper and to participate in all the other blessings of salvation which God has given to his Church, in the name of the Father and of the ✝ Son and of the Holy Spirit.**

4. As the hand of fellowship is extended, each person is called by name. After all have been received, the pastor says:

℘ **Peace be with you.**

℟ Amen

5. All return to their places.

Stand

6. The service continues with the prayers (or Litany) appropriate to the Divine Service, Matins or Morning Prayer, Vespers or Evening Prayer.

NOTES

General

▶ *In the case of an adult baptism, where instruction precedes the ministration of Holy Baptism, neither confirmation nor any other rite need be used, since this sacrament brings the individual into the full fellowship of the Church.*

ANNOUNCEMENT
OF EXCOMMUNICATION
AND OF REINSTATEMENT

Local custom will determine the time and place for these announcements.

EXCOMMUNICATION

P   Beloved in Christ, I am bound as a called and ordained servant of the Word to make known to you that our fellow member ____name____ was under discipline and, although repeatedly admonished from the Word of God, has refused to repent. Following the direction of our Lord in the Gospel according to St. Matthew, one and two or three members have pleaded with ____him/her____ on several occasions, but without success. Others have done likewise, but to no avail. Finally, ____name____ refuses also to hear the Church.

So that the seriousness of ____his/her____ sin may be more fully shown to ____him/her____ as a last effort to win ____him/her____ back to our Lord, I announce that ____he/she____ is excommunicated from the Church. ____He/She____ may not come to this or any other Christian altar until ____he/she____ repents. May the almighty and merciful God grant ____him/her____ grace to confess ____his/her____ sin and work in ____him/her____ repentance.

OR

P   Beloved in Christ, I am bound as a called and ordained servant of the Word to make known to you that our fellow member ____name____ has refused counsel from the Word of God to make confession of ____his/her____ sin and repent. ____name____ has therefore deprived us of the opportunity to admonish ____him/her____ as a ____brother/sister____, and we are constrained to commit ____his/her____ cause to him who judges rightly. ____He/She____ may not come to this or any other Christian altar until ____he/she____ repents. May the Lord in his great mercy grant ____him/her____ knowledge of ____his/her____ sin that ____he/she____ may repent and return.

118

P **Let us pray.**

Gracious heavenly Father, since you want all people to be saved and to come to the knowledge of the truth, grant that ____name____ may yet be led to repentance, receive forgiveness, and be restored to the life and health of your people to the praise and honor of your Son, our Savior, Jesus Christ. ⟨262⟩

C Amen

REINSTATEMENT

P **Beloved in Christ, because ____name____ , having been under excommunication for a time, has now by the grace of God given evidence of repentance to the Church, I joyfully announce that ____his/her____ excommunication is removed and that ____he/she____ is restored to Christian fellowship in this congregation.**

Let us pray.

We thank you, Father, that you have heard us, moving the heart of ____name____ to repent. Comfort ____him/her____ and be with ____him/her____ in all trial and temptation that ____he/she____ may continue steadfast in faith and godliness throughout ____his/her____ earthly life. Keep us from the pride of thinking that we cannot fall, and cause us to trust solely in the strength you give in Jesus Christ. ⟨263⟩

C Amen

MARRIAGE

1. This rite, with adaptation, may be set within the Divine Service, Matins or Morning Prayer, Vespers or Evening Prayer, where it will follow the Sermon. It may also be used as a separate service.

2. The Propers are those appointed on pages 124—26.

Stand

3. When the wedding party has come to the foot of the altar, the pastor says:

℗ **In the name of the Father and of the ✠ Son and of the Holy Spirit.**

℃ Amen

℗ **We are gathered here in the sight of God and of his Church to witness and bless the joining together of this man and this woman in holy marriage. This is an honorable estate, which God himself has instituted and blessed, and by which he gives us a picture of the very communion of Christ and his bride, the Church. God has both established and sanctified marriage and has promised to bless therein all who love and trust in him and who seek to give him their faithful worship and service, for the sake of our Lord Jesus Christ.**

The union of husband and wife in heart, body, and mind is intended by God for their mutual joy, for the help and comfort given one another in prosperity and adversity, and, when it is God's will, for the procreation of children and their nurture in the knowledge and love of the Lord. Therefore marriage is not to be entered into inadvisedly or lightly, but reverently, deliberately, and in accordance with the purposes for which it was instituted by God.

Sit

4. Appropriate portions of Holy Scripture are read.

Ⓟ The Lord God said, "It is not good for the man to be alone. I will make a helper suitable for him." Now the Lord God had formed out of the ground all the beasts of the field and all the birds of the air. He brought them to the man to see what he would name them; and whatever the man called each living creature, that was its name. So the man gave names to all the livestock, the birds of the air and all the beasts of the field. But for Adam no suitable helper was found. So the Lord God caused the man to fall into a deep sleep; and while he was sleeping, he took one of the man's ribs and closed up the place with flesh. Then the Lord God made a woman from the rib he had taken out of the man, and he brought her to the man. The man said, "This is now bone of my bones and flesh of my flesh; she shall be called 'woman,' for she was taken out of man." For this reason a man will leave his father and mother and be united to his wife, and they will become one flesh. (Gen. 2:18-24)

Submit to one another out of reverence for Christ. Wives, submit to your husbands as to the Lord. For the husband is the head of the wife as Christ is the head of the church, his body, of which he is the Savior. Now as the church submits to Christ, so also wives should submit to their husbands in everything. Husbands, love your wives, just as Christ loved the church and gave himself up for her to make her holy, cleansing her by the washing with water through the word, and to present her to himself as a radiant church, without stain or wrinkle or any other blemish, but holy and blameless. In this same way, husbands ought to love their wives as their own bodies. He who loves his wife loves himself. After all, no one ever hated his own body, but he feeds and cares for it, just as Christ does the church—for we are members of his body. "For this reason a man will leave his father and mother and be united to his wife, and the two will become one flesh." This is a profound mystery—but I am talking about Christ and the church. However, each one of you also must love his wife as he loves himself, and the wife must respect her husband. (Eph. 5:21-33)

[Jesus replied to the Pharisees, "Have you not read that] at the beginning the Creator 'made them male and female,' and said, 'For this reason a man will leave his father and mother and be united to his wife, and the two will become one flesh'? So they are no longer two, but one. Therefore what God has joined together, let man not separate." (Matt. 19:4-6)

5. An address may follow. A hymn may be sung.

6. If the bride and bridegroom have been seated for an address and/or a hymn, they now stand. The pastor asks the bridegroom:

121

P _____name_____ , **will you have this woman to be your wife, to live with her in holy marriage according to the Word of God? Will you love her, comfort her, honor her, and keep her in sickness and in health and, forsaking all others, be husband to her as long as you both shall live?**

R I will.

7. The pastor asks the bride:

P _____name_____ , **will you have this man to be your husband, to live with him in holy marriage according to the Word of God? Will you love him, comfort him, honor him, obey him, and keep him in sickness and in health and forsaking all others, be wife to him as long as you both shall live?**

R I will.

8. The pastor leads the bride and bridegroom to the altar.

9. The bridegroom, taking the right hand of the bride and facing her, says after the pastor:

I, _____name_____ , in the presence of God and these witnesses, take you, _____name_____ , to be my wife, to have and to hold from this day forward, for better, for worse, for richer, for poorer, in sickness and in health, to love and to cherish, until death parts us, and I pledge you my faithfulness.

10. The bride, in the same way, says after the pastor:

I, _____name_____ , in the presence of God and these witnesses, take you, _____name_____ , to be my husband, to have and to hold from this day forward, for better, for worse, for richer, for poorer, in sickness and in health, to love and to cherish, until death parts us, and I pledge you my faithfulness.

11. The bride and bridegroom exchange rings, saying:

Receive this ring as a pledge and token of wedded love and faithfulness.

12. The pastor may speak a blessing upon the pledging of their love with the exchange of rings.

P **Grant your blessing, O Lord, to your servants** _____name_____ **and** _____name_____ **that they may be ever mindful of their solemn pledge and, trusting in your mercy, abound evermore in love all their days; through Jesus Christ, our Lord.** ⟨264⟩

R Amen

122

13. The bride and bridegroom kneel, and the pastor says:

🅟 Now that _____name_____ and _____name_____ have consented together in holy marriage, have given themselves to each other by their solemn pledges, and have declared the same before God and these witnesses, I pronounce them to be husband and wife, in the name of the Father and of the ☩Son and of the Holy Spirit.

What God has joined together, let no one put asunder.

🅒 Amen

🅟 The almighty and gracious God abundantly grant you his favor and sanctify and bless you with the blessing given our first parents in paradise that you may please him in both body and soul and live together in holy love until your life's end.

🅒 Amen

Stand

🅟 Let us pray.

Almighty, everlasting God, our heavenly Father, grant that by your blessing _____name_____ and _____name_____ may live together according to your Word and promise. Strengthen them in faithfulness and love toward each other. Sustain and defend them in all trial and temptation. Help them to live in faith toward you in the communion of your holy Church and in loving service to each other that they may ever enjoy your heavenly blessing; through Jesus Christ, your Son, our Lord, who lives and reigns with you and the Holy Spirit, one God, now and forever. ⟨265⟩

🅒 Amen

🅒 Our Father who art in heaven,	OR	🅒 Our Father in heaven,
hallowed be thy name,		hallowed be your name,
thy kingdom come,		your kingdom come,
thy will be done		your will be done
on earth as it is in heaven.		on earth as in heaven.
Give us this day our daily bread;		Give us today our daily bread.
and forgive us our trespasses		Forgive us our sins
as we forgive those		as we forgive those
who trespass against us;		who sin against us.
and lead us not into temptation,		Lead us not into temptation,
but deliver us from evil.		but deliver us from evil.
For thine is the kingdom		For the kingdom, the power,
and the power and the glory		and the glory are yours
forever and ever. Amen		now and forever. Amen

14. The pastor pronounces the Blessing.

Ⓟ The eternal God, the Father of our Lord Jesus Christ, grant you his Holy Spirit, be with you, and richly bless you now and forever.

Ⓒ Amen

PROPERS

INTROIT

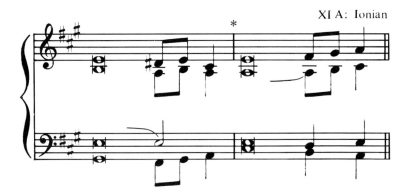

XI A: Ionian

The Lord is good and his love
endures forēver;*
　　his faithfulness continues through
　　all generātions.

Shout for joy to the Lord,*
　　all the earth.
Serve the Lord with gladness;*
　　come before him with joyful songs.
Know that the Lord is God.*
　　It is he who made us, and we are
　　his; we are his people, the sheep
　　of his pasture.
Enter his gates with thanksgiving
and his courts with praise;*
　　give thanks to him and praise his
　　name.

For the Lord is good and his love
endures forēver;*
　　his faithfulness continues through
　　all generātions.

Glory be to the Father and to the Son*
　　and to the Holy Spirit;
as it was in the beginning,*
　　is now, and will be forever. Āmen

The Lord is good and his love
endures forēver;*
　　his faithfulness continues through
　　all generātions.
　　(Antiphon, Ps. 100:5; Ps. 100)

COLLECT

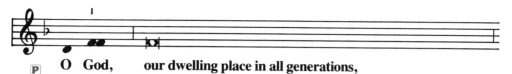

P O God,   our dwelling place in all generations,

look with favor upon the homes of our land. Embrace husbands and wives, parents and children, in the arms of your love. Bless our homes that they may ever be a shelter for the defenseless, a bulwark for the tempted, a resting place for the weary, and a foretaste of our eternal home with you;

through Jesus Christ, your Son, our Lord, who lives and reigns with you and the Holy Spirit, one God, now and for - ev   - er. ⟨266⟩

READINGS
Psalm 127
Genesis 2:18-24
Ephesians 5:21-33
Matthew 19:4-6

GRADUAL

XI A: Ionian

Blessed are all who fear the Lord, *
  who walk in his ways.
You will eat the fruit of your
labor; *
  blessings and prosperity will
  be yours. *(Ps. 128:1-2)*

VERSE

(Ps. 121:5)

Al - le - lu - ia, al - le - lu - ia. The Lord watches o - ver you—

the Lord is your shade at your right hand. Al - le - lu - ia.

NOTES

General

▶ *This marriage rite is designed for use in a variety of worship settings <1>.*

▶ *If this rite is set within the Divine Service with Holy Communion, the Communion must be open to the gathered congregation and not limited to the bride and bridegroom or the wedding party.*

▶ *When thus set within a formal service, except during the marriage itself, the wedding party may occupy the front pews or be provided special chairs in a convenient place near the altar.*

▶ *Because of the solemn character of Holy Week, it is inappropriate to schedule a marriage in that period.*

▶ *Music selected should embody high standards of quality and, in general, reflect the praise of God, God's steadfast love in Christ as the foundation and model for marriage, and the asking of God's presence and blessing. It should not becloud the content and mood of the service with musical triteness or associations bordering on sentimentality and should be within the ability of the performers to play or sing with assurance.*

▶ *A number of musical options are possible before the entrance procession: solo, ensemble, or choral pieces; organ or other instrumental music; music using a combination of these media.*

▶ *Organ music may be based on hymn or chorale tunes used within the marriage service. A printed wedding folder helps to establish such themes and relationships for the congregation. Instrumental music may be selected from chamber music literature or similar sources and should reflect the mood of joy and celebration. Voice(s) and instruments may be joined in solo or choral cantatas.*

The Service in Detail

4. ▶ In the case of the marriage of young persons, it may be desired that the respective parents of the bride and bridegroom be involved in giving their formal consent and pledge of support. In this circumstance, immediately before the reading of Holy Scripture, the pastor may ask the parents of each in turn:

P **Do you give your consent and approval to this marriage?**

R We do.

▶ The pastor may continue by asking both sets of parents:

P **Will you, as parents, support, encourage, and strengthen ____name(s)____ in their marriage, remembering at all times that God wants them to live in obedience to his holy ordinance until death parts them?**

R We will.

12. ▶ After the pastor's blessing, the parents may add their blessing with these or similar words:
May the Lord make you strong in faith and love, defend you on every side, and guide you in truth and peace.

9., 10. ▶ If an alternate pledge on the part of the bridegroom and bride is desired, the following may be said:
I take you, ____name____ , to be my wife (husband), and I pledge before God and the witnesses here present to be your faithful husband (wife), to share with you in plenty and in want, in joy and sorrow, in sickness and in health, to forgive and strengthen you, and to join with you that together we may serve God and others as long as we both shall live.

Propers

Additional Psalms and Readings
Psalm 67
Psalm 117
Psalm 127
Psalm 128

Genesis 1:26-31
1 Corinthians 12:31b—13:13
Mark 10:6-9, 13-16

BLESSING OF
A CIVIL MARRIAGE

1. This rite is intended for use as a separate service. It may, however, with adaptation, be set within the Divine Service, Matins or Morning Prayer, Vespers or Evening Prayer, where it will follow the Sermon.

Sit

2. The couple and those who may be attending them gather and stand at the foot of the altar. The pastor says:

ℙ **Dearly beloved** _____name_____ **and** _____name_____ **, you have come here today to receive the blessing of God on your marriage, in which you were united according to civil law, and to give your wholehearted pledges to live together as husband and wife according to his Word.**

Hear of our Creator God's institution of holy marriage.

The Lord God said, "It is not good for the man to be alone. I will make a helper suitable for him." (Gen. 2:18)

Our Lord Jesus Christ said:

"[Have you not read] that at the beginning the Creator 'made them male and female,' and said, 'For this reason a man will leave his father and mother and be united to his wife, and the two will become one flesh'? So they are no longer two, but one. Therefore what God has joined together, let man not separate." (Matt. 19:4-6)

Hear also these strengthening words of the apostle Paul.

Therefore, as God's chosen people, holy and dearly loved, clothe yourselves with

compassion, kindness, humility, gentleness and patience. Bear with each other and forgive whatever grievances you may have against one another. Forgive as the Lord forgave you. And over all these virtues put on love, which binds them all together in perfect unity. Let the peace of Christ rule in your hearts, since as members of one body you were called to peace. And be thankful. Let the word of Christ dwell in you richly as you teach and admonish one another with all wisdom, and as you sing psalms, hymns and spiritual songs with gratitude in your hearts to God. And whatever you do, whether in word or deed, do it all in the name of the Lord Jesus, giving thanks to God the Father through him. (Col. 3:12-17)

3. The pastor addresses the congregation:

P Let us now lift our hearts to the joy in which our Father would have _____ name _____ and _____ name _____ grow.

Stand

4. The Psalm is sung.

IX g²: Aeolian

The Lord is good and his love endures forêver;*	give thanks to him and praise his name.
his faithfulness continues through all generâtions.	For the Lord is good and his love endures forêver;*
Shout for joy to the Lord,*	his faithfulness continues through all generâtions.
all the earth.	
Serve the Lord with gladness;*	Glory be to the Father and to the Son*
come before him with joyful songs.	and to the Holy Spirit;
Know that the Lord is God.*	as it was in the beginning,*
It is he who made us, and we are his; we are his people, the sheep of his pasture.	is now, and will be forever. Amen
Enter his gates with thanksgiving and his courts with praise;*	The Lord is good and his love endures forêver;*
	his faithfulness continues through all generâtions.

(Antiphon, Ps. 100:5; Ps. 100)

Sit

5. An address may follow. A hymn may be sung.

6. If the husband and wife have been seated for an address and/or a hymn, they now stand. The pastor says:

P **Before God and his people give your wholehearted pledges that you will live your marriage in his name, according to his Word, within his favor, and without reservation, daily seeking his blessing on your union.**

7. The husband, taking the right hand of the wife and facing her, says after the pastor:

I, _____name_____ , pledge myself to you, _____name_____ , as your husband according to the Word and ordinance of God our Father. As God is my witness, I will never forsake you. I am your husband until death parts us.

8. The wife, in the same way, says after the pastor:

I, _____name_____ , pledge myself to you, _____name_____ , as your wife according to the Word and ordinance of God our Father. As God is my witness, I will never forsake you. I am your wife until death parts us.

Stand

9. The husband and wife kneel, and the pastor says:

P **Let us pray.**

Dear heavenly Father, of your generous goodness you created man and woman for each other that they might rejoice in their love within the bounty of your love and blessing. Grant _____name_____ and _____name_____ always to live within your love, your blessing, and your protection so that no sin or trial may separate them. Enable them by your Word and Spirit, and within the family of your Church, to live their life confessing you as Lord. May they through days of happiness and sorrow be drawn always closer to you and to each other, even to the fulfillment of all your promises in Jesus Christ, our Savior, who lives and reigns with you and the Holy Spirit, one God, now and forever. ⟨267⟩

C Amen

P **With all the family of our Lord we are bold to pray:**

131

⒞ Our Father who art in heaven,	OR	⒞ Our Father in heaven,
hallowed be thy name,		hallowed be your name,
thy kingdom come,		your kingdom come,
thy will be done		your will be done
on earth as it is in heaven.		on earth as in heaven.
Give us this day our daily bread;		Give us today our daily bread.
and forgive us our trespasses		Forgive us our sins
as we forgive those		as we forgive those
who trespass against us;		who sin against us.
and lead us not into temptation,		Lead us not into temptation,
but deliver us from evil.		but deliver us from evil.
For thine is the kingdom		For the kingdom, the power,
and the power and the glory		and the glory are yours
forever and ever. Amen		now and forever. Amen

10. *The pastor pronounces the Blessing.*

Ⓟ **The Lord bless you and keep you.**
The Lord make his face shine on you and be gracious to you.
The Lord lift up his countenance on you and ✠ give you peace.

⒞ Amen

NOTES

General

▶ *Because of the solemn character of Holy Week, it is inappropriate to schedule this rite in that period.*

▶ *Those who desire to have their civil marriage blessed should, in discussing their intent with the pastor beforehand, present official documentation confirming their marriage: date, place, time, and participants.*

▶ *The pastor will explain the nature of this rite, especially that its use not be construed as a remarriage.*

ANNIVERSARY
OF A MARRIAGE

1. This rite is intended for use in the Divine Service before the Prayer of the Church, or The Prayers.

2. When used in a separate anniversary celebration, it may be expanded with a psalm, hymns, Scripture readings, and an address.

Sit

3. Immediately before the Prayer of the Church, or The Prayers, the husband and wife present themselves before the altar. The pastor addresses the congregation with these or similar words:

P Dear friends in Christ, ____name____ and ____name____ have come today before the Lord to reaffirm and be renewed in their solemn marriage pledges made ___number___ year(s) ago, to offer thanks to the Lord for the many blessings he has showered upon them, and to seek the Lord's continued gracious care.

4. The pastor asks the husband:

P ____name____ , do you in the presence of God and of this congregation reaffirm the pledge you made when you took to yourself ___name___ as your wife?

R I do.

5. The pastor asks the wife:

P   ____ name ____ , do you in the presence of God and of this congregation reaffirm the pledge you made when you took to yourself _____ name ____ as your husband?

R   I do.

6. The husband and wife kneel, and the pastor prays on their behalf.

P   Lord God, heavenly Father, we give thanks for the fatherly love and grace that you have shown to _____ name _____ and _____ name _____ during the year(s) of their marriage. You have accompanied them with loving-kindness and tender mercy, strengthened them in sorrow and sickness, and crowned their life with untold blessings. To you alone belong all honor and praise. Continue to be with them in the future. Be their light though the light in their eyes begins to dim. Be their strength though their strength departs. Be their health in sickness and infirmity. Be their refuge and their life in the hour of death, and graciously bring them to the marriage supper of the Lamb, Jesus Christ, our Lord, where we all will feast with you and forever rejoice in your presence. Amen ⟨268⟩

OR

P   Most gracious God, we give thanks for the joy and blessings that you have granted _____ name _____ and _____ name _____ . Assist them always with your grace that with true fidelity and steadfast love they may ever honor and keep their promises, grow in love toward you and for each other, and come at last to the eternal joys that you have promised; through Jesus Christ, our Lord, who lives and reigns with you and the Holy Spirit, one God, now and forever. Amen ⟨269⟩

Stand

7. The pastor turns to the congregation and says:

P   **Let us pray.**

Almighty and most gracious Father, continue to send your blessing upon _____ name ____ and _____ name ____ , who have here reaffirmed their pledges to each other. Grant them your grace that they may never cease to love, honor, and cherish each other in faithfulness and patience, in wisdom and true godliness. May their lives together be a witness to your love and forgiveness and their home a haven of blessing and peace; through Jesus Christ, your Son, our Lord, who lives and reigns with you and the Holy Spirit, one God, now and forever. ⟨270⟩

C   Amen

8. The pastor blesses the anniversary couple.

135

P **May God, who has sustained and blessed you by his grace in your wedded life, continue to grant his divine protection and blessing and cause your hearts to remain united in faithful love as long as you both shall live. Depart in peace.**

C Amen

9. *The husband and wife return to their places.*

10. *The service continues with the Prayer of the Church, or The Prayers.*

NOTES

General

▶ *This rite may be adapted and used as an act of reconciliation after consultation with those concerned.*

SERVICE OF CORPORATE CONFESSION AND ABSOLUTION

1. A HYMN may be sung.

Stand

P **In the name of the Father and of the ☩ Son and of the Holy Spirit.**

C Amen

2. The pastor says the following or another appropriate prayer:

P **Father of mercies and God of all consolation, come to the aid of your people, turning us from our sin to live for you alone. Give us the power of your Holy Spirit that we may attend to your Word, confess our sins, receive your forgiveness, and grow into the fullness of your Son Jesus Christ, our Lord and our Redeemer.** (203)

C Amen

3. PSALM 51 or another appropriate psalm is sung or said.

Sit

4. Then may follow a CONFESSIONAL ADDRESS or an EXHORTATION after the following manner:

P **Dearly beloved, since it is our intention to come to the Holy Supper of our Lord Jesus Christ, it is proper that we diligently examine ourselves as St. Paul tells us to do, for this Holy Sacrament has been instituted for the special comfort** and strengthening of those who humbly confess their sins and hunger and thirst for righteousness.

But if we thus examine ourselves, we shall find nothing in us but sin and death, from which we cannot set ourselves free. Therefore our Lord Jesus Christ has had mercy on us and has taken on himself our nature that he might fulfill for us the whole will and law of God and for us and for our deliverance suffer death and all that we by our sins have deserved. And that we should the more confidently believe this and be strengthened by our faith in cheerful obedience to his holy will, he has instituted the Holy Sacrament of his Supper, in which he feeds us with his body and gives us to drink of his blood.

Therefore whoever eats of this bread and drinks of this cup, firmly believing the words of Christ, dwells in Christ, and Christ in him, and has eternal life.

We should do this also in remembrance of him, showing his death, that he was delivered for our offenses and raised again for our justification and, giving him our most hearty thanks, take up our cross and follow him and according to his commandment love one another as he has loved us. For we are all one body, even as we all eat of his body and drink of his blood.

P Humble yourselves before God, confess your sins to him, and implore his forgiveness.

Kneel/Stand

C O almighty God, merciful Father, I, a poor, miserable sinner, confess to you all my sins and iniquities with which I have ever offended you and justly deserved your punishment now and forever. But I am heartily sorry for them and sincerely repent of them, and I pray you of your boundless mercy and for the sake of the holy, innocent, bitter sufferings and death of your beloved Son, Jesus Christ, to be gracious and merciful to me, a poor sinful being. Forgive me all my sins and grant me the power of your Holy Spirit that I may amend my sinful life.

5. The pastor stands and says to the penitents:

P **God be gracious to you and strengthen your faith.**

C Amen

6. The pastor shall preferably absolve the penitents individually at the altar, laying his hand on each and pronouncing the following absolution, or he may absolve all the penitents corporately from the altar.

℗ **In the stead and by the command of my Lord Jesus Christ I forgive you all your sins in the name of the Father and of the** ✝ **Son and of the Holy Spirit.**

C Amen

℗ **The God of peace will sanctify you wholly and keep your spirit, soul, and body sound and blameless at the coming of our Lord Jesus Christ. He who calls you is faithful, and he will do it. Go in** ✝ **peace.**

C Amen

NOTES

General

▶ *Consult the* General *notes on Individual Confession and Absolution, page 144.*

▶ *From the historical standpoint this service of Corporate Confession and Absolution might well be considered as one step removed from Individual Confession and Absolution. Despite the widespread salutary use of individual confession and absolution in numerous 16th-century Lutheran Church orders as well as the approbation of it and advocacy for it by the foremost dogmaticians in the period of Lutheran orthodoxy, group (corporate) confession gradually supplanted the former and became more closely connected to the reception of the Lord's Supper. Although this development was due in part to a false understanding of the power of the keys and the nature of sin by pietism and rationalism, nevertheless, this type of confession and absolution, based on good historic models, can serve a useful and salutary purpose in the life of a congregation.*

▶ *This service is intended for use at confessional services apart from the Holy Communion. It envisions the presence of only those penitents who have specifically come to make confession and who are desirous of receiving the personal application and comfort of the indicative-operative absolution. If, on the other hand, this service is used immediately prior to the Divine Service (with Holy Communion), it may supplant the general confession and absolution or declaration of grace in the respective Divine Service. When used thus, it is appropriate that there be an interval of silence before the Introit of the Day, the appointed Psalm, or an Entrance Hymn.*

▶ *This service of corporate confession should not appear as another form of general or public confession. It should reflect the fact that the pastor is here dealing with a restricted group of Christians, not an unidentifiable group as is often the case in public worship.*

▶ *It is inappropriate for anyone not ordained to preside at this service.*

Preparation for the Service

▶ *When the number of people is small, they should be requested to sit in the front pews.*

▶ *Appropriate vestments for the pastor are alb, or surplice, and stole in the color of the day or season.*

The Service in Detail

1. ▶ A refrain/antiphon for Psalm 51, if desired, is:
   Create in me a pure heart, O God,*
   and renew a steadfast spirit within me.

4. ▶ When there is a confessional address, the pastor may emphasize the gravity of sin or the need to accept the responsibility for sin and its consequences. Primarily, however, he will direct his people to the unfailing mercy and grace of God in Jesus Christ and the comforting words of absolution. In connection with the latter, such Scripture passages as Matthew 16:19; 18:18; and John 20:22-23 will be useful.

6. ▶ The historical and theological thrust of this service is in the absolution imparted to the individual. When the group is small, the people should be invited to come forward and kneel near the altar or at the chancel rail, there individually to receive the absolution. In the case of a larger group, the people may approach the altar in continuous fashion, filling the empty places at the rail when those who have received the laying on of the hand and the absolution have returned to their places.

INDIVIDUAL CONFESSION
AND ABSOLUTION

1. When, during consultation with the pastor, a person desires individual confession and absolution, the following order may be used. The confession made by the penitent is protected from disclosure. The pastor is at all times obligated to respect the confidential nature of a confession.

2. The penitent, who may kneel, says:

Dear pastor, hear my confession.

3. The pastor responds:

Ⓟ **Let us begin in the name of God, to whom all hearts are open and from whom no secrets are hid.**

The pastor and penitent say:

In the name of God, the Father, the Son, and the Holy Spirit.
Hear my prayer, O Lord; let my cry for help come to you.
Do not hide your face from me when I am in distress.
Turn your ear to me; when I call, answer me quickly. (Ps. 102:1-2)

Have mercy on me, O God, according to your unfailing love;
    according to your great compassion blot out my transgressions.
Wash away all my iniquity and cleanse me from my sin.
For I know my transgressions, and my sin is always before me.
Against you, you only, have I sinned and done what is evil in your sight.
(Ps. 51:1-4a)

The penitent continues:

I have lived as if God did not matter and as if I mattered most.

My Lord's name I have not honored as I should; my worship and prayers have faltered.

I have not let his love have its way with me; and so my love for others has failed.

There are those whom I have hurt, and those whom I failed to help.

My thoughts and deeds have been soiled with sin.

What troubles me particularly is that . . .

4. Here the penitent confesses those sins which are known and those which disturb or grieve him/her.

5. The pastor may then offer admonition and comfort from Holy Scripture. Then they say together:

Create in me a clean heart, O God,
  and renew a right spirit within me.
Cast me not away from your presence,
  and take not your Holy Spirit from me.
Restore to me the joy of your salvation,
  and uphold me with your free Spirit. (Ps. 51:10-12)

The penitent continues:

O almighty God, merciful Father, I, a poor, miserable sinner, confess to you all my sins and iniquities with which I have ever offended you and justly deserved your punishment now and forever. But I am heartily sorry for them and sincerely repent of them, and I pray you of your boundless mercy and for the sake of the holy, innocent, bitter sufferings and death of your beloved Son, Jesus Christ, to be gracious and merciful to me, a poor sinful being.

6. The pastor stands and says:

Ⓟ **Do you believe that the word of Christ's forgiveness I speak to you is from the Lord himself?**

Ⓡ Yes, I do.

7. The pastor lays his hand on the head of the penitent and says:

Ⓟ **Receive the forgiveness Christ won for you by his Passion, death, and resurrection. By the command of our Lord Jesus Christ I, a called and ordained servant of the Word, forgive you your sins in the name of the Father and of the ✠ Son and of the Holy Spirit.**

Ⓡ Amen

142

The penitent and pastor continue:

Sing to the Lord, you saints of his; praise his holy name. For his anger lasts only a moment, but his favor lasts a lifetime; weeping may remain for a night, but rejoicing comes in the morning. O Lord my God, I will give you thanks forever. (Ps. 30:4-5, 12b)

8. The pastor says:

℗ Go in the strength, the peace, and the joy of the Lord, and come soon to receive Christ's body and blood and, being joined to him, live toward the work and the beauty he would fulfill in you for himself and for others. Go, you are free.

NOTES

General

▶ *This is the type of confession of which the Lutheran Confessions, or Symbols, speak and which they value highly in pastoral care allowing it to be called a Sacrament in the strict sense (Apology, XIII, 4), particularly in view of the theological importance of the indicative-operative absolution: "I forgive you all your sins . . . ." As in Holy Baptism and the Lord's Supper, the forgiveness of sins is here applied to the individual and appropriated by that individual's faith in the forgiveness of sins earned by Jesus Christ. The certainty and power of this direct absolution are based on the power of the keys (Matthew 16:19; 18:18; John 20:22-23), exercised through God's called servants of the Word in the office of the public ministry.*

▶ *Individual confession with its comforting absolution stands in its own right as a function of pastoral care and the exercise of the divinely ordained Office of the Keys (in the strict sense). No rule should be made that it become an indispensable presupposition for the reception of the Lord's Supper.*

▶ *It is helpful if regular times are posted when the pastor is available in a designated place to hear individual confession. Counseling sessions will frequently lead to individual confession and absolution. In such situations the pastor should provide an appropriate transition.*

▶ *The confidentiality of confession, commonly known as the seal of confession, must under no circumstances be broken by the pastor.*

Preparation for the Rite

▶ *Confession may be made in the church, at or near the altar (chancel rail). The pastor may kneel with the penitent, or may sit in a chair placed on the opposite side of the rail, thus sitting at right angles to the kneeling penitent. Care should be taken to ensure that no one overhears or disturbs the penitent.*

▶ *When a counseling session leads to individual confession, the confession will most frequently take place in the pastor's private office or study.*

▶ *Appropriate vestments for the pastor are alb, or surplice, and stole in the color of the day or season.*

▶ *When confessions are heard at regularly appointed times, it is helpful to provide devotional aids for those waiting in the nave.*

▶ *If penitents are uncomfortable with this actual form of confession, they should be encouraged to use their own words.*

144

MINISTRY TO THE SICK
AND INFIRM

1. Members of the congregation are encouraged to notify the pastor when a member is sick that prayer may be offered and that by the ministry of Word and Sacrament the afflicted may be strengthened in faith and hope.

2. By means of the Word of God the pastor will instruct his people, especially in time of sickness, to trust in God, confident that, according to his gracious promise, in all things he works for the good of those who love him.

3. When the pastor is called to minister to an unbeliever, he will seek to speak the Word of God to him/her that he/she may be moved to repentance and faith in Christ.

4. The pastor is encouraged to assess the sick person's spiritual condition and adapt this ministration accordingly. Ordinarily it will include a reading from Holy Scripture and a brief meditation on it, Confession and Absolution, Intercessory Prayer, Lord's Prayer, and Benediction.

5. The pastor may begin with the following or some other greeting:

℗ **Peace be to this house (place) and all who dwell here.**

℟ Amen

6. The pastor may read any of the following portions of Holy Scripture and give words of comfort based on them.

145

INVOCATION AND CONSOLATION

"Those who suffer he delivers in their suffering; he speaks to them in their affliction." (Job 36:15)

All my longings lie open before you, O Lord; my sighing is not hidden from you. O Lord, do not forsake me; be not far from me, O my God. Come quickly to help me, O Lord my Savior. (Ps. 38:9, 21-22)

Hear my prayer, O Lord; let my cry for help come to you. Do not hide your face from me when I am in distress. (Ps. 102:1-2)

Out of the depths I cry to you, O Lord; O Lord, hear my voice. Let your ears be attentive to my cry for mercy. If you, O Lord, kept a record of sins, O Lord, who could stand? But with you there is forgiveness; therefore you are feared. I wait for the Lord, my soul waits, and in his word I put my hope. (Ps. 130:1-5)

Is any one of you sick? He should call the elders of the church to pray over him and anoint him with oil in the name of the Lord. And the prayer offered in faith will make the sick person well; the Lord will raise him up. If he has sinned, he will be forgiven. Therefore confess your sins to each other and pray for each other so that you may be healed. The prayer of a righteous man is powerful and effective. (James 5:14-16)

O Lord, you have searched me and you know me. You know when I sit and when I rise; you perceive my thoughts from afar. You discern my going out and my lying down; you are familiar with all my ways. Before a word is on my tongue you know it completely, O Lord. You hem me in—behind and before; you have laid your hand upon me. Such knowledge is too wonderful for me, too lofty for me to attain. Where can I go from your Spirit? Where can I flee from your presence? If I go up to the heavens, you are there; if I make my bed in the depths, you are there. If I rise on the wings of dawn, if I settle on the far side of the sea, even there your hand will guide me, your right hand will hold me fast. If I say, "Surely the darkness will hide me and the light become night around me," even the darkness will not be dark to you; the night will shine like the day, for darkness is as light to you. Search me, O God, and know my heart; test me and know my anxious thoughts. See if there is any offensive way in me, and lead me in the way everlasting. (Ps. 139:1-12, 23-24)

Because of the Lord's great love we are not consumed, for his compassions never fail. They are new every morning; great is your faithfulness. I say to myself, "The Lord is my portion; therefore I will wait for him." The Lord is good to those whose hope is in him, to the one who seeks him; it is good to wait quietly for the salvation of the Lord. (Lam. 3:22-26)

"Come, let us return to the Lord. He has torn us to pieces but he will heal us; he has injured us but he will bind up our wounds." (Hos. 6:1)

"God did not send his Son into the world to condemn the world, but to save the world through him." (John 3:17)

[Jesus said,] "Whoever comes to me I will never drive away." (John 6:37b)

God demonstrates his own love for us in this: While we were still sinners, Christ died for us. Since we have now been justified by his blood, how much more shall we be saved from God's wrath through him! (Rom. 5:8-9)

Therefore, since we are surrounded by such a great cloud of witnesses, let us throw off everything that hinders and the sin that so easily entangles, and let us run with perseverance the race marked out for us. Let us fix our eyes on Jesus, the author and perfecter of our faith, who for the joy set before him endured the cross, scorning its shame, and sat down at the right hand of the throne of God. Consider him who endured such opposition from sinful men, so that you will not grow weary and lose heart. In your struggle against sin, you have not yet resisted to the point of shedding your blood. (Heb. 12:1-4)

FORGIVENESS AND REDEMPTION

Blessed is he whose transgressions are forgiven, whose sins are covered. Blessed is the man whose sin the Lord does not count against him and in whose spirit is no deceit. When I kept silent, my bones wasted away through my groaning all day long. For day and night your hand was heavy upon me; my strength was sapped as in the heat of summer. Then I acknowledged my sin to you and did not cover up my iniquity. I said, "I will confess my transgressions to the Lord"—and you forgave the guilt of my sin. (Ps. 32:1-5)

I waited patiently for the Lord; he turned to me and heard my cry. He lifted me out of the slimy pit, out of the mud and mire; he set my feet on a rock and gave me a firm place to stand. He put a new song in my mouth, a hymn of praise to our God. Many will see and fear and put their trust in the Lord. (Ps. 40:1-3)

"Call upon me in the day of trouble; I will deliver you, and you will honor me." (Ps. 50:15)

A few days later, when Jesus again entered Capernaum, the people heard that he had come home. So many gathered that there was no room left, not even outside the door, and he preached the word to them. Some men came, bringing to him a paralytic, carried by four of them. Since they could not get him to Jesus because of the crowd, they made an opening in the roof above Jesus and, after digging through it, lowered the mat the paralyzed man was lying on. When Jesus saw their faith, he said to the paralytic, "Son, your sins are forgiven." Now some teachers of the law were sitting there, thinking to themselves, "Why does this fellow talk like that? He's blaspheming! Who can forgive sins but God alone?" Immediately Jesus knew in his spirit that this was what they were thinking in their hearts, and he said to them, "Why are you thinking these things? Which is easier: to say to the paralytic, 'Your sins are forgiven,' or to say, 'Get up, take your mat and walk'? But that you may know that the Son of Man has authority on earth to forgive sins . . . ." He said to the paralytic, "I tell you, get up, take your mat and go home." He got up, took his mat and walked out in full view of them all. This amazed everyone and they praised God, saying, "We have never seen anything like this!" (Mark 2:1-12)

The Lord is compassionate and gracious, slow to anger, abounding in love. He will not always accuse, nor will he harbor his anger forever; he does not treat us as our sins deserve or repay us according to our iniquities. For as high as the heavens are above the earth, so great is his love for those who fear him; as far as the east is from the west, so far has he removed our transgressions from us. (Ps. 103:8-12)

Jesus said, "It is not the healthy who need a doctor, but the sick. But go and learn what this means: 'I desire mercy, not sacrifice.' For I have not come to call the righteous, but sinners." (Matt. 9:12-13)

"Come to me, all you who are weary and burdened, and I will give you rest. Take my yoke upon you and learn from me, for I am gentle and humble in heart, and you will find rest for your souls. For my yoke is easy and my burden is light." (Matt. 11:28-30)

If anyone is in Christ, he is a new creation; the old has gone, the new has come! All this is from God, who reconciled us to himself through Christ and gave us the ministry of reconciliation: that God was reconciling the world to himself in Christ, not counting men's sins against them. And he has committed to us the message of reconciliation. (2 Cor. 5:17-19)

Praise be to the God and Father of our Lord Jesus Christ, who has blessed us in the heavenly realms with every spiritual blessing in Christ. For he chose us in him before the creation of the world to be holy and blameless in his sight. In love he predestined us to be adopted as his sons through Jesus Christ, in accordance with his pleasure and will—to the praise of his glorious grace, which he has freely given us in the One he loves. In him we have redemption through his blood, the forgiveness of sins, in accordance with the riches of God's grace . . . . (Eph. 1:3-7)

This is how God showed his love among us: He sent his one and only Son into the world that we might live through him. This is love: not that we loved God, but that he loved us and sent his Son as an atoning sacrifice for our sins. (1 John 4:9-10)

PEACE AND HOPE

You have made known to me the path of life; you will fill me with joy in your presence, with eternal pleasures at your right hand. (Ps. 16:11)

The Lord is my shepherd; I shall not want. He maketh me to lie down in green pastures: he leadeth me beside the still waters. He restoreth my soul: he leadeth me in the paths of righteousness for his name's sake. Yea, though I walk through the valley of the shadow of death, I will fear no evil: for thou art with me; thy rod and thy staff they comfort me. Thou preparest a table before me in the presence of mine enemies: thou anointest my head with oil; my cup runneth over. Surely goodness and mercy shall follow me all the days of my life: and I will dwell in the house of the Lord for ever. (Ps. 23 KJV)

The Lord is my shepherd, I shall lack nothing. He makes me lie down in green pastures, he leads me beside quiet waters, he restores my soul. He guides me in paths of righteousness for his name's sake. Even though I walk through the valley of the shadow of death, I will fear no evil, for you are with me; your rod and your staff, they comfort me. You prepare a table before me in the presence of my enemies. You anoint my head with oil; my cup overflows. Surely goodness and love will follow me all the days of my life, and I will dwell in the house of the Lord forever. (Ps. 23 NIV)

The Lord is my light and my salvation—whom shall I fear? The Lord is the stronghold of my life—of whom shall I be afraid? (Ps. 27:1)

How priceless is your unfailing love! Both high and low among men find refuge in the shadow of your wings. They feast on the abundance of your house; you give them drink from your river of delights. For with you is the fountain of life; in your light we see light. (Ps. 36:7-9)

Trust in the Lord with all your heart and lean not on your own understanding; in all your ways acknowledge him, and he will make your paths straight. Do not be wise in your own eyes; fear the Lord and shun evil. This will bring health to your body and nourishment to your bones. (Prov. 3:5-8)

You did not receive a spirit that makes you a slave again to fear, but you received the Spirit of sonship. And by him we cry, "Abba, Father." The Spirit himself testifies with our spirit that we are God's children. Now if we are children, then we are heirs—heirs of God and co-heirs with Christ, if indeed we share in his sufferings in order that we may also share in his glory. (Rom. 8:15-17)

Do not throw away your confidence; it will be richly rewarded. You need to persevere so that when you have done the will of God, you will receive what he has promised. For in just a very little while, "He who is coming will come and will not delay. But my righteous one will live by faith." (Heb. 10:35-38a)

Praise be to the God and Father of our Lord Jesus Christ! In his great mercy he has given us new birth into a living hope through the resurrection of Jesus Christ from the dead, and into an inheritance that can never perish, spoil or fade—kept in heaven for you, who through faith are shielded by God's power until the coming of the salvation that is ready to be revealed in the last time. In this you greatly rejoice, though now for a little while you may have had to suffer grief in all kinds of trials. These have come so that your faith—of greater worth than gold, which perishes even though refined by fire—may be proved genuine and may result in praise, glory and honor when Jesus Christ is revealed. Though you have not seen him, you love him; and even though you do not see him now, you believe in him and are filled with an inexpressible and glorious joy, for you are receiving the goal of your faith, the salvation of your souls. (1 Peter 1:3-9)

Humble yourselves, therefore, under God's mighty hand, that he may lift you up in due time. Cast all your anxiety on him because he cares for you. Be self-controlled and alert. Your enemy the devil prowls around like a roaring lion looking for someone to devour. Resist him, standing firm in the faith, because you know that your brothers throughout the world are undergoing the same kind of sufferings. And the God of all grace, who called you to his eternal glory in Christ, after you have suffered a little while, will himself restore you and make you strong, firm and steadfast. To him be the power for ever and ever. Amen. (1 Peter 5:6-11)

How great is the love the Father has lavished on us, that we should be called children of God! And that is what we are! The reason the world does not know us is that it did not know him. Dear friends, now we are children of God, and what we will be has not yet been made known. But we know that when he appears, we shall be like him, for we shall see him as he is. (1 John 3:1-2)

7. If the sick person desires to make individual, or private, confession, the pastor requests others present to leave the room. Otherwise the pastor leads the sick person and others present in the general confession.

℗ O almighty God, merciful Father, I, a poor, miserable sinner, confess to you all my sins and iniquities with which I have ever offended you and justly deserved your punishment now and forever. But I am heartily sorry for them and sincerely repent of them, and I pray you of your boundless mercy and for the sake of the holy, innocent, bitter sufferings and death of your beloved Son, Jesus Christ, to be gracious and merciful to me, a poor sinful being.

The pastor lays his hand on the head of the penitent and says:

℗ Receive the forgiveness Christ won for you by his Passion, death, and resurrection. By the command of our Lord Jesus Christ I, a called and ordained servant of the Word, forgive you all your sins in the name of the Father and of the ✠ Son and of the Holy Spirit.

℟ Amen

OR

℗ Most merciful God, we confess that we are by nature sinful and unclean. We have sinned against you in thought, word, and deed, by what we have done and by what we have left undone. We have not loved you with our whole heart; we have not loved our neighbors as ourselves. We justly deserve your present and eternal punishment. For the sake of your Son, Jesus Christ, have mercy on us. Forgive us, renew us, and lead us, so that we may delight in your will and walk in your ways to the glory of your holy name.

℟ Amen

The pastor lays his hand on the head of the penitent and says:

℗ Almighty God in his mercy has given his Son to die for you and for his sake forgives you all your sins. As a called and ordained servant of the Word I therefore forgive you all your sins in the name of the Father and of the ✠ Son and of the Holy Spirit.

℟ Amen

8. *The Prayer Sentences (Preces) may be said.*

℗ **O Lord, save your servant,**

℟ who trusts in you.

℗ **Send your servant help from your holy sanctuary,**

151

Ⓡ and strength from your holy dwelling.

Ⓟ **Look upon __his/her__ affliction and pain,**

Ⓡ and forgive all __his/her__ sins.

Ⓟ **O Lord, hear our prayer,**

Ⓡ and let our cry come to you.

9. One of the following or another appropriate Prayer is said.

Ⓟ **O Lord, look down from heaven; behold, visit, and relieve your servant __name__ for whom we pray. Look upon __him/her__ with the eyes of your mercy and give __him/her__ comfort and sure confidence in you. Defend __him/her__ from every danger to body and soul and keep __him/her__ in peace and safety; through Jesus Christ, our Lord, who lives and reigns with you and the Holy Spirit, one God, now and forever.** ⟨271⟩

Ⓡ Amen

OR

Ⓟ **Father of all mercy, you never fail to help those who call on you for help. Give strength and confidence to your __son/daughter__ in __his/her__ time of great need that __he/she__ may know that you are near and that underneath are your everlasting arms. Grant that, resting on your protection, __he/she__ may fear no evil, for you are with __him/her__ to comfort and deliver __him/her__ ; through Jesus Christ, our Lord, who lives and reigns with you and the Holy Spirit, one God, now and forever.** ⟨272⟩

Ⓡ Amen

10. The Lord's Prayer is said.

Ⓐ Our Father who art in heaven,	OR	Ⓐ Our Father in heaven,
hallowed be thy name,		hallowed be your name,
thy kingdom come,		your kingdom come,
thy will be done		your will be done
on earth as it is in heaven.		on earth as in heaven.

Give us this day our daily bread;
and forgive us our trespasses
   as we forgive those
     who trespass against us;
and lead us not into temptation,
   but deliver us from evil.
For thine is the kingdom
   and the power and the glory
   forever and ever. Amen

Give us today our daily bread.
Forgive us our sins
   as we forgive those
     who sin against us.
Lead us not into temptation,
   but deliver us from evil.
For the kingdom, the power,
   and the glory are yours
   now and forever. Amen

11. The Benediction is said.

P **The Lord bless you and keep you.**
The Lord make his face shine on you and be gracious to you.
The Lord lift up his countenance on you and ✠ give you peace.

R Amen

153

COMMUNION OF THE SICK
AND HOMEBOUND

1. The Lord's Supper is given only to those in the communion of the Church who repent and believe that the true body and blood of Jesus Christ are present in the bread and wine for the forgiveness of their sins.

2. The table used for the celebration of the Sacrament is covered with a clean white cloth. Two lighted candles (unless oxygen is being administered) and a crucifix or cross may be placed on the table.

3. If the entire service cannot be used, it may be shortened to the following: Confession and Absolution, Collect, Reading, Offertory, Preface, Lord's Prayer, Words of Institution, Distribution, and Benediction.

4. The pastor may begin with the following or some other greeting.

℗   **Peace be to this house (place) and all who dwell here.**

℟   Amen

5. The pastor may engage in conversation the person being visited and others present, thus establishing a pastoral relationship with them.

6. If the sick person desires to make individual, or private, confession, the pastor requests others present to leave the room. Otherwise the pastor leads the sick person and others present in the general confession.

154

P O almighty God, merciful Father, I, a poor, miserable sinner, confess to you all my sins and iniquities with which I have ever offended you and justly deserved your punishment now and forever. But I am heartily sorry for them and sincerely repent of them, and I pray you of your boundless mercy and for the sake of the holy, innocent, bitter sufferings and death of your beloved Son, Jesus Christ, to be gracious and merciful to me, a poor sinful being.

The pastor lays his hand on the head of the penitent and says:

P Receive the forgiveness Christ won for you by his Passion, death, and resurrection. By the command of our Lord Jesus Christ I, a called and ordained servant of the Word, forgive you all your sins in the name of the Father and of the ✠ Son and of the Holy Spirit.

R Amen

OR

P Most merciful God, we confess that we are by nature sinful and unclean. We have sinned against you in thought, word, and deed, by what we have done and by what we have left undone. We have not loved you with our whole heart; we have not loved our neighbors as ourselves. We justly deserve your present and eternal punishment. For the sake of your Son, Jesus Christ, have mercy on us. Forgive us, renew us, and lead us, so that we may delight in your will and walk in your ways to the glory of your holy name.

R Amen

The pastor lays his hand on the head of the penitent and says:

P Almighty God in his mercy has given his Son to die for you and for his sake forgives you all your sins. As a called and ordained servant of the Word I therefore forgive you all your sins in the name of the Father and of the ✠ Son and of the Holy Spirit.

R Amen

7. The Collect of the Day or one of the following Collects is said.

P Let us pray.

[P] O God, the strength of the weak and the consolation of all who put their trust in you, mercifully accept our prayers on behalf of your servant _____name_____ that by your power ____his/her____ sickness may be turned to health and our sorrow to joy; through Jesus Christ, your Son, our Lord, who lives and reigns with you and the Holy Spirit, one God, now and forever. ⟨273⟩

[R] Amen

OR

[P] Gracious Father, you have assured us that we shall receive strength for every day of our lives. Grant your servant _____name_____ , who is homebound, both the desire and the will to spend ____his/her____ days as an obedient child, trusting in your goodness and remembering with thankfulness your mercies, which are new every morning; through Jesus Christ, your Son, our Lord, who lives and reigns with you and the Holy Spirit, one God, now and forever. ⟨274⟩

[R] Amen

OR

[P] O God, in accordance with your infinite wisdom you have permitted your servant _____name_____ to be homebound for many days and perhaps for the rest of ____his/her____ earthly life. Grant ____him/her____ a special measure of grace to accept this confinement not as punishment but as a sign of loving care from you; through Jesus Christ, your Son, our Lord, who lives and reigns with you and the Holy Spirit, one God, now and forever. ⟨275⟩

[R] Amen

8. The Old Testament Reading, Epistle, and Holy Gospel of the Day may be read or the following Readings. The pastor may briefly comment on the reading(s).

[P] But now, this is what the Lord says—he who created you, O Jacob, he who formed you, O Israel: "Fear not, for I have redeemed you; I have called you by name; you are mine. When you pass through the waters, I will be with you; and when you pass through the rivers, they will not sweep over you. When you walk through the fire, you will not be burned; the flames will not set you ablaze. For I am the Lord, your God, the Holy One of Israel, your Savior." (Is. 43:1-3a)

Praise be to the God and Father of our Lord Jesus Christ, the Father of compassion and the God of all comfort, who comforts us all in our troubles, so that we can comfort those in any trouble with the comfort we ourselves have received from God. For just as the sufferings of Christ flow over into our lives, so also through Christ our comfort overflows. (2 Cor. 1:3-5)

Some men brought to him a paralytic, lying on a mat. When Jesus saw their faith, he said to the paralytic, "Take heart, son; your sins are forgiven." At this, some of the teachers of the law said to themselves, "This fellow is blaspheming!" Knowing their thoughts, Jesus said, "Why do you entertain evil thoughts in your hearts? Which is easier: to say, 'Your sins are forgiven,' or to say, 'Get up and walk'? But so that you may know that the Son of Man has authority on earth to forgive sins . . ." Then he said to the paralytic, "Get up, take your mat and go home." And the man got up and went home. When the crowd saw this, they were filled with awe; and they praised God, who had given such authority to men. (Matt. 9:2-8)

"If anyone loves me, he will obey my teaching. My Father will love him, and we will come to him and make our home with him." (John 14:23)

9. The table is prepared and the Offertory is said.

Ⓐ Create in me a clean heart, O God, and renew a right spirit within me. Cast me not away from your presence, and take not your Holy Spirit from me. Restore to me the joy of your salvation, and uphold me with your free spirit. Amen

10. The Preface is said.

Ⓟ **The Lord be with you.**

Ⓡ And with your spirit.

Ⓟ **Lift up your hearts.**

Ⓡ We lift them to the Lord.

Ⓟ **Let us give thanks to the Lord, our God.**

Ⓡ It is good and right so to do.

Ⓟ **It is truly good, right, and salutary that we should at all times and in all places give thanks to you, holy Lord, almighty Father, everlasting God, through Jesus Christ, our Lord, who overcame death and the grave and by his glorious resurrection opened to us the way of everlasting life. Therefore with angels and**

157

archangels and with all the company of heaven we laud and magnify your glorious name, evermore praising you and saying:

🄰 Holy, holy, holy Lord, God of Sabaoth. Heaven and earth are full of your glory. Hosanna in the highest. Blessed is he who comes in the name of the Lord. Hosanna in the highest.

🄿 **Lord of heaven and earth, we praise and thank you for having had mercy on those whom you created, sending your only-begotten Son into our flesh to bear our sin and be our Savior. With repentant joy we receive the salvation accomplished for us by the all-availing sacrifice of his body and his blood on the cross.**

Gathered in the name and the remembrance of Jesus, we beg you, O Lord, to forgive, renew, and strengthen us with your Word and Spirit. Grant us faithfully to eat his body and drink his blood as he bids us to do in his own testament. Hear us as we pray in his name and as he has taught us. (162)

11. The Lord's Prayer is said.

🄰 Our Father who art in heaven,
    hallowed be thy name,
    thy kingdom come,
    thy will be done
        on earth as it is in heaven.
Give us this day our daily bread;
and forgive us our trespasses
    as we forgive those
        who trespass against us;
and lead us not into temptation,
    but deliver us from evil.
For thine is the kingdom
    and the power and the glory
    forever and ever. Amen

OR

🄰 Our Father in heaven,
    hallowed be your name,
    your kingdom come,
    your will be done
        on earth as in heaven.
Give us today our daily bread.
Forgive us our sins
    as we forgive those
        who sin against us.
Lead us not into temptation,
    but deliver us from evil.
For the kingdom, the power,
    and the glory are yours
    now and forever. Amen

12. The Words of Institution are said.

🄿 **Our Lord Jesus Christ, on the night when he was betrayed, took bread, and when he had given thanks, he broke it and gave it to the disciples and said: Take, eat; this is my ✠body, which is given for you. This do in remembrance of me. In the same way also he took the cup after supper, and when he had given thanks, he gave it to them, saying: Drink of it, all of you; this is my ✠blood of the new testament, which is shed for you for the forgiveness of sins. This do, as often as you drink it, in remembrance of me.**

13. The Peace is said.

P **The peace of the Lord be with you always.**

R Amen

OR

P **The peace of the Lord be with you always.**

R And also with you.

Those present may greet one another in the name of the Lord.

Peace be with you.   R Peace be with you.

14. The Agnus Dei may be said.

All O Christ, the Lamb of God, who takes away the sin of the world, have mercy on us and grant us your peace. Amen

15. The Distribution. It is appropriate that the pastor receive the body and blood of the Lord, together with those present who have previously been admitted to the Lord's Table.

Take, eat; this is the true body of our Lord and Savior Jesus Christ, given into death for your sins. Take, drink; this is the true blood of our Lord and Savior Jesus Christ, shed for the forgiveness of your sins.	**OR** Take, eat; this is the very body of Christ, given for you. Take, drink; this is the very blood of Christ, shed for you.

16. After all have communed, the pastor says:

159

P **The body and blood of our Lord strengthen and preserve you steadfast in the true faith to life everlasting.**

R Amen

17. One of the following Post-Communion Collects is said.

P **Let us pray.**

P **Almighty God, heavenly Father, we give thanks that you have refreshed us with the body and blood of your dear Son, Jesus Christ, and we pray that this heavenly food which we have received will strengthen our faith that we may bear all crosses, sickness, and trials with patience and trust until you grant us deliverance, peace, and health; through Jesus Christ, our Lord, who lives and reigns with you and the Holy Spirit, one God, now and forever.** ⟨276⟩

R Amen

OR

P **We give thanks to you, almighty God, that you have refreshed us through this salutary gift, and we implore you that of your mercy you would strengthen us through the same in faith toward you and in fervent love toward one another; through Jesus Christ, your Son, our Lord, who lives and reigns with you and the Holy Spirit, one God, now and forever.** (163)

R Amen

18. The Benedicamus and Benediction conclude the service.

P **Bless we the Lord.**

R Thanks be to God.

P **The Lord bless you and keep you.**
The Lord make his face shine on you and be gracious to you.
The Lord lift up his countenance on you and✠ give you peace.

R Amen

NOTES

General

▶ *If a person desires to receive Holy Communion, but, because of extreme illness or physical disability, is unable to eat and drink the body and blood of the Lord, the pastor is to assure the person that in Holy Baptism he/she has received all the blessings of Christ's atonement.*

COMMENDATION
OF THE DYING

1. When a member of the Church is near death, the pastor should be called. In the absence of the pastor, members of the family may use this rite.

2. When death appears imminent, the rite may best be limited to the use of rubrics 5, 6, 8, 10, and 11.

3. In some circumstances it may be appropriate that the pastor spend a prolonged period of time with the dying person and the family. The full rite may then be used, with its parts paced to the condition of the dying person.

4. The pastor may begin with the following or some other greeting.

℗ **Peace be to this house (place) and all who dwell here.**

℟ Amen

5. The Kyrie and the Lord's Prayer are said.

🅰 Lord have mercy;
Christ have mercy;
Lord have mercy.

🅰 Our Father who art in heaven,
   hallowed be thy name,
   thy kingdom come,
   thy will be done
     on earth as it is in heaven.

OR

🅰 Our Father in heaven,
   hallowed be your name,
   your kingdom come,
   your will be done
     on earth as in heaven.

Give us this day our daily bread;
and forgive us our trespasses
    as we forgive those
      who trespass against us;
and lead us not into temptation,
    but deliver us from evil.
For thine is the kingdom
    and the power and the glory
    forever and ever. Amen

Give us today our daily bread.
Forgive us our sins
    as we forgive those
      who sin against us.
Lead us not into temptation,
    but deliver us from evil.
For the kingdom, the power,
    and the glory are yours
    now and forever. Amen

6. The pastor says:

P **Lord God, heavenly Father, look with favor upon your child** ___name___ **, forgive** ___him/her___ **all** ___his/her___ **sins, and comfort** ___him/her___ **with the promise of resurrection to life everlasting; through your Son Jesus Christ, our Lord, who lives and reigns with you and the Holy Spirit, one God, now and forever.** ⟨277⟩

R Amen

7. One or more of the following Psalms are said. Other psalms may be used instead.

PSALM 16

1 Keep me safe, O God, *
    for in you I take refuge.

2 I said to the Lord, "You are my
Lord; *
    apart from you I have no good
    thing."

3 As for the saints who are in the
land,*
    they are the glorious ones
    in whom is all my delight.

4 The sorrows of those will increase
who run after other gods.*
    I will not pour out their
    libations of blood or take up
    their names on my lips.

5 Lord, you have assigned me my
portion and my cup;*
    you have made my lot secure.

6 The boundary lines have fallen
for me in pleasant places; *
    surely I have a delightful
    inheritance.

7 I will praise the Lord, who
counsels me; *
    even at night my heart
    instructs me.

8 I have set the Lord always
before me.*
    Because he is at my right
    hand, I will not be shaken.

9 Therefore my heart is glad
and my tongue rejoices;*
    my body also will rest secure,

10 because you will not abandon me
to the grave,*
    nor will you let your Holy One
    see decay.

11 You have made known to me
the path of life; *
    you will fill me with joy
    in your presence,
    with eternal pleasures
    at your right hand.

Glory be to the Father and to the Son *
    and to the Holy Spirit;
as it was in the beginning, *
    is now, and will be forever. Amen

PSALM 23 (KJV)

OR

PSALM 23 (NIV)

1 The Lord is my shepherd; *
    I shall not want.

2 He maketh me to lie down
in green pastures; *
    he leadeth me beside
    the still waters.

3 He restoreth my soul; *
    he leadeth me in the
    paths of righteousness
    for his name's sake.

4 Yea, though I walk through
the valley of the shadow
of death, I will fear no
evil; *
    for thou art with me;
    thy rod and thy staff,
    they comfort me.

5 Thou preparest a table before
me in the presence of mine
enemies; *
    thou anointest my head with
    oil; my cup runneth over.

6 Surely goodness and mercy
shall follow me all the days
of my life; *
    and I will dwell in the
    house of the Lord for ever.

Glory be to the Father and
to the Son; *
    and to the Holy Spirit;
as it was in the beginning, *
    is now, and will be forever.
    Amen

1 The Lord is my shepherd, *
    I shall lack nothing.

2 He makes me lie down
in green pastures, *
    he leads me beside
    quiet waters,

3 he restores my soul. *
    He guides me in
    paths of righteousness
    for his name's sake.

4 Even though I walk through
the valley of the shadow
of death, I will fear no
evil, *
    for you are with me;
    your rod and your staff,
    they comfort me.

5 You prepare a table before me
in the presence of my
enemies. *
    You anoint my head with
    oil; my cup overflows.

6 Surely goodness and love
will follow me all the days
of my life, *
    and I will dwell in the
    house of the Lord forever.

Glory be to the Father and
to the Son *
    and to the Holy Spirit;
as it was in the beginning, *
    is now, and will be forever.
    Amen

PSALM 90

1 Lord, you have been our dwelling place *
  throughout all generations.

2 Before the mountains were born
or you brought forth the earth
and the world, *
  from everlasting to everlasting
  you are God.

3 You turn men back to dust, saying, *
  "Return to dust, O sons of men."

4 For a thousand years in your sight
are like a day that has just gone by, *
  or like a watch in the night.

5 You sweep men away in the sleep
of death; *
  they are like the new grass
  of the morning—

6 though in the morning it springs up
new, *
  by evening it is dry and withered.

7 We are consumed by your anger *
  and terrified by your indignation.

8 You have set our iniquities
before you, *
  our secret sins in the light
  of your presence.

9 All our days pass away
under your wrath; *
  we finish our years with a moan.

10 The length of our days is seventy
years—or eighty, if we have the
strength; *

yet their span is but trouble and
sorrow, for they quickly pass, and
we fly away.

11 Who knows the power of your anger? *
  For your wrath is as great as the
  fear that is due you.

12 Teach us to number our days aright, *
  that we may gain a heart of
  wisdom.

13 Relent, O Lord! How long will it
be? *
  Have compassion on your servants.

14 Satisfy us in the morning
with your unfailing love, *
  that we may sing for joy
  and be glad all our days.

15 Make us glad for as many days
as you have afflicted us, *
  for as many years
  as we have seen trouble.

16 May your deeds be shown to your
servants, *
  your splendor to their children.

17 May the favor of the Lord our God
rest upon us; *
  establish the work of our hands
  for us—yes, establish the work
  of our hands.

Glory be to the Father and to the Son *
  and to the Holy Spirit;
as it was in the beginning, *
  is now, and will be forever. Amen

8. One or more of the following portions of Holy Scripture are read.

Ⓟ **When the Sabbath was over, Mary Magdalene, Mary the mother of James, and Salome bought spices so that they might go to anoint Jesus' body. Very early on the first day of the week, just after sunrise, they were on their way to the tomb and they asked each other, "Who will roll the stone away from the entrance of the tomb?" But when they looked up, they saw that the stone, which was very large, had been rolled away. As they entered the tomb, they saw a** young man dressed in a white robe sitting on the right side, and they were alarmed. "Don't be alarmed," he said. "You are looking for Jesus the Nazarene, who was crucified. He has risen! He is not here. See the place where they laid him. But go, tell his disciples and Peter, 'He is going ahead of you into Galilee. There you will see him, just as he told you.'" Trembling and bewildered, the women went out and fled from the tomb. They said nothing to anyone, because they were afraid. (Mark 16:1-8)

"God so loved the world that he gave his one and only Son, that whoever believes in him shall not perish but have eternal life. For God did not send his Son into the world to condemn the world, but to save the world through him. Whoever believes in him is not condemned, but whoever does not believe stands condemned already because he has not believed in the name of God's one and only Son. This is the verdict: Light has come into the world, but men loved darkness instead of light because their deeds were evil. Everyone who does evil hates the light, and will not come into the light for fear that his deeds will be exposed. But whoever lives by the truth comes into the light, so that it may be seen plainly that what he has done has been done through God." (John 3:16-21)

Early on the first day of the week, while it was still dark, Mary of Magdala went to the tomb and saw that the stone had been removed from the entrance. So she came running to Simon Peter and the other disciple, the one Jesus loved, and said, "They have taken the Lord out of the tomb, and we don't know where they have put him!" So Peter and the other disciple started for the tomb. Both were running, but the other disciple outran Peter and reached the tomb first. He bent over and looked in at the strips of linen lying there but did not go in. Then Simon Peter, who was behind him, arrived and went into the tomb. He saw the strips of linen lying there, as well as the burial cloth that had been around Jesus' head. The cloth was folded up by itself, separate from the linen. Finally the other disciple, who had reached the tomb first, also went inside. He saw and believed. (They still did not understand from Scripture that Jesus had to rise from the dead.) Then the disciples went back to their homes, but Mary stood outside the tomb crying. As she wept, she bent over to look into the tomb and saw two angels in white, seated where Jesus' body had been, one at the head and the other at the foot. They asked her, "Woman, why are you crying?" "They have taken my Lord away," she said, "and I don't know where they have put him." At this, she turned around and saw Jesus standing there, but she did not realize that it was Jesus. "Woman," he said, "why are you crying? Who is it you are looking for?" Thinking he was the gardener, she said, "Sir, if you have carried him away, tell me where you have put him, and I will get him." Jesus said to her, "Mary." She turned toward him and cried out in Aramaic, "Rabboni!" (which means Teacher). Jesus said, "Do not hold on to me, for I have not yet returned to the Father. Go instead to my brothers and tell them, 'I am returning to my Father and your Father, to my God and your God.'" Mary of Magdala went to the disciples with the news: "I have seen the Lord!" And she told them that he had said these things to her. (John 20:1-18)

After this I looked and there before me was a great multitude that no one could count, from every nation, tribe, people and language, standing before the throne and in front of the Lamb. They were wearing white robes and were holding palm branches in their hands. And they cried out in a loud voice: "Salvation belongs to our God, who sits on the throne, and to the Lamb." All the angels were standing around the throne and around the elders and the four living creatures. They fell down on their faces before the throne and worshiped God, saying: "Amen! Praise and glory and wisdom and thanks and honor and power and strength be to our God for ever and ever. Amen!" (Rev. 7:9-12)

9. When death is near, one or both of the following Canticles may be said or sung. The Magnificat, the Te Deum, The Litany, or other canticles or hymns may also be used.

Ⓐ Lamb of God, you take away the sin of the world;
have mercy on us.
Lamb of God, you take away the sin of the world;
have mercy on us.
Lamb of God, you take away the sin of the world;
grant us peace.

OR

Ⓐ Lord, now you let your servant go in peace; your word has been fulfilled. My own eyes have seen the salvation which you have prepared in the sight of every people: A light to reveal you to the nations and the glory of your people Israel. Glory be to the Father and to the Son and to the Holy Spirit; as it was in the beginning, is now, and will be forever. Amen.

10. The pastor lays his hand on the head of the dying Christian and says:

Ⓟ **Go in peace, ___name___. May God the Father, who created you, may God the Son, who redeemed and saved you with his blood, may God the Holy Spirit, who sanctified you in the water of Holy Baptism, receive you into the company of saints and angels to live in the light of his glory forevermore.**

Ⓡ Amen

℗ **The Lord bless you and keep you.**
The Lord make his face shine on you and be gracious to you.
The Lord lift up his countenance on you and ✠ give you peace.

℟ Amen

11. *The pastor may continue:*

℗ **Then let at last your angels come,**
To Abram's bosom bear me home
That I may die unfearing.
Within my earthen chamber keep
My body safe in peaceful sleep
Until your reappearing.
And then from death awaken me
That my own eyes with joy may see,
O Son of God, your glorious face,
My Savior and my ground of grace!
Lord Jesus Christ,
Oh, hear my prayer; oh, hear my prayer,
Your love surround me ev'rywhere!

12. *Should death occur, the following Prayer may be said:*

℗ **O God the Father, fountain and source of all blessings, we give thanks that you have kept our ___brother/sister___ in the faith and have taken ___him/her___ to yourself. Comfort us with your holy Word and give us strength that when our last hour comes we may peacefully fall asleep in you; through Jesus Christ, our Lord, who lives and reigns with you and the Holy Spirit, one God, now and forever.** ⟨278⟩

℟ Amen

13. *The rite concludes:*

℗ **The Lord bless us, defend us from all evil, and bring us to everlasting life.**

℟ Amen

BURIAL OF THE DEAD

1. This service is intended for the burial of those who departed this life in the Christian faith.

2. The ceremonies or tributes of social or other societies have no place within or after the service of the Church.

3. Baptized members are properly buried from the church.

AT THE HOME OR THE MORTUARY

4. The pastor greets the bereaved.

P **Grace to you and peace from God our Father and the Lord Jesus Christ.**

R Amen

5. A PSALM is read.

PSALM 23 (KJV)	OR	PSALM 23 (NIV)
[1] The Lord is my shepherd;* I shall not want.		[1] The Lord is my shepherd,* I shall lack nothing.

[2] He maketh me to lie down
 in green pastures;*
  he leadeth me beside
  the still waters.
		[2] He makes me lie down
		 in green pastures,*
		  he leads me beside
		  quiet waters,

³ He restoreth my soul;[*]
 he leadeth me in the
 paths of righteousness
 for his name's sake.

⁴ Yea, though I walk through
 the valley of the shadow
 of death, I will fear no
 evil;[*]
 for thou art with me;
 thy rod and thy staff,
 they comfort me.

⁵ Thou preparest a table before
 me in the presence of mine
 enemies;[*]
 thou anointest my head with
 oil; my cup runneth over.

⁶ Surely goodness and mercy
 shall follow me all the days
 of my life;[*]
 and I will dwell in the
 house of the Lord for ever.

Glory be to the Father and
to the Son[*]
 and to the Holy Spirit;
as it was in the beginning,[*]
 is now, and will be forever.
 Amen

³ he restores my soul.[*]
 He guides me in
 paths of righteousness
 for his name's sake.

⁴ Even though I walk through
 the valley of the shadow
 of death, I will fear no
 evil,[*]
 for you are with me;
 your rod and your staff,
 they comfort me.

⁵ You prepare a table before me
 in the presence of my
 enemies.[*]
 You anoint my head with
 oil; my cup overflows.

⁶ Surely goodness and love
 will follow me all the days
 of my life,[*]
 and I will dwell in the
 house of the Lord forever.

Glory be to the Father and
to the Son[*]
 and to the Holy Spirit;
as it was in the beginning,[*]
 is now, and will be forever.
 Amen

PSALM 90

¹ Lord, you have been our dwelling
 place[*]
 throughout all generations.

² Before the mountains were born
 or you brought forth the earth
 and the world,[*]
 from everlasting to everlasting
 you are God.

³ You turn men back to dust, saying,[*]
 "Return to dust, O sons of men."

⁴ For a thousand years in your sight
 are like a day that has just gone
 by,[*]
 or like a watch in the night.

⁵ You sweep men away in the sleep
 of death;[*]
 they are like the new grass
 of the morning—

⁶ though in the morning it springs up
 new,[*]
 by evening it is dry
 and withered.

⁷ We are consumed by your anger[*]
 and terrified by your indignation.

⁸ You have set our iniquities
 before you,[*]
 our secret sins in the light
 of your presence.

9 All our days pass away under your
    wrath;∗
        we finish our years with a moan.

10 The length of our days is seventy
    years—or eighty, if we have the
    strength;∗
        yet their span is but trouble and
        sorrow, for they quickly pass,
        and we fly away.

11 Who knows the power of your anger?∗
        For your wrath is as great as the
        fear that is due you.

12 Teach us to number our days aright,∗
        that we may gain a heart of
        wisdom.

13 Relent, O Lord! How long will it be?∗
        Have compassion on your servants.

14 Satisfy us in the morning with your
    unfailing love,∗

        that we may sing for joy and be
        glad all our days.

15 Make us glad for as many days
    as you have afflicted us,∗
        for as many years as we have seen
        trouble.

16 May your deeds be shown to your
    servants,∗
        your splendor to their children.

17 May the favor of the Lord our God
    rest upon us;∗
        establish the work of our hands
        for us—yes, establish the work
        of our hands.

    Glory be to the Father
    and to the Son∗
        and to the Holy Spirit;
    as it was in the beginning,∗
        is now, and will be forever. Amen

PSALM 130

1 Out of the depths∗
        I cry to you, O Lord;

2 O Lord, hear my voice.∗
        Let your ears be attentive
        to my cry for mercy.

3 If you, O Lord, kept a record of
    sins,∗
        O Lord, who could stand?

4 But with you there is forgiveness;∗
        therefore you are feared.

5 I wait for the Lord, my soul waits,∗
        and in his word I put my hope.

6 My soul waits for the Lord more
    than watchmen wait for the morning,∗

        more than watchmen wait for the
        morning.

7 O Israel, put your hope in the
    Lord,∗
        for with the Lord is unfailing
        love and with him is full
        redemption.

8 He himself will redeem Israel∗
        from all their sins.

    Glory be to the Father
    and to the Son∗
        and to the Holy Spirit;
    as it was in the beginning,∗
        is now, and will be forever. Amen

*6. A READING from Holy Scripture is announced, and one of the following
portions is read.*

Ⓟ Hear the Word of God from the _____ chapter of _____ .

Brothers, we do not want you to be ignorant about those who fall asleep, or to grieve like the rest of men, who have no hope. We believe that Jesus died and rose again and so we believe that God will bring with Jesus those who have fallen asleep in him. According to the Lord's own word, we tell you that we who are still alive, who are left till the coming of the Lord, will certainly not precede those who have fallen asleep. For the Lord himself will come down from heaven, with a loud command, with the voice of the archangel and with the trumpet call of God, and the dead in Christ will rise first. After that, we who are still alive and are left will be caught up with them in the clouds to meet the Lord in the air. And so we will be with the Lord forever. Therefore encourage each other with these words. (1 Thess. 4:13-18)

"I tell you the truth, whoever hears my word and believes him who sent me has eternal life and will not be condemned; he has crossed over from death to life." (John 5:24)

"My sheep listen to my voice; I know them, and they follow me. I give them eternal life, and they shall never perish; no one can snatch them out of my hand. My Father, who has given them to me, is greater than all; no one can snatch them out of my Father's hand." (John 10:27-29)

"Do not let your hearts be troubled. [Believe] in God; [believe] also in me. In my Father's house are many rooms; if it were not so, I would have told you. I am going there to prepare a place for you. And if I go and prepare a place for you, I will come back and take you to be with me that you also may be where I am. You know the way to the place where I am going." Thomas said to him, "Lord, we [do not] know where you are going, so how can we know the way?" Jesus answered, "I am the way and the truth and the life. No one comes to the Father except through me." (John 14:1-6)

Ⓟ This is the Word of the Lord.

7. The COLLECT is said.

Ⓟ Almighty and most merciful God, you bring us through suffering and death with our Lord Jesus Christ to enter with him into glory. Grant us grace at all times to acknowledge and accept your holy and gracious will, to remain in true faith, and to find peace and joy in the resurrection of the dead and the glory of everlasting life; through Jesus Christ, your Son, our Lord, who lives and reigns with you and the Holy Spirit, one God, now and forever. ⟨279⟩

Ⓡ Amen

172

8. The LORD'S PRAYER is said.

Our Father who art in heaven,
    hallowed be thy name,
    thy kingdom come,
    thy will be done
        on earth as it is in heaven.
Give us this day our daily bread;
and forgive us our trespasses
    as we forgive those
        who trespass against us;
and lead us not into temptation,
    but deliver us from evil.
For thine is the kingdom
    and the power and the glory
    forever and ever. Amen

OR

Our Father in heaven,
    hallowed be your name,
    your kingdom come,
    your will be done
        on earth as in heaven.
Give us today our daily bread.
Forgive us our sins
    as we forgive those
        who sin against us.
Lead us not into temptation,
    but deliver us from evil.
For the kingdom, the power,
    and the glory are yours
    now and forever. Amen

9. The pastor blesses the bereaved.

P   **The grace of our Lord Jesus Christ and the love of God and the communion of the Holy Spirit ✠ be with you all.**

R   Amen

AT THE CHURCH

10. This service may be used as a memorial service by omitting rubrics 11, 12, 13, 14, and 32.

11. The pastor, in his customary vestments, meets the coffin, the pallbearers, and the bereaved at the entrance to the church.

12. The pastor greets the bereaved:

173

℗ Grace and peace to you from God our Father and the Lord Jesus Christ. I always thank God for you because of his grace given you in Christ Jesus. For in him you have been enriched in every way—in all your speaking and in all your knowledge. (1 Cor. 1:3-5)

℟ Thanks be to God.

OR

℗ Blessed be the God and Father of our Lord Jesus Christ, the source of all mercy and the God of all consolation. He comforts us in all our sorrows so that we can comfort others in their sorrows with the consolation we ourselves have received from God.

℟ Thanks be to God.

13. The coffin is covered with a pall to recall Holy Baptism. The pastor says:

℗ [Do you not] know that all of us who were baptized into Christ Jesus were baptized into his death? We were therefore buried with him through baptism into death in order that, just as Christ was raised from the dead through the glory of the Father, we too may live a new life. If we have been united with him in his death, we will certainly also be united with him in his resurrection. (Rom. 6:3-5)

Stand

14. The procession forms and enters the church, the pastor and assisting minister(s) going before the coffin.

15. A HYMN is sung, or one or more of the following PSALMS may be sung or said.

PSALM 39

XI E: Ionian

1 I said, "I will watch my ways and
  keep my tongue from sin;*
    I will put a muzzle on my mouth
    as long as the wicked are in my
    presence."

2 But when I was silent and still,
  not even saying anything good,*
    my anguish increased.

3 My heart grew hot within me, and as
  I meditated, the fire burned;*
    then I spoke with my tongue:

4 "Show me, O Lord, my life's end
  and the number of my days;*
    let me know how fleeting is my
    life.

5 You have made my days a mere
  handbreadth; the span of my years
  is as nothing before you.*
    Each man's life is but a breath.

6 Man is a mere phantom as he goes
  to and fro: He bustles about,
  but only in vain;*
    he heaps up wealth, not knowing
    who will get it.

7 "But now, Lord, what do I look for?*
    My hope is in you.

8 Save me from all my transgressions;*
    do not make me the scorn of fools.

9 I was silent; I would not open my
  mouth,*
    for you are the one who has done
    this.

10 Remove your scourge from me;*
    I am overcome by the blow
    of your hand.

11 You rebuke and discipline men for
  their sin; you consume their wealth
  like a moth—*
    each man is but a breath.

12 "Hear my prayer, O Lord, listen to
  my cry for help; be not deaf to my
  weeping.*
    For I dwell with you as an alien,
    a stranger, as all my fathers
    were.

13 Look away from me, that I may
  rejoice again*
    before I depart and am no more."

Glory be to the Father
and to the Son*
    and to the Holy Spirit;
as it was in the beginning,*
    is now, and will be forever. Amen

PSALM 46

XI Bb: Ionian

1 God is our refuge and strength,*
    an ever present help in trouble.

2 Therefore we will not fear,
    though the earth give way*

and the mountains fall into
the heart of the sea,

3 though its waters roar and foam*
and the mountains quake
with their surging.

4 There is a river whose streams make
glad the city of God;*
the holy place where the Most High
dwells.

5 God is within her, she will not fail;*
God will help her at break of day.

6 Nations are in uproar, kingdoms
fall;*
he lifts his voice, the earth melts.

7 The Lord Almighty is with us;*
the God of Jacob is our fortress.

8 Come and see the works
of the Lord,*

the desolations he has brought
on the earth.

9 He makes wars cease to the ends
of the earth;*
he breaks the bow and shatters the
spear, he burns the shields with
fire.

10 "Be still, and know that I am God;*
I will be exalted among the nations,
I will be exalted in the earth."

11 The Lord Almighty is with us;*
the God of Jacob is our fortress.

Glory be to the Father
and to the Son*
and to the Holy Spirit;
as it was in the beginning,*
is now, and will be forever. Amen

PSALM 90

XI C: Ionian

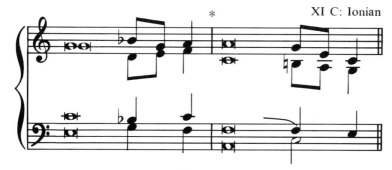

1 Lord, you have been our dwelling
place*
throughout all generations.

2 Before the mountains were born
or you brought forth the earth
and the world,*
from everlasting to everlasting
you are God.

3 You turn men back to dust, saying,*
"Return to dust, O sons of men."

4 For a thousand years in your
sight are like a day that has
just gone by,*
or like a watch in the night.

5 You sweep men away in the sleep
of death;*
they are like the new grass
of the morning—

6 though in the morning it springs
up new,*
by evening it is dry and withered.

7 We are consumed by your anger *
   and terrified by your indignation.

8 You have set our iniquities
   before you, *
      our secret sins in the light
      of your presence.

9 All our days pass away under your
   wrath; *
      we finish our years with a moan.

10 The length of our days is seventy
    years—or eighty, if we have the
    strength; *
       yet their span is but trouble and
       sorrow, for they quickly pass,
       and we fly away.

11 Who knows the power of your anger? *
    For your wrath is as great as the
    fear that is due you.

12 Teach us to number our days aright; *
    that we may gain a heart of
    wisdom.

13 Relent, O Lord! How long will it
    be? *

Have compassion on your servants.

14 Satisfy us in the morning with your
    unfailing love, *
       that we may sing for joy and be
       glad all our days.

15 Make us glad for as many days
    as you have afflicted us, *
       for as many years as we have seen
       trouble.

16 May your deeds be shown to your
    servants, *
       your splendor to their children.

17 May the favor of the Lord our God
    rest upon us; *
       establish the work of our hands
       for us—yes, establish the work
       of our hands.

Glory be to the Father
and to the Son *
   and to the Holy Spirit;
as it was in the beginning, *
   is now, and will be forever. Amen

PSALM 121

IX g^2 : Aeolian

1 I lift up my eyes to the hills— *
   where does my help come from?

2 My help comes from the Lord, *
   the Maker of heaven and earth.

3 He will not let your foot slip— *
   he who watches over you
   will not slumber;

4 indeed, he who watches over Israel *
   will neither slumber nor sleep.

5 The Lord watches over you— *
   the Lord is your shade at your
   right hand;

6 the sun will not harm you by day, *
   nor the moon by night.

7 The Lord will keep you
from all harm—*
    he will watch over your life;

8 the Lord will watch over your
coming and going*
    both now and forevermore.

Glory be to the Father
and to the Son*
    and to the Holy Spirit;
as it was in the beginning,*
    is now, and will be forever. Amen

PSALM 139

V E♭: Lydian

1 O Lord, you have searched me*
    and you know me.

2 You know when I sit and when I
rise;*
    you perceive my thoughts from
    afar.

3 You discern my going out and my
lying down;*
    you are familiar with all my ways.

4 Before a word is on my tongue*
    you know it completely, O Lord.

5 You hem me in, behind and before;*
    you have laid your hand upon me.

6 Such knowledge is too wonderful
for me,*
    too lofty for me to attain.

7 Where can I go from your Spirit?*
Where can I flee from your
presence?

8 If I go up to the heavens, you are
there;*
    if I make my bed in the depths,
    you are there.

9 If I rise on the wings of the dawn,*
    if I settle on the far side of the sea,

10 even there your hand will guide me,*
    your right hand will hold me fast.

11 If I say, "Surely the darkness
will hide me*
    and the light become night
    around me,"

12 even the darkness will not be dark
to you;*
    the night will shine like the day,
    for darkness is as light to you.

13 For you created my inmost being;*
    you knit me together in my
    mother's womb.

14 I praise you because I am fearfully
and wonderfully made;*
    your works are wonderful,
    I know that full well.

15 My frame was not hidden from you
when I was made in the secret
place.*
    When I was woven together
    in the depths of the earth,

16 your eyes saw my unformed body.*
    All the days ordained for me
    were written in your book
    before one of them came to be.

17 How precious to me are your
    thoughts, O God!*
        How vast is the sum of them!

18 Were I to count them, they would
    outnumber the grains of sand.*
        When I awake,
        I am still with you.

19 If only you would slay the wicked,
    O God!*
        Away from me, you bloodthirsty
        men!

20 They speak of you with evil intent;*
    your adversaries misuse your name.

21 Do I not hate those who hate you,
    O Lord,*
        and abhor those who rise up
        against you?

22 I have nothing but hatred for them;*
    I count them my enemies.

23 Search me, O God, and know my
    heart;*
        test me and know my anxious
        thoughts.

24 See if there is any offensive way
    in me,*
        and lead me in the way
        everlasting.

Glory be to the Father
and to the Son*
    and to the Holy Spirit;
as it was in the beginning,*
    is now, and will be forever. Amen

16. The COLLECT is chanted or said; the Salutation may precede it.

P The Lord be with you.

C And with your spir - it.

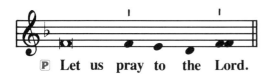

P Let us pray to the Lord.

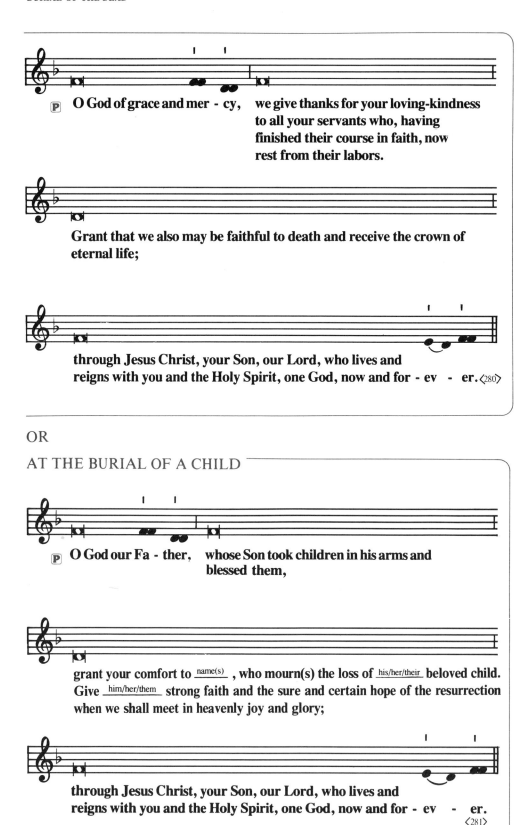

℗ O God of grace and mer - cy, we give thanks for your loving-kindness
to all your servants who, having
finished their course in faith, now
rest from their labors.

Grant that we also may be faithful to death and receive the crown of
eternal life;

through Jesus Christ, your Son, our Lord, who lives and
reigns with you and the Holy Spirit, one God, now and for - ev - er. ⟨280⟩

OR

AT THE BURIAL OF A CHILD

℗ O God our Fa - ther, whose Son took children in his arms and
blessed them,

grant your comfort to _name(s)_ , who mourn(s) the loss of _his/her/their_ beloved child.
Give _him/her/them_ strong faith and the sure and certain hope of the resurrection
when we shall meet in heavenly joy and glory;

through Jesus Christ, your Son, our Lord, who lives and
reigns with you and the Holy Spirit, one God, now and for - ev - er.
⟨281⟩

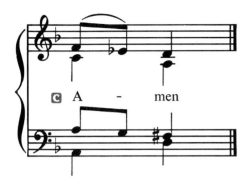

Sit

17. The OLD TESTAMENT READING is announced, and one of the following portions of Holy Scripture is read.

Ⓐ **The Old Testament Reading is from the _____ chapter of _____ .**

"Have pity on me, my friends, have pity, for the hand of God has struck me. Why do you pursue me as God does? Will you never get enough of my flesh? Oh, that my words were recorded, that they were written on a scroll, that they were inscribed with an iron tool on lead, or engraved in rock forever! I know that my Redeemer lives, and that in the end he will stand upon the earth. And after my skin has been destroyed, yet in my flesh I will see God; I myself will see him with my own eyes—I, and not another. How my heart yearns within me!" (Job 19:21-27)

On this mountain the Lord Almighty will prepare a feast of rich food for all peoples, a banquet of aged wine—the best of meats and the finest of wines. On this mountain he will destroy the shroud that enfolds all peoples, the sheet that covers all nations; he will swallow up death forever. The Sovereign Lord will wipe away the tears from all faces; he will remove the disgrace of his people from all the earth. The Lord has spoken. In that day they will say, "Surely this is our God; we trusted in him, and he saved us. This is the Lord, we trusted in him; let us rejoice and be glad in his salvation." (Is. 25:6-9)

The Spirit of the Sovereign Lord is on me, because the Lord has anointed me to preach good news to the poor. He has sent me to bind up the brokenhearted, to proclaim freedom for the captives and release for the prisoners, to proclaim the year of the Lord's favor and the day of vengeance of our God, to comfort all who mourn, and provide for those who grieve in Zion—to bestow on them a crown of beauty instead of ashes, the oil of gladness instead of mourning, and a garment of praise instead of a spirit of despair. They will be called oaks of righteousness, a planting of the Lord for the display of his splendor. (Is. 61:1-3)

181

Because of the Lord's great love we are not consumed, for his compassions never fail. They are new every morning; great is your faithfulness. I say to myself, "The Lord is my portion; therefore I will wait for him." The Lord is good to those whose hope is in him, to the one who seeks him; it is good to wait quietly for the salvation of the Lord. It is good for a man to bear the yoke while he is young. Let him sit alone in silence, for the Lord has laid it on him. Let him bury his face in the dust—there may yet be hope. Let him offer his cheek to one who would strike him, and let him be filled with disgrace. For men are not cast off by the Lord forever. Though he brings grief, he will show compassion, so great is his unfailing love. For he does not willingly bring affliction or grief to the children of men. (Lam. 3:22-33)

18. After the reading the assisting minister chants or says:

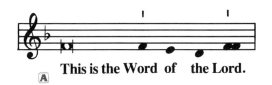

This is the Word of the Lord.

Thanks be to God.

19. The GRADUAL is sung or said.

IX g² : Aeolian

I lift up my eyes to the hills—*
  where does my help come from?
My help comes from the Lord,*
  the Maker of heaven and earth.
He will not let your foot slip—*
  he who watches over you will not
  slumber.   *(Ps. 121:1-3)*

20. The EPISTLE is announced, and one of the following portions of Holy Scripture is read.

Ⓐ **The Epistle is from the _____ chapter of _____ .**

What, then, shall we say in response to this? If God is for us, who can be against us? He who did not spare his own Son, but gave him up for us all—how will he not also, along with him, graciously give us all things? Who will bring any charge against those whom God has chosen? It is God who justifies. Who is he that condemns? Christ Jesus, who died—more than that, who was raised to life—is at the right hand of God and is also interceding for us. Who shall separate us from the love of Christ? Shall trouble or hardship or persecution or famine or nakedness or danger or sword? As it is written: "For your sake we face death all day long; we are considered as sheep to be slaughtered." No, in all these things we are more than conquerors through him who loved us. For I am convinced that neither death nor life, neither angels nor demons, neither the present nor the future, nor any powers, neither height nor depth, nor anything else in all creation, will be able to separate us from the love of God that is in Christ Jesus our Lord. (Rom. 8:31-39)

Now, brothers, I want to remind you of the gospel I preached to you, which you received and on which you have taken your stand. By this gospel you are saved, if you hold firmly to the word I preached to you. Otherwise, you have believed in vain. For what I received I passed on to you as of first importance: that Christ died for our sins according to the Scriptures, that he was buried, that he was raised on the third day according to the Scriptures, and that he appeared to Peter, and then to the Twelve. After that, he appeared to more than five hundred of the brothers at the same time, most of whom are still living, though some have fallen asleep. Then he appeared to James, then to all the apostles, and last of all he appeared to me also, as to one abnormally born. For I am the least of the apostles and do not even deserve to be called an apostle, because I persecuted the church of God. But by the grace of God I am what I am, and his grace to me was not without effect. No, I worked harder than all of them—yet not I, but the grace of God that was with me. Whether, then, it was I or they, this is what we preach, and this is what you believed. But if it is preached that Christ has been raised from the dead, how can some of you say that there is no

resurrection of the dead? If there is no resurrection of the dead, then not even Christ has been raised. And if Christ has not been raised, our preaching is useless and so is your faith. More than that, we are then found to be false witnesses about God, for we have testified about God that he raised Christ from the dead. But he did not raise him if in fact the dead are not raised. For if the dead are not raised, then Christ has not been raised either. And if Christ has not been raised, your faith is futile; you are still in your sins. Then those also who have fallen asleep in Christ are lost. If only for this life we have hope in Christ, we are to be pitied more than all men. But Christ has indeed been raised from the dead, the firstfruits of those who have fallen asleep. For since death came through a man, the resurrection of the dead comes also through a man. For as in Adam all die, so in Christ all will be made alive. But each in his own turn: Christ, the firstfruits; then, when he comes, those who belong to him. Then the end will come, when he hands over the kingdom to God the Father after he has destroyed all dominion, authority and power. For he must reign until he has put all his enemies under his feet. The last enemy to be destroyed is death. (1 Cor. 15:1-26)

But someone may ask, "How are the dead raised? With what kind of body will they come?" How foolish! What you sow does not come to life unless it dies. When you sow, you do not plant the body that will be, but just a seed, perhaps of wheat or of something else. But God gives it a body as he has determined, and to each kind of seed he gives its own body. All flesh is not the same: Men have one kind of flesh, animals have another, birds another and fish another. There are also heavenly bodies and there are earthly bodies; but the splendor of the heavenly bodies is one kind, and the splendor of the earthly bodies is another. The sun has one kind of splendor, the moon another and the stars another; and star differs from star in splendor. So will it be with the resurrection of the dead. The body that is sown is perishable, it is raised imperishable; it is sown in dishonor, it is raised in glory; it is sown in weakness, it is raised in power; it is sown a natural body, it is raised a spiritual body. If there is a natural body, there is also a spiritual body. So it is written: "The first man Adam became a living being"; the last Adam, a life-giving spirit. The spiritual did not come first, but the natural, and after that the spiritual. The first man was of the dust of the earth, the second man from heaven. As was the earthly man, so are those who are of the earth; and as is the man from heaven, so also are those who are of heaven. And just as we have borne the likeness of the earthly man, so shall we bear the likeness of the man from heaven. I declare to you, brothers, that flesh and blood cannot inherit the kingdom of God, nor does the perishable inherit the imperishable. Listen, I tell you a mystery: We will not all sleep, but we will all be changed—in a flash, in the twinkling of an eye, at the last trumpet. For the trumpet will sound, the dead will be raised imperishable, and we will be changed. For the perishable must clothe itself with the imperishable, and the mortal with immortality. When the perishable has been clothed with the imperishable, and the mortal with immortality, then the saying that is written will come true: "Death has been swallowed up in victory." "Where, O death, is your victory? Where, O death, is your sting?" The sting of death is sin, and the power of sin is the law. But thanks be to God! He gives us the victory through our Lord Jesus Christ. (1 Cor. 15:35-57)

Listen, I tell you a mystery: We will not all sleep, but we will all be changed—in a flash, in the twinkling of an eye, at the last trumpet. For the trumpet will sound, the dead will be raised imperishable, and we will be changed. For the perishable must clothe itself with the imperishable, and the mortal with immortality. When the perishable has been clothed with the imperishable, and the mortal with immortality, then the saying that is written will come true: "Death has been swallowed up in victory." "Where, O Death, is your victory? Where, O death, is your sting?" The sting of death is sin, and the power of sin is the law. But thanks be to God! He gives us the victory through our Lord Jesus Christ. (1 Cor. 15:51-57)

Praise be to the God and Father of our Lord Jesus Christ! In his great mercy he has given us new birth into a living hope through the resurrection of Jesus Christ from the dead, and into an inheritance that can never perish, spoil or fade—kept in heaven for you, who through faith are shielded by God's power until the coming of the salvation that is ready to be revealed in the last time. In this you greatly rejoice, though now for a little while you may have had to suffer grief in all kinds of trials. These have come so that your faith—of greater worth than gold, which perishes even though refined by fire—may be proved genuine and may result in praise, glory and honor when Jesus Christ is revealed. Though you have not seen him, you love him; and even though you do not see him now, you believe in him and are filled with an inexpressible and glorious joy, for you are receiving the goal of your faith, the salvation of your souls. (1 Peter 1:3-9)

How great is the love the Father has lavished on us, that we should be called children of God! And that is what we are! The reason the world does not know us is that it did not know him. Dear friends, now we are children of God, and what we will be has not yet been made known. But we know that when he appears, we shall be like him, for we shall see him as he is. (1 John 3:1-2)

After this I looked and there before me was a great multitude that no one could count, from every nation, tribe, people and language, standing before the throne and in front of the Lamb. They were wearing white robes and were holding palm branches in their hands. And they cried out in a loud voice: "Salvation belongs to our God, who sits on the throne, and to the Lamb." All the angels were standing around the throne and around the elders and the four living creatures. They fell down on their faces before the throne and worshiped God, saying: "Amen! Praise and glory and wisdom and thanks and honor and power and strength be to our God for ever and ever. Amen!" Then one of the elders asked me, "These in white robes—who are they, and where did they come from?" I answered, "Sir, you know." And he said, "These are they who have come out of the great tribulation; they have washed their robes and made them white in the blood of the Lamb. Therefore, they are before the throne of God and serve him day and night in his temple; and he who sits on the throne will spread his tent over them. Never again will they hunger; never again will they thirst. The sun will not beat upon them, nor any scorching heat. For the Lamb at the center of the throne will be their shepherd; he will lead them to springs of living water. And God will wipe away every tear from their eyes." (Rev. 7:9-17)

I saw the Holy City, the new Jerusalem, coming down out of heaven from God, prepared as a bride beautifully dressed for her husband. And I heard a loud voice from the throne saying, "Now the dwelling of God is with men, and he will live with them. They will be his people, and God himself will be with them and be their God. He will wipe every tear from their eyes. There will be no more death or mourning or crying or pain, for the old order of things has passed away." He who was seated on the throne said, "I am making everything new!" Then he said, "Write this down, for these words are trustworthy and true." He said to me: "It is done. I am the Alpha and the Omega, the Beginning and the End. To him who is thirsty I will give to drink without cost from the spring of the water of life. He who overcomes will inherit all this, and I will be his God and he will be my son." (Rev. 21:2-7)

21. After the reading the assisting minister chants or says:

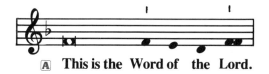

Ⓐ This is the Word of the Lord.

Stand

22. The choir responds with the appropriate VERSE.

(Adapt. from Col. 1:18)

Al - le - lu - ia, al - le - lu - ia.

Jesus Christ is the firstborn of the dead; to him be glory

and power for - ev - er. Al - le - lu - ia.

OR

LENT

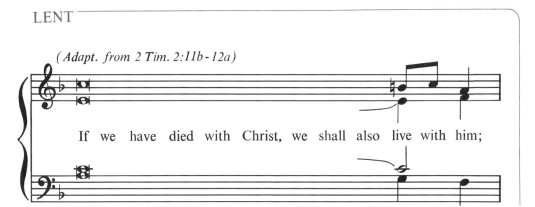

(Adapt. from 2 Tim. 2:11b-12a)

If we have died with Christ, we shall also live with him;

187

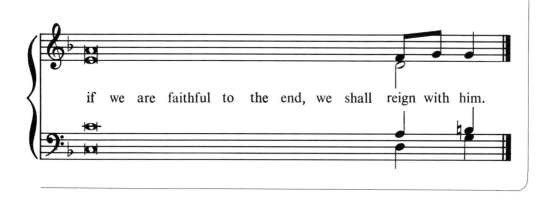

if we are faithful to the end, we shall reign with him.

23. The HOLY GOSPEL is announced, and one of the following portions of Holy Scripture is read.

Ⓟ **The Holy Gospel according to St. _____ , the _____ chapter.**

Ⓒ Glo-ry to you, O Lord.

"I tell you the truth, whoever hears my word and believes him who sent me has eternal life and will not be condemned; he has crossed over from death to life. I tell you the truth, a time is coming and has now come when the dead will hear the voice of the Son of God and those who hear will live. For as the Father has life in himself, so he has granted the Son to have life in himself. And he has given him authority to judge because he is the Son of Man." (John 5:24-27)

"All that the Father gives me will come to me, and whoever comes to me I will never drive away. For I have come down from heaven not to do my will but to do the will of him who sent me. And this is the will of him who sent me, that I shall lose none of all that he has given me, but raise them up at the last day. For my Father's will is that everyone who looks to the Son and believes in him shall have eternal life, and I will raise him up at the last day." (John 6:37-40)

"I am the good shepherd. The good shepherd lays down his life for the sheep. The hired hand is not the shepherd who owns the sheep. So when he sees the wolf coming, he abandons the sheep and runs away. Then the wolf attacks the flock and scatters it. The man runs away because he is a hired hand and cares nothing for the sheep. I am the good shepherd; I know my sheep and my sheep know me—just as the Father knows me and I know the Father—and I lay down my life for the sheep. I have other sheep that are not of this sheep pen. I must bring them also. They too will listen to my voice, and there shall be one flock and one shepherd." (John 10:11-16)

"Lord," Martha said to Jesus, "if you had been here, my brother would not have died. But I know that even now God will give you whatever you ask." Jesus said to her, "Your brother will rise again." Martha answered, "I know he will rise again in the resurrection at the last day." Jesus said to her, "I am the resurrection and the life. He who believes in me will live, even though he dies; and whoever lives and believes in me will never die. Do you believe this?" "Yes, Lord," she told him, "I believe that you are the Christ, the Son of God, who was to come into the world." (John 11:21-27)

"Do not let your hearts be troubled. Trust in God; trust also in me. In my Father's house are many rooms; if it were not so, I would have told you. I am going there to prepare a place for you. And if I go and prepare a place for you, I will come back and take you to be with me that you also may be where I am. You know the way to the place where I am going." Thomas said to him, "Lord, we [do not] know where you are going, so how can we know the way?" Jesus answered, "I am the way and the truth and the life. No one comes to the Father except through me." (John 14:1-6)

People were bringing little children to Jesus to have him touch them, but the disciples rebuked them. When Jesus saw this, he was indignant. He said to them, "Let the little children come to me, and do not hinder them, for the kingdom of God belongs to such as these. I tell you the truth, anyone who will not receive the kingdom of God like a little child will never enter it." And he took the children in his arms, put his hands on them and blessed them. (Mark 10:13-16)

24. After the reading the pastor chants or says:

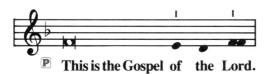

℗ This is the Gospel of the Lord.

℗ **God has made us his people through our Baptism into Christ. Living together in trust and hope, we confess our faith.**

25. The APOSTLES' CREED is said.

℃ I believe in God, the Father Almighty,
   maker of heaven and earth.

   And in Jesus Christ, his only Son, our Lord,
      who was conceived by the Holy Spirit,
      born of the virgin Mary,
      suffered under Pontius Pilate,
      was crucified, died and was buried.
      He descended into hell.
      The third day he rose again from the dead.
      He ascended into heaven
         and sits at the right hand of God the Father Almighty.
      From thence he will come to judge the living and the dead.

   I believe in the Holy Spirit,
      the holy Christian Church,*
      the communion of saints,
      the forgiveness of sins,
      the resurrection of the body,
      and the life everlasting. Amen

* The ancient text: the holy catholic Church

Sit

26. A HYMN is sung.

27. The SERMON

Stand
190

28. The PRAYERS are said. Other appropriate prayers may be used instead.

Ⓐ **Let us pray.**

Almighty God, you have knit your chosen people together in one communion, in the mystical body of your Son, Jesus Christ our Lord. Give to your whole Church in heaven and on earth your light and your peace.

Ⓒ Hear us, O Lord.

Ⓐ **Grant that all who have been baptized into Christ's death and resurrection may die to sin and rise to newness of life and that through the gate of death and the grave we may pass with him to our joyful resurrection.**

Ⓒ Hear us, O Lord.

Ⓐ **Grant to us who are still in our pilgrimage, and who walk as yet by faith, your Holy Spirit that he may lead us in holiness and righteousness all our days.**

Ⓒ Hear us, O Lord.

Ⓐ **Grant to your faithful people pardon and peace that we may be cleansed from all our sins and serve you with a quiet mind.**

Ⓒ Hear us, O Lord.

Ⓐ **Grant to all who mourn a sure confidence in your loving care that, casting all their sorrow on you, they may know the consolation of your love.**

Ⓒ Hear us, O Lord.

Ⓐ **Give courage and faith to the bereaved that they may have strength to meet the days ahead in the assurance of a holy and certain hope, in the communion of your Church, and in the joyful expectation of eternal life with those they love who have departed in the faith.**

Ⓒ Hear us, O Lord.

Ⓐ **Help us, we pray, in the midst of things we cannot understand, to believe in and find comfort in the communion of saints, the forgiveness of sins, the resurrection of the body, and the life everlasting.**

Ⓒ Hear us, O Lord.

29. The pastor concludes the intercessions with the following prayer.

℗ God of all grace, you sent your Son, our Savior Jesus Christ, to bring life and immortality to light. We give you thanks that by his death he destroyed the power of death and by his resurrection opened the kingdom of heaven to all believers. Strengthen us in the confidence that because he lives we shall live also and that neither death nor life nor things present nor things to come will be able to separate us from your love which is in Christ Jesus our Lord, who lives and reigns with you and the Holy Spirit, one God, now and forever. ⟨282⟩

C Amen

30. When there is Holy Communion, the service continues with an OFFERTORY, or an appropriate hymn or psalm may be sung. When there is no Communion, the service continues with the LORD'S PRAYER.

C Our Father who art in heaven,
    hallowed be thy name,
    thy kingdom come,
    thy will be done
        on earth as it is in heaven.
Give us this day our daily bread;
and forgive us our trespasses
    as we forgive those
        who trespass against us;
and lead us not into temptation,
    but deliver us from evil.
For thine is the kingdom
    and the power and the glory
    forever and ever. Amen

OR

C Our Father in heaven,
    hallowed be your name,
    your kingdom come,
    your will be done
        on earth as in heaven.
Give us today our daily bread.
Forgive us our sins
    as we forgive those
        who sin against us.
Lead us not into temptation,
    but deliver us from evil.
For the kingdom, the power,
    and the glory are yours
    now and forever. Amen

31. The pastor takes his place at the coffin and blesses the congregation.

℗ **The Lord bless you and keep you.**
The Lord make his face shine on you and be gracious to you.
The Lord lift up his countenance on you and ☩ give you peace.

C Amen

32. The procession forms and leaves the church, the pastor and assisting minister(s) going before the coffin.

THE COMMITTAL

33. The pastor and assisting minister(s) go before the coffin to the place of interment. During the procession one or more of the following verses may be said.

Ⓐ Lord, you know the secrets of our hearts; shut not your ears to our prayers, but spare us, Lord most holy, O God most mighty, O holy and merciful Savior, O most worthy judge eternal. Do not let the pains of death turn us away from you at our last hour. (Liturgical verse)

In my anguish I cried to the Lord, and he answered by setting me free.

It is better to take refuge in the Lord than to trust in man.
It is better to take refuge in the Lord than to trust in princes.

I was pushed back and about to fall, but the Lord helped me.

Shouts of joy and victory resound in the tents of the righteous: "The Lord's right hand has done mighty things! The Lord's right hand is lifted high; the Lord's right hand has done mighty things!" I will not die but live, and will proclaim what the Lord has done.

Open for me the gates of righteousness; I will enter and give thanks to the Lord. This is the gate of the Lord through which the righteous may enter. (Ps. 118:5, 8-9, 13, 15-17, 19-20)

"I know that my Redeemer lives, and that in the end he will stand upon the earth. And after my skin has been destroyed, yet in my flesh I will see God. (Job 19:25-26)

For none of us lives to himself alone and none of us dies to himself alone. If we live, we live to the Lord; and if we die, we die to the Lord. So, whether we live or die, we belong to the Lord. (Rom. 14:7-8)

[Jesus said,] "I am the resurrection and the life. He who believes in me will live, even though he dies; and whoever lives and believes in me will never die." (John 11:25-26 a)

34. When all have arrived at the place of interment, the following Prayer may be said.

Ⓟ Merciful Father and Lord of life, with whom live the spirits of those who depart in the faith, we thank you for the blessings of body and soul that you granted this departed _____brother/sister_____ , whose earthly remains we now lay to rest. Above all we rejoice at your gracious promise to all your servants, living and departed, that we shall rise again at the coming of our Lord Jesus Christ, who lives and reigns with you and the Holy Spirit, one God, now and forever. ⟨283⟩

Ⓒ Amen

35. One or both of the following portions of Holy Scripture are read.

P Jesus [said], "The hour has come for the Son of Man to be glorified. I tell you the truth, unless a kernel of wheat falls to the ground and dies, it remains only a single seed. But if it dies, it produces many seeds. The man who loves his life will lose it, while the man who hates his life in this world will keep it for eternal life. Whoever serves me must follow me; and where I am, my servant also will be. My Father will honor the one who serves me." (John 12:23-26)

Listen, I tell you a mystery: We will not all sleep, but we will all be changed—in a flash, in the twinkling of an eye, at the last trumpet. For the trumpet will sound, the dead will be raised imperishable, and we will be changed. For the perishable must clothe itself with the imperishable, and the mortal with immortality. When the perishable has been clothed with the imperishable, and the mortal with immortality, then the saying that is written will come true: "Death has been swallowed up in victory." "Where, O death, is your victory? Where, O death, is your sting?" The sting of death is sin, and the power of sin is the law. But thanks be to God! He gives us the victory through our Lord Jesus Christ. (1 Cor. 15:51-57)

36. The coffin is lowered into the grave or placed in its resting place. Earth may be cast on the coffin as the pastor says:

P We now commit _____his/her_____ body to ____the ground/the deep/its resting place____ ; earth to earth, ashes to ashes, dust to dust, in the sure and certain hope of the resurrection to eternal life through our Lord Jesus Christ, who will change our lowly bodies so that they will be like his glorious body, by the power that enables him to subdue all things to himself.

May God the Father, who created this body, may God the ✝ Son, who by his blood redeemed this body, may God the Holy Spirit, who by Holy Baptism sanctified this body to be his temple, keep these remains to the day of the resurrection of all flesh.

C Amen

P Lord, remember us in your kingdom and teach us to pray:

C Our Father who art in heaven,	OR	**C** Our Father in heaven,
hallowed be thy name,		hallowed be your name,
thy kingdom come,		your kingdom come,
thy will be done		your will be done
on earth as it is in heaven.		on earth as in heaven.
Give us this day our daily bread;		Give us today our daily bread.

and forgive us our trespasses
   as we forgive those
      who trespass against us;
and lead us not into temptation,
   but deliver us from evil.
For thine is the kingdom
   and the power and the glory
   forever and ever. Amen

Forgive us our sins
   as we forgive those
      who sin against us.
Lead us not into temptation,
   but deliver us from evil.
For the kingdom, the power,
   and the glory are yours
   now and forever. Amen

Ⓟ **Almighty God, by the death of your Son Jesus Christ you destroyed death, by his rest in the tomb you sanctified the graves of your saints, and by his glorious resurrection you brought life and immortality to light so that all who die in him abide in peace and hope. Receive our thanks for the victory over death and the grave which he won for us. Keep us in everlasting fellowship with all that wait for him on earth and with all in heaven who are with him who is the resurrection and the life, Jesus Christ, our Lord.** ⟨284⟩

Ⓒ Amen

37. The pastor blesses the people.

Ⓟ **The God of peace, who brought again from the dead our Lord Jesus Christ, the great shepherd of the sheep, through the blood of the everlasting covenant, make you perfect in every good work to do his will, working in you that which is well pleasing in his sight; through Jesus Christ, to whom be glory forever and ever.**

Ⓒ Amen

38. The pastor may dismiss the people with these words.

Ⓟ **Christ is risen.**

Ⓒ He is risen indeed.

Ⓟ **Let us go forth in peace**

Ⓒ in the name of the Lord.

NOTES

General

▶ *The death of a member of the Church should immediately be reported to the pastor. No arrangements should be made without consultation with him.*
▶ *Hymns and music selected should be of high quality and, in general, reflect the spirit of Christian confidence, trust, and hope in the resurrection and life everlasting.*

The Service in Detail

10. ▶ The service At the Church may be used as a memorial service by omitting rubrics 11, 12, 13, 14, and 32.
14. ▶ The procession into the church may be in this order: cross, paschal candle or torches, pastor, assisting ministers, pallbearers and coffin, the bereaved.
    ▶ The coffin is placed before the altar at right angles to it.
    ▶ The paschal candle is placed on its stand at the head of the coffin. When torches are used instead, they are placed at the head and at the foot of the coffin. The cross is put in its customary place.
32. ▶ Where feasible, the procession forms in the same order as before (see the note on rubric 14 above).
    ▶ The pall may be removed from the coffin at the church door and left in the church. The paschal candle remains in the church. The processional cross and torches may be taken to the place of interment.
33. ▶ Where feasible, the procession forms in the same order as before (see the note on rubric 14 above). Where not feasible, at least the pastor should precede the coffin to the place of interment.
    ▶ When the body has been willed for medical research, the Committal, with appropriate modifications, may be used in the presence of the bereaved before the body is removed.
    ▶ If the body is to be cremated, the ashes of the deceased are interred later using, with appropriate modifications, the Committal.

Propers

Additional Psalms

Psalm 16
Psalm 71

BURIAL OF THE STILLBORN

1. This service may be adapted for the burial of an unbaptized child of Christian parents.

AT THE HOME

2. The pastor greets the bereaved.

P **Grace to you and peace from God our Father and the Lord Jesus Christ.**

R Amen

3. The PSALM is read.

PSALM 23 (KJV)	OR	PSALM 23 (NIV)

[1] The Lord is my shepherd; *
    I shall not want.
		[1] The Lord is my shepherd, *
		    I shall lack nothing.

[2] He maketh me to lie down
  in green pastures; *
    he leadeth me beside
    the still waters.
		[2] He makes me lie down
		  in green pastures, *
		    he leads me beside
		    quiet waters,

[3] He restoreth my soul; *
    he leadeth me in the
    paths of righteousness
    for his name's sake.
		[3] he restores my soul. *
		    He guides me in
		    paths of righteousness
		    for his name's sake.

[4] Yea, though I walk through
  the valley of the shadow
  of death, I will fear no
  evil; *
		[4] Even though I walk through
		  the valley of the shadow
		  of death, I will fear no
		  evil, *

for thou art with me;
thy rod and thy staff,
they comfort me.

5 Thou preparest a table before
me in the presence of mine
enemies;*
    thou anointest my head with
    oil; my cup runneth over.

6 Surely goodness and mercy
shall follow me all the days
of my life;*
    and I will dwell in the
    house of the Lord for ever.

Glory be to the Father and
to the Son*
    and to the Holy Spirit;
as it was in the beginning,*
    is now, and will be forever.
    Amen

for you are with me;
your rod and your staff,
they comfort me.

5 You prepare a table before me
in the presence of my
enemies.*
    You anoint my head with
    oil; my cup overflows.

6 Surely goodness and love
will follow me all the days
of my life,*
    and I will dwell in the
    house of the Lord forever.

Glory be to the Father and
to the Son*
    and to the Holy Spirit;
as it was in the beginning,*
    is now, and will be forever.
    Amen

4. A READING from Holy Scripture is announced, and one of the following portions is read.

Ⓐ **Hear the Word of God from the _____ chapter of _____ .**

"My sheep listen to my voice; I know them, and they follow me. I give them eternal life, and they shall never perish; no one can snatch them out of my hand. My Father, who has given them to me, is greater than all; no one can snatch them out of my Father's hand." (John 10:27-29)

People were bringing little children to Jesus to have him touch them, but the disciples rebuked them. When Jesus saw this, he was indignant. He said to them, "Let the little children come to me, and do not hinder them, for the kingdom of God belongs to such as these. I tell you the truth, anyone who will not receive the kingdom of God like a little child will never enter it." (Mark 10:13-15)

Peter [said], "Repent and be baptized, every one of you, in the name of Jesus Christ so that your sins may be forgiven. And you will receive the gift of the Holy Spirit. The promise is for you and your children." (Acts 2:38-39a)

Ⓐ **This is the Word of the Lord.**

5. The pastor may read the following or speak other suitable words:

℗ When God in his will for us changes our anticipation and joy into disappointment and grief, we turn to him for comfort and reassurance, which can come only from him. He does not explain to us why he has allowed the circumstance that saddens us, but he does call us through it to a faith which again acknowledges him to be our heavenly Father, who has given us his first and best in Christ Jesus and through him will work always for good in the lives of those who love him, who are called according to his purpose.

In love God has blessed his people also with the washing of Holy Baptism, through which he gives rebirth in the power of the Holy Spirit to us and to our children. When in his will God allows the sadness of stillbirth [the sudden death of a child before Baptism], we trust that he himself is not bound to the means of grace that he has provided for our conscientious use. So we look in faith and hope to him who alone is the source of our faith and hope, trusting that in his grace he has received this child to himself for the sake of his Son Jesus Christ.

6. The COLLECT is said.

℗ Let us pray.

Almighty and eternal God, our hopes have been turned to sorrow. You gave, and you have taken away. As the heavens are higher than the earth, so are your ways higher than our ways and your thoughts higher than our thoughts. Help us, Father, also in this time of sadness, to trust in you. Strengthen the faith of these parents into whose life you have allowed this sorrow to come. Teach them to depend on your boundless mercy and to trust that their little one has been invited into the arms of your Son. Grant that they, and all of us, may also come at last into the heavenly kingdom of Jesus Christ, our Lord, who lives and reigns with you and the Holy Spirit, one God, now and forever. ⟨285⟩

℟ Amen

7. The LORD'S PRAYER is said.

𝔸 Our Father who art in heaven,
    hallowed be thy name,
    thy kingdom come,
    thy will be done
        on earth as it is in heaven.
	OR	𝔸 Our Father in heaven,
		    hallowed be your name,
		    your kingdom come,
		    your will be done
		        on earth as in heaven.

<table>
<tr>
<td>
Give us this day our daily bread;
and forgive us our trespasses
   as we forgive those
      who trespass against us;
and lead us not into temptation,
   but deliver us from evil.
For thine is the kingdom
   and the power and the glory
   forever and ever. Amen
</td>
<td>
Give us today our daily bread.
Forgive us our sins
   as we forgive those
      who sin against us.
Lead us not into temptation,
   but deliver us from evil.
For the kingdom, the power,
   and the glory are yours
   now and forever. Amen
</td>
</tr>
</table>

8. The pastor blesses the bereaved.

P The grace of our Lord Jesus Christ and the love of God and the communion of the Holy Spirit ✛ be with you all.

R Amen

THE COMMITTAL

9. When the coffin is lowered into the grave or placed in its resting place, the pastor says:

P The Lord gave, and the Lord has taken away. Blessed be the name of the Lord.

The holy apostle instructs us about the resurrection of the dead:

The body that is sown is perishable, it is raised imperishable; it is sown in dishonor, it is raised in glory; it is sown in weakness, it is raised in power; it is sown a natural body, it is raised a spiritual body. If there is a natural body, there is also a spiritual body. When the perishable has been clothed with the imperishable, and the mortal with immortality, then the saying that is written will come true: "Death has been swallowed up in victory. Where, O death, is your victory? Where, O death, is your sting?" The sting of death is sin, and the power of sin is the law. But thanks be to God! He gives us the victory through our Lord Jesus Christ. (1 Cor. 15:42-44, 54-57)

10. The pastor continues:

P It has pleased our heavenly Father in his wise providence to call this child to himself. We now commit ___his/her___ body to ___the ground/its resting place___ ; earth to earth, ashes to ashes, dust to dust, in the sure and certain hope of the resurrection to eternal life through our Lord Jesus Christ, who will change our lowly bodies so that they will be like his glorious body, by the power that enables him to subdue all things to himself.

R Amen

℗ **Lord, remember us in your kingdom, and teach us to pray:**

🄰 Our Father who art in heaven,
   hallowed be thy name,
   thy kingdom come,
   thy will be done
     on earth as it is in heaven.
   Give us this day our daily bread;
   and forgive us our trespasses
    as we forgive those
     who trespass against us;
   and lead us not into temptation,
    but deliver us from evil.
   For thine is the kingdom
    and the power and the glory
    forever and ever. Amen

OR

🄰 Our Father in heaven,
   hallowed be your name,
   your kingdom come,
   your will be done
     on earth as in heaven.
   Give us today our daily bread.
   Forgive us our sins
    as we forgive those
     who sin against us.
   Lead us not into temptation,
    but deliver us from evil.
   For the kingdom, the power,
    and the glory are yours
    now and forever. Amen

℗ **Almighty God, by the death of your dear Son you overcame death and redeemed and saved little children no less than others, by your rising from death you restored everlasting life that by the power of your resurrection our mortal bodies may also be raised from the dead to eternal life. Grant that we may ever confidently believe this and finally with all your saints be partakers of this joyful resurrection; through Jesus Christ, our Lord, who lives and reigns with you and the Holy Spirit, one God, now and forever.** ⟨286⟩

℞ Amen

11. The pastor blesses the people.

℗ **The God of peace, who brought again from the dead our Lord Jesus Christ, the great shepherd of the sheep, through the blood of the everlasting covenant, make you perfect in every good work to do his will, working in you that which is well pleasing in his sight; through Jesus Christ, to whom be glory forever and ever.**

℞ Amen

12. The pastor may dismiss the people with these words:

℗ **Christ is risen.**

℞ He is risen indeed.

℗ **Let us go forth in peace**

℞ in the name of the Lord.

FAREWELL AND GODSPEED
TO A CANDIDATE
FOR ORDINATION

1. This rite is used to bid farewell and Godspeed to the son of a congregation who has been declared a candidate for ordination and has accepted his first call.

Sit

2. Immediately before the Prayer of the Church, or The Prayers, in the Divine Service, the candidate presents himself before the altar. The pastor addresses the congregation with these or similar words:

℗ **Dear brothers and sisters in Christ, ___name___, a son of this congregation, who has been aided in his preparation for the office of the public ministry by your encouragement, your gifts, and your prayers, has accepted a call according to the Church's usual order to his first field of service. At this time of farewell and Godspeed we look to the Word of our Lord for encouragement, strength, and guidance.**

Stand

3. The following selected portions of Psalmody are read responsively:

℗ **Glorify the Lord with me; let us exalt his name together. Know that the Lord is God.**

ᑕ It is he who made us, and we are his; we are his people, the sheep of his pasture.

℗ **Enter his gates with thanksgiving and his courts with praise; give thanks to him and praise his name.**

ᑕ For the Lord is good and his love endures forever; his faithfulness continues through all generations.

202

℗ **O Lord Almighty, blessed are those who dwell in your house.**

℃ O Lord Almighty, blessed is the man who trusts in you.

℗ **Blessed is the man who does not walk in the counsel of the wicked or stand in the way of sinners or sit in the seat of mockers.**

℃ But his delight is in the law of the Lord, and on his law he meditates day and night.

℗ **He is like a tree planted by streams of water, which yields its fruit in season and whose leaf does not wither. Whatever he does prospers.** (Ps. 34:3; 100:3-5; 84:1b, 4a, 12; 1:1-3)

℃ Glory be to the Father and to the Son and to the Holy Spirit; as it was in the beginning, is now, and will be forever. Amen

4. The Prayer is said.

℗ **Let us pray.**

O Lord God, merciful and gracious Father, we give thanks for all the blessings you have bestowed on ___ name ___ in his preparation for the holy ministry. By your Holy Spirit grant him grace in his first field of service, readiness and steadfastness in his ministry, patience, understanding, and great zeal. Support and strengthen him that by your Word your Church may be built and increased; through your Son, our great High Priest, Jesus Christ, our Lord. ⟨287⟩

℃ Amen

5. The pastor dismisses and blesses the candidate.

℗ **Go, then, in peace and joy. The almighty and most merciful God, the Father, the ✠ Son, and the Holy Spirit, go with you, bless and strengthen you for faithful service in his name.**

℃ Amen

6. The candidate returns to his place.

Sit

7. The congregation sings "Forth in Your Name, O Lord, I Go," Hymn 380, or "God of the Prophets, Bless the Prophets' Sons," Hymn 258.

Stand

8. *The service continues with the Prayer of the Church, or The Prayers.*

NOTES

Preparation for the Rite

▶ *A chair is provided near the chancel for the seating of the candidate for ordination.*

ORDINATION

1. This rite is administered, according to the Church's usual order, by those so authorized for such candidates as have been adjudged by the Church to be ready and prepared to enter the office of the public ministry and who have received a regular call to minister in the Church.

2. The ordination takes place in the Divine Service before the Prayer of the Church, or The Prayers. The Propers are those appointed on pages 218—20.

3. In addition to the presiding minister, it is fitting that other pastors serve as assisting ministers, according to local custom and the direction of the presiding minister.

4. Before the service begins, the presiding minister gathers all who will take part in it in some convenient place for the Word of God and prayer. Then all enter the church together, the candidate, vested in an alb or surplice, going before the assisting ministers, and the presiding minister last of all.

Sit

5. When the time for the ordination has come, the candidate presents himself before the altar. The presiding minister, standing before the altar, says:

℗ **In the name of the Father and of the ☩ Son and of the Holy Spirit.**

◉ Amen

6. The minister addresses the congregation:

P Dear brothers and sisters in Christ, ⸻name⸻ has been called by the Lord of the Church into the office of the public ministry of the Word of God and the sacraments of our Lord Jesus Christ. He has prepared himself for this ministry by prayer and careful study. He has been examined and declared ready and prepared to undertake this sacred responsibility and, by the guidance of God the Holy Spirit, he has in the Church's usual order been called to be ⸻ministry and place⸻ . According to apostolic use, he is now presented to be ordained and consecrated to this office established by God.

7. *The candidate kneels. The minister chants or says:*

8. *The Hymn, "Creator Spirit, Heavenly Dove," Hymn 156, or "Come, Holy Ghost, Our Souls Inspire," Hymn 157, is sung.*

Stand

9. *The Salutation and Collect are chanted or said. Instead, The Litany may be chanted or said.*

P The Lord be with you.

C And with your spir - it.

P Let us pray to the Lord.

10. *An assisting minister prays:*

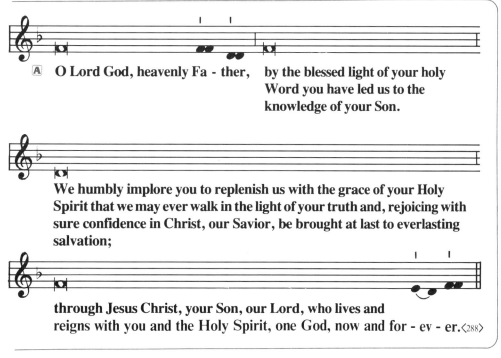

A O Lord God, heavenly Fa - ther,   by the blessed light of your holy
Word you have led us to the
knowledge of your Son.

We humbly implore you to replenish us with the grace of your Holy
Spirit that we may ever walk in the light of your truth and, rejoicing with
sure confidence in Christ, our Savior, be brought at last to everlasting
salvation;

through Jesus Christ, your Son, our Lord, who lives and
reigns with you and the Holy Spirit, one God, now and for - ev - er. ⟨288⟩

OR

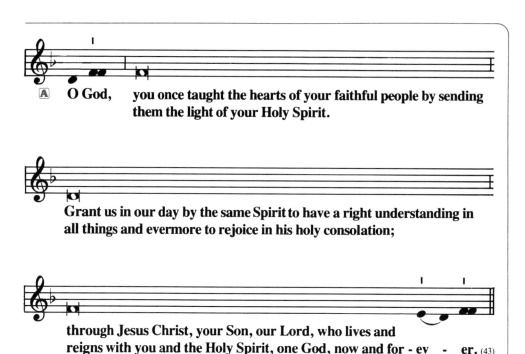

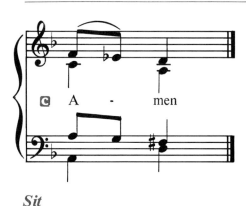

Sit

11. The ministers and candidate stand. An assisting minister turns to the candidate and says:

Ⓐ **Hear what Holy Scripture says concerning the office of the public ministry.**

12. The assisting ministers read one or more portions of Holy Scripture from each of the following sections.

THE INSTITUTION OF THE OFFICE
OF THE PUBLIC MINISTRY

Ⓐ **Then Jesus came to them and said, "All authority in heaven and on earth has been given to me. Therefore go and make disciples of all nations, baptizing them** in the name of the Father and of the Son and of the Holy Spirit, and teaching them to obey everything I have commanded you. And surely I will be with you always, to the very end of the age." (Matt. 28:18-20)

Again Jesus said, "Peace be with you! As the Father has sent me, I am sending you." And with that he breathed on them and said, "Receive the Holy Spirit. If you forgive anyone his sins, they are forgiven; if you do not forgive them, they are not forgiven." (John 20:21-23)

When they had finished eating, Jesus said to Simon Peter, "Simon son of John, do you truly love me more than these?" "Yes, Lord," he said, "you know that I love you." Jesus said, "Feed my lambs." Again Jesus said, "Simon son of John, do you truly love me?" He answered, "Yes, Lord, you know that I love you." Jesus said, "Take care of my sheep." The third time he said to him, "Simon son of John, do you love me?" Peter was hurt because Jesus asked him the third time, "Do you love me?" He said, "Lord, you know all things; you know that I love you." Jesus said, "Feed my sheep." (John 21:15-17)

THE RESPONSIBILITIES OF THE OFFICE OF THE PUBLIC MINISTRY

A "You did not choose me, but I chose you to go and bear fruit—fruit that will last. Then the Father will give you whatever you ask in my name."(John 15:16)

Do not neglect your gift, which was given you through a prophetic message when the body of elders laid their hands on you. Be diligent in these matters; give yourself wholly to them, so that everyone may see your progress. Watch your life and doctrine closely. Persevere in them, because if you do, you will save both yourself and your hearers. (1 Tim. 4:14-16)

So then, men ought to regard us as servants of Christ and as those entrusted with the secret things of God. Now it is required that those who have been given a trust must prove faithful. (1 Cor. 4:1-2)

Such confidence as this is ours through Christ before God. Not that we are competent to claim anything for ourselves, but our competence comes from God. (2 Cor. 3:4-5)

Therefore, if anyone is in Christ, he is a new creation; the old has gone, the new has come! All this is from God, who reconciled us to himself through Christ and gave us the ministry of reconciliation: that God was reconciling the world to himself in Christ, not counting men's sins against them. And he has committed to us the message of reconciliation. We are therefore Christ's ambassadors, as though God were making his appeal through us. We implore you on Christ's behalf: Be reconciled to God. God made him who had no sin to be sin for us, so that in him we might become the righteousness of God. (2 Cor. 5:17-21)

In the presence of God and of Christ Jesus, who will judge the living and the dead, and in view of his appearing and his kingdom, I give you this charge: Preach the Word; be prepared in season and out of season; correct, rebuke and encourage—with great patience and careful instruction. For the time will come when men will not put up with sound doctrine. Instead, to suit their own desires, they will gather around them a great number of teachers to say what their itching ears want to hear. They will turn their ears away from the truth and turn aside to myths. But you, keep your head in all situations, endure hardship, do the work of an evangelist, discharge all the duties of your ministry. (2 Tim. 4:1-5)

Here is a trustworthy saying: If anyone sets his heart on being an overseer, he desires a noble task. Now the overseer must be above reproach, the husband of but one wife, temperate, self-controlled, respectable, hospitable, able to teach, not given to much wine, not violent but gentle, not quarrelsome, not a lover of money. He must manage his own family well and see that his children obey him with proper respect. (If anyone does not know how to manage his own family, how can he take care of God's church?) He must not be a recent convert, or he may become conceited and fall under the same judgment as the devil. He must also have a good reputation with outsiders, so that he will not fall into disgrace and into the devil's trap. (1 Tim. 3:1-7)

"Remain in me, and I will remain in you. No branch can bear fruit by itself; it must remain in the vine. Neither can you bear fruit unless you remain in me. I am the vine; you are the branches. If a man remains in me and I in him, he will bear much fruit; apart from me you can do nothing." (John 15:4-5)

It was he who gave some to be apostles, some to be prophets, some to be evangelists, and some to be pastors and teachers, to prepare God's people for works of service, so that the body of Christ may be built up. (Eph. 4:11-12)

[Guard] yourselves and all the flock of which the Holy Spirit has made you overseers. Be shepherds of the church of God, which he bought with his own blood. (Acts 20:28)

Be shepherds of God's flock that is under your care, serving as overseers—not because you must, but because you are willing, as God wants you to be; not greedy for money, but eager to serve; not lording it over those entrusted to you, but being examples to the flock. And when the Chief Shepherd appears, you will receive the crown of glory that will never fade away. (1 Peter 5:2-4)

THE STRENGTH AND PROMISE IN THE OFFICE OF THE PUBLIC MINISTRY

Ⓐ "You are the salt of the earth. But if the salt loses its saltiness, how can it be made salty again? It is no longer good for anything, except to be thrown out and trampled by men. You are the light of the world. A city on a hill cannot be hidden. Neither do people light a lamp and put it under a bowl. Instead they put it on its stand, and it gives light to everyone in the house. In the same way, let your light shine before men, that they may see your good deeds and praise your Father in heaven." (Matt. 5:13-16)

"Let him who boasts boast in the Lord." For it is not the one who commends himself who is approved, but the one whom the Lord commends. (2 Cor. 10:17-18)

But as for you, continue in what you have learned and have become convinced of, because you know those from whom you learned it, and how from infancy you have known the holy Scriptures, which are able to make you wise for salvation through faith in Christ Jesus. All Scripture is God-breathed and is useful for teaching, rebuking, correcting and training in righteousness, so that the man of God may be thoroughly equipped for every good work. (2 Tim. 3:14-17)

13. The minister addresses the candidate:

℗ God gathers his Church by and around his holy Word and also grants it growth and increase. That this may be done, he has established the office of the public ministry into which you have been called and are now to be ordained and consecrated by prayer and the laying on of hands.

In the presence of God and of this congregation I now ask you:

℗ Do you believe the canonical books of the Old and New Testaments to be the inspired Word of God and the only infallible rule of faith and practice?

℞ I do.

℗ Do you accept the three Ecumenical Creeds, namely, the Apostles', the Nicene, and the Athanasian Creeds, as faithful testimonies to the truth of the Holy Scriptures, and do you reject all the errors which they condemn?

℞ I do.

℗ Do you believe that the Unaltered Augsburg Confession is a true exposition of the Word of God and a correct exhibition of the doctrine of the Evangelical Lutheran Church; that the Apology of the Augsburg Confession, the Small and Large Catechisms of Martin Luther, the Smalcald Articles, the Treatise on the Authority and Primacy of the Pope, and the Formula of Concord—as these are contained in the *Book of Concord*—are also in agreement with this one scriptural faith?

℞ I do.

℗ **Do you solemnly promise that you will perform the duties of your office in accordance with these Confessions, or Symbols, and that all your teaching and your administration of the sacraments will be in conformity with the Holy Scriptures and with the aforementioned Symbols?**

℞ I do.

℗ **Will you faithfully instruct both young and old in the chief articles of Christian doctrine; will you forgive the sins of those who repent, and will you promise never to divulge the sins confessed to you; will you minister faithfully to the sick and dying; will you demonstrate to the Church a constant and ready ministry, admonishing the people to a lively confidence in Christ and holy living?**

℞ I will with the help of God.

℗ **Finally, will you adorn the office of the public ministry with a holy life?**

℞ I will, the Lord helping me through the power and grace of his Holy Spirit.

14. The candidate kneels. The minister lays both his hands on the head of the candidate and says:

℗ _____name_____ , **I ordain and consecrate you to the holy office of the public ministry in the one, holy, Christian, and apostolic Church, in the name of the Father and of the ☩ Son and of the Holy Spirit.**

15. The congregation joins in praying the Lord's Prayer.

ℭOur Father who art in heaven,
    hallowed be thy name,
    thy kingdom come,
    thy will be done
        on earth as it is in heaven.
Give us this day our daily bread;
and forgive us our trespasses
    as we forgive those
        who trespass against us;
and lead us not into temptation,
    but deliver us from evil.
	OR ℭ Our Father in heaven,
	        hallowed be your name,
	        your kingdom come,
	        your will be done
	            on earth as in heaven.
	    Give us today our daily bread.
	    Forgive us our sins
	        as we forgive those
	            who sin against us.
	    Lead us not into temptation,
	        but deliver us from evil.

> For thine is the kingdom
>   and the power and the glory
>   forever and ever. Amen

> For the kingdom, the power,
>   and the glory are yours
>   now and forever. Amen

16. The assisting ministers lay their hands on the newly ordained, adding an appropriate blessing from the Word of God.

17. The newly ordained rises and may be vested with a stole; he may also be vested with a chasuble.

18. The minister and the newly ordained turn to face the congregation. The minister says:

℗ Will you, assembled here as God's people and speaking for the whole Church, receive _____name_____ as a servant of Christ, a minister of Word and Sacrament, given the Church to serve God's people with the Gospel of grace and salvation? If so, answer: We will.

℃ We will.

Stand

19. The ministers and the newly ordained kneel. The presiding minister prays:

℗ O eternal, merciful God, you have spoken through your own dear Son, saying that the harvest is plentiful but the laborers few and that we should ask you, the Lord of the harvest, to send laborers into your harvest. Hear now our prayer on behalf of him who this day is ordained and consecrated to be your minister in the Church. Strengthen him mightily to take up the word of truth and faithfully to administer your holy sacraments.

O Lord Jesus Christ, our great High Priest, who gave your own life to be a holy and perfect sacrifice for us and for our salvation, grant him a heart zealous for your people and boldness to guide, comfort, admonish, and serve your congregation with gentleness and wisdom. Fill him, your undershepherd, with your love that in your name he will seek the straying and bear up the weak. Give him the heart never to grow weary in the service of your flock.

O Holy Spirit, strengthen and keep him in the Word of truth and life, and support him in every time of trouble and distress. Grant fruit to his labors and, when the day of labor is ended, grant him to come with rejoicing before your presence to receive with all the saints his portion in eternal salvation.

213

And to you, God the Father, Son, and Holy Spirit, be all glory and honor, both now and forever. ⟨289⟩

C Amen

20. When the installation of a pastor takes place at ordination, the service continues below ⟨26⟩. ▶

21. When the installation of a missionary or chaplain takes place at ordination, the service continues on page 216 ⟨26⟩. ▶

22. The minister dismisses and blesses the newly ordained.

P **Go, therefore, and be a shepherd of the Good Shepherd's flock. Proclaim the Word of God, administer the holy sacraments, offer prayer for all God's people, instruct, watch over, and guide the flock over which the Holy Spirit has placed you. Do it not for earthly gain but with great joy, for you have been called not to lordship but to serve his flock. And when the Chief Shepherd appears, you will receive the crown of glory that will never fade away.**

The almighty and most merciful God, the Father, the ✝ Son, and the Holy Spirit, bless and preserve you.

C Amen

23. The Hymn, "To God the Holy Spirit Let Us Pray," Hymn 155, may be sung.

24. The service continues with the Prayer of the Church, or The Prayers.

25. The newly ordained presides at the Holy Communion.

INSTALLATION OF A PASTOR AT ORDINATION

26. ▶ *When the installation of a pastor takes place at ordination, the following is used immediately after the prayer ⟨19⟩ in the rite of Ordination.*

Sit

27. The ministers and the newly ordained stand. The presiding minister addresses the congregation:

P **Dear brothers and sisters in Christ, the Reverend _____name_____ has been called to be (a) pastor of _____name(s)_____ congregation(s). I ask you now, in the presence of**

214

God: Will you receive him, show him that love, honor, and obedience in the Lord which you owe to the shepherd and teacher placed over you by your Lord Jesus Christ, and will you support him by your gifts and fervent prayer? If so, answer: We will with the help of God.

ⓒ We will with the help of God.

ⓟ The almighty and most merciful God strengthen and assist you always.

28. The minister asks the pastor-elect:

ⓟ Are you willing and ready to assume this trust and responsibility?

ⓡ I am.

ⓟ ___name___ , I install you as (a) pastor of ___name(s)___ congregation(s), in the name of the Father and of the ☩ Son and of the Holy Spirit.

May the God of peace, who through the blood of the eternal covenant brought back from the dead our Lord Jesus, that great Shepherd of the sheep, equip you with everything good for doing his will, and may he work in you what is pleasing to him, through Jesus Christ, to whom be glory for ever and ever. (Heb. 13:20-21)

ⓒ Amen

Stand

ⓟ Let us pray.

29. One or both of the following Prayers are said.

ⓟ Merciful God and Father, you have graciously promised that through the preaching of the crucified Christ those who believe in him will be saved. By your Holy Spirit grant grace to ___name___ , whom you have given to be pastor of this (these) congregation(s). Grant him readiness and steadfastness in this ministry, patience, understanding, and great zeal. Support and strengthen him in your service that by your Word your Church may be built and increased; through your Son, our great High Priest, Jesus Christ, our Lord. ⟨290⟩

ⓒ Amen

OR

P Almighty and most merciful God and Father, through your only-begotten Son, Jesus Christ, you have established your Church to be a temple and dwelling place of the Holy Spirit. We give thanks that you continue to provide shepherds to feed and serve your flock over which the Holy Spirit has made them overseers. We humbly implore you ever to strengthen the labors of your ministers that through their ministry of Word and Sacrament your people may bear fruit in your knowledge and service and grow up into him who is the head, Jesus Christ, to whom, with you and the Holy Spirit, be glory now and forever. ⟨291⟩

C Amen

30. The service continues with the dismissal and blessing ⟨22⟩ in the rite of Ordination.

INSTALLATION OF A MISSIONARY OR CHAPLAIN AT ORDINATION

26. ▶ When the installation of a missionary or chaplain takes place at ordination, the following is used immediately after the prayer ⟨19⟩ in the rite of Ordination.

Sit

27. The ministers and newly ordained stand. The presiding minister addresses the congregation:

P Dear brothers and sisters in Christ, the Reverend _____name_____ has been called by the _____name_____ board of _____name_____ to serve as (a) _____missionary/chaplain_____ in _____place/institution/branch of armed forces_____ . I ask you now, in the presence of God: Will you support him by your gifts and fervent prayer? If so, answer: We will with the help of God.

C We will with the help of God.

P The almighty and most merciful God strengthen and assist you always.

28. The minister asks the missionary or chaplain being installed:

P Are you ready and willing to assume this trust and responsibility?

R I am.

216

Ⓟ _____ , I install you as (a) _missionary/chaplain_ **in** _place/institution/branch of armed forces_ ,
     name

in the name of the Father and of the ✠ **Son and of the Holy Spirit.**

May the God of peace, who through the blood of the eternal covenant brought back from the dead our Lord Jesus, that great Shepherd of the sheep, equip you with everything good for doing his will, and may he work in you what is pleasing to him, through Jesus Christ, to whom be glory forever and ever. (Heb. 13:20-21)

Ⓒ Amen

Stand

29. The assisting minister says:

Ⓐ **Let us pray.**

MISSIONARY

Ⓐ **Almighty and merciful God, our heavenly Father, guide and bless your servant _____ , sent forth to be a witness to _____ . Graciously look with favor upon him for the sake of your Son, our Savior, Jesus Christ. Grant him confidence and great boldness; uphold and sustain him in hardship; and grant him faithfulness in all his labors that through the speaking of your Word the nations may come to worship before your throne in spirit and in truth; through Jesus Christ, our Lord, who lives and reigns with you and the Holy Spirit, one God, now and forever.**⟨292⟩

Ⓒ Amen

INSTITUTIONAL CHAPLAIN

Ⓐ **Most merciful God, give to your called servant _____ a special measure of compassion and patience that he may effectively minister to the sick and suffering and to the aged, whose increasing years bring them weakness, anxiety, distress, or loneliness. Grant that through him your Word and Spirit may heal, strengthen, and comfort them with the message of forgiveness of sins, life, and salvation; through Jesus Christ, your Son, our Lord, who lives and reigns with you and the Holy Spirit, one God, now and forever.** ⟨293⟩

Ⓒ Amen

OR

Ⓐ **O Lord, God of justice and mercy, your Son directed that in our works of mercy we also visit those in prison. Grant grace and power to _____ as he** proclaims your Law to the impenitent and the comforting message of forgiveness to those who repent. Bless him with wisdom and discernment as he ministers to prisoners, giving them a right understanding of themselves and their lot as well as of your heavenly promises through Jesus Christ. May your servant ever comfort the distressed and give aid to the innocent. Grant that through his ministry they may, by the Holy Spirit, be set free from the bondage of sin and be brought to the glorious liberty of your children; through Jesus Christ, our Lord, who lives and reigns with you and the Holy Spirit, one God, now and forever. ⟨294⟩

C Amen

MILITARY CHAPLAIN

A O Lord God of hosts, we thank you for calling your servant ____name____ for ministry in your name to the armed forces of our nation. Grant him grace and zeal that he may faithfully perform the work of an evangelist and pastor and set an example for all in speech, in life, in love, in faith, and in purity. Stretch forth your almighty arm to protect those who serve in the armed forces. Give them courage and loyalty, and keep them from temptation and harm; through Jesus Christ, your Son, our Lord, who lives and reigns with you and the Holy Spirit, one God, now and forever. ⟨295⟩

C Amen

30. The service continues with the dismissal and blessing ⟨22⟩ in the rite of Ordination.

PROPERS

INTROIT

IX g² : Aeolian

218

I proclaim righteousness in the great assembly; I speak of your faithfulness and salvation. *

    I do not conceal your love and your truth.

I waited patiently for the Lord; *

    he turned to me and heard my cry.

He put a new song in my mouth,
a hymn of praise to our God. *

    Many will see and fear and put their trust in the Lord.

Blessed is the man who makes the Lord his trust, *

    who does not look to the proud, to those who turn aside to false gods.

May all who seek you rejoice and be glad in you; *

    may those who love your salvation always say: "The Lord be exalted!"

Glory be to the Father and to the Son *

    and to the Holy Spirit.

As it was in the beginning *

    is now, and will be for ever. Amen

I proclaim righteousness in the great assembly; I speak of your faithfulness and salvation. *

    I do not conceal your love and your truth.

(Antiphon, Ps. 40:9a, 10b, 10c; Ps. 40:1, 3-4, 16)

COLLECT

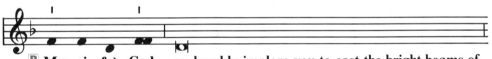

P **Mer-ci-ful God,** we humbly implore you to cast the bright beams of your light upon your Church that we, being instructed by the doctrine of the blessed apostles, may walk in the light of your truth and at length attain to the light of everlasting life;

through Jesus Christ, your Son, our Lord, who lives and reigns with you and the Holy Spirit, one God, now and for-ev-er. (107)

READINGS

Psalm 99
Jeremiah 15:19-21
2 Corinthians 3:4-11
John 20:21-23
or John 10:1-16

GRADUAL

Praise the name of the Lord;*
  praise him, you servants of the Lord,
you who minister in the house of the
Lord,*
  in the courts of the house of our God. (*Ps. 135:1b-2*)

VERSE

PREFACE: Pentecost

COLOR: red

220

NOTES

General

▶ *Because of the solemn character of Holy Week, it is inappropriate to schedule an ordination in that period.*

Preparation for the Rite

▶ *The one(s) to be ordained should be vested in an alb or in a cassock with surplice.*
▶ *A chair is provided near the chancel for the seating of the one(s) to be ordained.*
▶ *If there is no Communion rail, a kneeling desk may be provided for the convenience of the one(s) to be ordained.*

The Rite in Detail

6. ▶ While mention of both Christian name and surname is appropriate here, in other places only the Christian name of the candidate, the name given in Baptism, is used.
13. ▶ When several persons are being ordained, each answers in turn.
14. ▶ The presiding minister lays both his hands on the head of the candidate. The service book is held by an assisting minister. Other clergy, as assisting ministers, lay their right hands on the newly ordained. If the number of such clergy is large, a few may function on behalf of all.
18. ▶ Whether in the sermon, by an announcement, or by a note in the service folder, the congregation should be made aware that it is here speaking for the entire Church.

INSTALLATION
OF A PASTOR

1. This rite is used by those so authorized to install a pastor when he has been called according to the Church's usual order to a new field of service.

2. The installation is set within the Divine Service before the Prayer of the Church, or The Prayers. The Propers are those of the Sunday or festival on which the installation takes place or those appointed on pages 218—20.

3. In addition to the presiding minister, other pastors may serve as assisting ministers.

4. Before the service begins, the presiding minister gathers all who will take part in it in some convenient place for the Word of God and prayer. Then all enter the church together, the pastor-elect going before the assisting ministers, and the presiding minister last of all.

Sit

5. When the time for the installation has come, the pastor-elect presents himself before the altar. The presiding minister, standing before the altar, says:

℗ **In the name of the Father and of the ✠Son and of the Holy Spirit.**

℃ Amen

6. The minister addresses the congregation:

℗ **Dear brothers and sisters in Christ, the Reverend _____name_____ has been called to be (a) pastor of ____name(s)____ congregation(s). Hear now what Holy Scripture says concerning the office of the public ministry.**

222

7. The assisting ministers read one or more portions of Holy Scripture from each of the following sections.

THE INSTITUTION OF THE OFFICE
OF THE PUBLIC MINISTRY

A **Then Jesus came to them and said, "All authority in heaven and on earth has been given to me. Therefore go and make disciples of all nations, baptizing them in the name of the Father and of the Son and of the Holy Spirit, and teaching them to obey everything I have commanded you. And surely I will be with you always, to the very end of the age." (Matt. 28:18-20)**

When they had finished eating, Jesus said to Simon Peter, "Simon son of John, do you truly love me more than these?" "Yes, Lord," he said, "you know that I love you." Jesus said, "Feed my lambs." Again Jesus said, "Simon son of John, do you truly love me?" He answered, "Yes, Lord, you know that I love you." Jesus said, "Take care of my sheep." The third time he said to him, "Simon son of John, do you love me?" Peter was hurt because Jesus asked him the third time, "Do you love me?" He said, "Lord, you know all things; you know that I love you." Jesus said, "Feed my sheep." (John 21:15-17)

Again Jesus said, "Peace be with you! As the Father has sent me, I am sending you." And with that he breathed on them and said, "Receive the Holy Spirit. If you forgive anyone his sins, they are forgiven; if you do not forgive them, they are not forgiven." (John 20:21-23)

THE RESPONSIBILITIES OF THE OFFICE
OF THE PUBLIC MINISTRY

A **We do not preach ourselves, but Jesus Christ as Lord, and ourselves as your servants for Jesus' sake. For God, who said, "Let light shine out of darkness," made his light shine in our hearts to give us the light of the knowledge of the glory of God in the face of Christ. (2 Cor. 4:5-6)**

Now if the ministry that brought death, which was engraved in letters on stone, came with glory, so that the Israelites could not look steadily at the face of Moses because of its glory, fading though it was, will not the ministry of the Spirit be even more glorious? (2 Cor. 3:7-8)

The Lord's servant must not quarrel; instead, he must be kind to everyone, able to teach, not resentful. Those who oppose him he must gently instruct, in the hope that God will grant them repentance leading them to a knowledge of the truth. (2 Tim. 2:24-25)

Watch your life and doctrine closely. Persevere in them, because if you do, you will save both yourself and your hearers. (1 Tim. 4:16)

Preach the Word; be prepared in season and out of season; correct, rebuke and encourage—with great patience and careful instruction. (2 Tim. 4:2)

So then, men ought to regard us as servants of Christ and as those entrusted with the secret things of God. Now it is required that those who have been given a trust must prove faithful. (1 Cor. 4:1-2)

It was he who gave some to be apostles, some to be prophets, some to be evangelists, and some to be pastors and teachers, to prepare God's people for works of service, so that the body of Christ may be built up. (Eph. 4:11-12)

THE STRENGTH AND PROMISE IN THE OFFICE OF THE PUBLIC MINISTRY

Ⓐ **"So you also, when you have done everything you were told to do, should say, 'We are unworthy servants; we have only done our duty.' "** (Luke 17:10)

Therefore I do not run like a man running aimlessly; I do not fight like a man beating the air. No, I beat my body and make it my slave so that after I have preached to others, I myself will not be disqualified for the prize. (1 Cor. 9:26-27)

Do not throw away your confidence; it will be richly rewarded. You need to persevere so that when you have done the will of God, you will receive what he has promised. (Heb. 10:35-36)

Therefore, my dear brothers, stand firm. Let nothing move you. Always give yourselves fully to the work of the Lord, because you know that your labor in the Lord is not in vain. (1 Cor. 15:58)

Be shepherds of God's flock that is under your care, serving as overseers—not because you must, but because you are willing, as God wants you to be; not greedy for money, but eager to serve; not lording it over those entrusted to you, but being examples to the flock. And when the Chief Shepherd appears, you will receive the crown of glory that will never fade away. (1 Peter 5:2-4)

8. The minister addresses the pastor-elect:

Ⓟ **Dear brother in Christ, the Lord grant that you receive and keep these words in your heart that you may be strengthened and encouraged in your labors.**

224

God gathers his Church by and around his holy Word and also grants it growth and increase. That this may be done, he has established the office of the public ministry into which you were ordained. It is fitting that you should again acknowledge the responsibilities of this holy office in which you are to serve this (these) congregation(s).

In the presence of God and of this congregation I now ask you:

Ⓟ Do you believe the canonical books of the Old and New Testaments to be the inspired Word of God and the only infallible rule of faith and practice?

Ⓡ I do.

Ⓟ Do you accept the three Ecumenical Creeds, namely, the Apostles', the Nicene, and the Athanasian Creeds, as faithful testimonies to the truth of the Holy Scriptures, and do you reject all the errors which they condemn?

Ⓡ I do.

Ⓟ Do you believe that the Unaltered Augsburg Confession is a true exposition of the Word of God and a correct exhibition of the doctrine of the Evangelical Lutheran Church; that the Apology of the Augsburg Confession, the Small and Large Catechisms of Martin Luther, the Smalcald Articles, the Treatise on the Authority and Primacy of the Pope, and the Formula of Concord—as these are contained in the *Book of Concord*—are also in agreement with this one scriptural faith?

Ⓡ I do.

Ⓟ Do you solemnly promise that you will perform the duties of your office in accordance with these Confessions, or Symbols, and that all your teaching and your administration of the sacraments will be in conformity with the Holy Scriptures and with the aforementioned Symbols?

Ⓡ I do.

Ⓟ Will you faithfully instruct both young and old in the chief articles of Christian doctrine; will you forgive the sins of those who repent, and will you promise never to divulge the sins confessed to you; will you minister faithfully to the sick and dying; will you demonstrate to the Church a constant and ready ministry, admonishing the people to a lively confidence in Christ and holy living?

Ⓡ I will with the help of God.

P Finally, will you adorn the office of the public ministry with a holy life?

R I will, the Lord helping me through the power and grace of his Holy Spirit.

9. The minister addresses the congregation:

P **You have heard the solemn promise of him called to be your pastor. Will you now receive him, show him that love, honor, and obedience in the Lord which you owe to the shepherd and teacher placed over you in your Lord Jesus Christ, and will you support him by your gifts and pray for him always that in his labors he may retain a cheerful spirit and that his ministry among you may be abundantly blessed? If so, answer: We will with the help of God.**

C We will with the help of God.

P **The almighty and most merciful God strengthen and assist you always.**

10. The minister asks the pastor-elect:

P **Are you willing and ready to assume this trust and responsibility?**

R I am.

11. The pastor-elect kneels. The minister continues:

P _____name_____ , I install you as (a) pastor of _____name_____ congregation(s), in the name of the Father and of the ✠ Son and of the Holy Spirit.

May the God of peace, who through the blood of the eternal covenant brought back from the dead our Lord Jesus, that great Shepherd of the sheep, equip you with everything good for doing his will, and may he work in you what is pleasing to him, through Jesus Christ, to whom be glory for ever and ever. (Heb. 13:20-21)

C Amen

Stand

P **Let us pray.**

12. One or both of the following Prayers are said.

P **Merciful God and Father, you have graciously promised that through the preaching of the crucified Christ those who believe in him will be saved. By your**

Holy Spirit grant grace to your servant whom you have given to be pastor of this (these) congregation(s). Grant him readiness and steadfastness in this ministry, patience, understanding, and great zeal. Support and strengthen him in your service that by your Word your Church may be built and increased; through your Son, our great High Priest, Jesus Christ, our Lord. ⟨290⟩

C Amen

OR

P Almighty and most merciful God and Father, through your only-begotten Son, Jesus Christ, you have established your Church to be a temple and dwelling place of the Holy Spirit. We give thanks that you continue to provide shepherds to feed and serve your flock over which the Holy Spirit has made them overseers. We humbly implore you ever to strengthen the labors of your ministers that through their ministry of Word and Sacrament your people may bear fruit in your knowledge and service and grow up into him who is the head, Jesus Christ, to whom, with you and the Holy Spirit, be glory now and forever. ⟨291⟩

C Amen

13. The Hymn, "To God the Holy Spirit Let Us Pray," Hymn 155, may be sung.

14. The service continues with the Prayer of the Church, or The Prayers.

15. The newly installed presides at the Holy Communion.

NOTES

Preparation for the Rite

▶ *A chair is provided near the chancel for the seating of the pastor to be installed.*

INSTALLATION OF
A MISSIONARY
OR CHAPLAIN

1. This rite is used by those so authorized to install a missionary or chaplain when he has been called according to the Church's usual order to a specific field of service.

2. The installation is set within the Divine Service before the Prayer of the Church, or The Prayers. The Propers are those of the Sunday or festival on which the installation takes place or those appointed on pages 235—37.

3. In addition to the presiding minister, other pastors may serve as assisting ministers.

4. Before the service begins, the presiding minister gathers all who will take part in it in some convenient place for the Word of God and prayer. Then all enter the church together, the one to be installed going before the assisting ministers, and the presiding minister last of all.

Sit

5. When the time for the installation has come, the one to be installed presents himself before the altar. The presiding minister, standing before the altar, says:

P **In the name of the Father and of the ✠ Son and of the Holy Spirit.**

C Amen

6. The minister addresses the congregation:

P **Dear brothers and sisters in Christ, the Reverend ____name____ has been called by the ____name____ board of ____name____ to serve as __missionary/chaplain__ to**

228

<u>place/institution/branch of armed forces</u> . I ask you now in the presence of God: Will you support him by your gifts and fervent prayer? If so, answer: We will with the help of God.

C We will with the help of God.

P Hear what Holy Scripture says concerning the office of the public ministry.

7. The assisting ministers read one or more portions of Holy Scripture from each of the following sections.

THE INSTITUTION OF THE OFFICE OF THE PUBLIC MINISTRY

A Then Jesus came to them and said, "All authority in heaven and on earth has been given to me. Therefore go and make disciples of all nations, baptizing them in the name of the Father and of the Son and of the Holy Spirit, and teaching them to obey everything I have commanded you. And surely I will be with you always, to the very end of the age." (Matt. 28:18-20)

Again Jesus said, "Peace be with you! As the Father has sent me, I am sending you." And with that he breathed on them and said, "Receive the Holy Spirit. If you forgive anyone his sins, they are forgiven; if you do not forgive them, they are not forgiven." (John 20:21-23)

When they had finished eating, Jesus said to Simon Peter, "Simon son of John, do you truly love me more than these?" "Yes, Lord," he said, "you know that I love you." Jesus said, "Feed my lambs." Again Jesus said, "Simon son of John, do you truly love me?" He answered, "Yes, Lord, you know that I love you." Jesus said, "Take care of my sheep." The third time he said to him, "Simon son of John, do you love me?" Peter was hurt because Jesus asked him the third time, "Do you love me?" He said, "Lord, you know all things; you know that I love you." Jesus said, "Feed my sheep." (John 21:15-17)

THE RESPONSIBILITIES OF THE OFFICE OF THE PUBLIC MINISTRY

A "You did not choose me, but I chose you to go and bear fruit—fruit that will last. Then the Father will give you whatever you ask in my name." (John 15:16)

Do not neglect your gift, which was given you through a prophetic message when the body of elders laid their hands on you. Be diligent in these matters; give yourself wholly to them, so that everyone may see your progress. Watch your life and doctrine closely. Persevere in them, because if you do, you will save both yourself and your hearers. (1 Tim. 4:14-16)

So then, men ought to regard us as servants of Christ and as those entrusted with the secret things of God. Now it is required that those who have been given a trust must prove faithful. (1 Cor. 4:1-2)

Such confidence as this is ours through Christ before God. Not that we are competent to claim anything for ourselves, but our competence comes from God. (2 Cor. 3:4-5)

Therefore, if anyone is in Christ, he is a new creation; the old has gone, the new has come! All this is from God, who reconciled us to himself through Christ and gave us the ministry of reconciliation: that God was reconciling the world to himself in Christ, not counting men's sins against them. And he has committed to us the message of reconciliation. We are therefore Christ's ambassadors, as though God were making his appeal through us. We implore you on Christ's behalf: Be reconciled to God. God made him who had no sin to be sin for us, so that in him we might become the righteousness of God. (2 Cor. 5:17-21)

In the presence of God and of Christ Jesus, who will judge the living and the dead, and in view of his appearing and his kingdom, I give you this charge: Preach the Word; be prepared in season and out of season; correct, rebuke and encourage—with great patience and careful instruction. For the time will come when men will not put up with sound doctrine. Instead, to suit their own desires, they will gather around them a great number of teachers to say what their itching ears want to hear. They will turn their ears away from the truth and turn aside to myths. But you, keep your head in all situations, endure hardship, do the work of an evangelist, discharge all the duties of your ministry. (2 Tim. 4:1-5)

Here is a trustworthy saying: If anyone sets his heart on being an overseer, he desires a noble task. Now the overseer must be above reproach, the husband of but one wife, temperate, self-controlled, respectable, hospitable, able to teach, not given to much wine, not violent but gentle, not quarrelsome, not a lover of money. He must manage his own family well and see that his children obey him with proper respect. (If anyone does not know how to manage his own family, how can he take care of God's church?) He must not be a recent convert, or he may become conceited and fall under the same judgment as the devil. He must also have a good reputation with outsiders, so that he will not fall into disgrace and into the devil's trap. (1 Tim. 3:1-7)

It was he who gave some to be apostles, some to be prophets, some to be evangelists, and some to be pastors and teachers, to prepare God's people for works of service, so that the body of Christ may be built up. (Eph. 4:11-12)

[Guard] yourselves and all the flock of which the Holy Spirit has made you overseers. Be shepherds of the church of God, which he bought with his own blood. (Acts 20:28)

Be shepherds of God's flock that is under your care, serving as overseers—not because you must, but because you are willing, as God wants you to be; not greedy for money, but eager to serve; not lording it over those entrusted to you, but being examples to the flock. And when the Chief Shepherd appears, you will receive the crown of glory that will never fade away. (1 Peter 5:2-4)

THE STRENGTH AND PROMISE IN THE OFFICE OF THE PUBLIC MINISTRY

Ⓐ "You are the salt of the earth. But if the salt loses its saltiness, how can it be made salty again? It is no longer good for anything, except to be thrown out and trampled by men. You are the light of the world. A city on a hill cannot be hidden. Neither do people light a lamp and put it under a bowl. Instead they put it on its stand, and it gives light to everyone in the house. In the same way, let your light shine before men, that they may see your good deeds and praise your Father in heaven." (Matt. 5:13-16)

"Remain in me, and I will remain in you. No branch can bear fruit by itself; it must remain in the vine. Neither can you bear fruit unless you remain in me. I am the vine; you are the branches. If a man remains in me and I in him, he will bear much fruit; apart from me you can do nothing." (John 15:4-5)

"Let him who boasts boast in the Lord." For it is not the one who commends himself who is approved, but the one whom the Lord commends. (2 Cor. 10:17-18)

But as for you, continue in what you have learned and have become convinced of, because you know those from whom you learned it, and how from infancy you have known the holy Scriptures, which are able to make you wise for salvation through faith in Christ Jesus. All Scripture is God-breathed and is useful for teaching, rebuking, correcting and training in righteousness, so that the man of God may be thoroughly equipped for every good work. (2 Tim. 3:14-17)

8. The minister addresses the one being installed:

Ⓟ Dear brother in Christ, the Lord grant that you receive and keep these words in your heart that you may be strengthened and encouraged in your labors.

God gathers his Church by and around his holy Word and also grants it growth and increase. That this may be done, he has established the office of the public ministry into which you were ordained. It is fitting, in accordance with the call extended you, that you should again acknowledge the responsibilities of this holy office.

In the presence of God and of this congregation I now ask you:

℗ Do you believe the canonical books of the Old and New Testaments to be the inspired Word of God and the only infallible rule of faith and practice?

℞ I do.

℗ Do you accept the three Ecumenical Creeds, namely, the Apostles', the Nicene, and the Athanasian Creeds, as faithful testimonies to the truth of the Holy Scriptures, and do you reject all the errors which they condemn?

℞ I do.

℗ Do you believe that the Unaltered Augsburg Confession is a true exposition of the Word of God and a correct exhibition of the doctrine of the Evangelical Lutheran Church; that the Apology of the Augsburg Confession, the Small and Large Catechisms of Martin Luther, the Smalcald Articles, the Treatise on the Authority and Primacy of the Pope, and the Formula of Concord—as these are contained in the *Book of Concord*—are also in agreement with this one scriptural faith?

℞ I do.

℗ Do you solemnly promise that you will perform the duties of your office in accordance with these Confessions, or Symbols, and that all your teaching and your administration of the sacraments will be in conformity with the Holy Scriptures and with the aforementioned Symbols?

℞ I do.

℗ Will you faithfully instruct both young and old in the chief articles of Christian doctrine; will you forgive the sins of those who repent, and do you promise never to divulge the sins confessed to you; will you minister faithfully to the sick and dying; will you demonstrate to the Church a constant and ready ministry, admonishing the people to a lively confidence in Christ and holy living?

℞ I will with the help of God.

℗ Finally, will you adorn the office of the public ministry with a holy life?

℞ I will, the Lord helping me through the power and grace of his Holy Spirit.

Ⓟ **Are you willing and ready to assume this trust and responsibility?**

Ⓡ I am.

9. The one being installed kneels. The minister continues:

Ⓟ ____name____ , **I install you as (a)** ___missionary/chaplain___ **in** ___place/institution/branch of armed forces___ **, in the name of the Father and of the ☩ Son and of the Holy Spirit.**

May the God of peace, who through the blood of the eternal covenant brought back from the dead our Lord Jesus, that great Shepherd of the sheep, equip you with everything good for doing his will, and may he work in you what is pleasing in him, through Jesus Christ, to whom be glory forever and ever. (Heb. 13:20-21)

Ⓒ Amen

Stand

10. The minister says:

Ⓟ **Let us pray.**

MISSIONARY

Ⓟ **Almighty and merciful God, our heavenly Father, guide and bless your servant** ____name____ **, sent forth to be a witness to** ___place___ **. Graciously look with favor upon him for the sake of your Son, our Savior, Jesus Christ. Grant him confidence and great boldness; uphold and sustain him in hardship; and grant him faithfulness in all his labors that through the speaking of your Word many may come to worship before your throne in spirit and in truth; through Jesus Christ, our Lord, who lives and reigns with you and the Holy Spirit, one God, now and forever.** ⟨292⟩

Ⓒ Amen

INSTITUTIONAL CHAPLAIN

Ⓟ **Most merciful God, give to your called servant** ___name___ **a special measure of compassion and patience that he may effectively minister to the sick and suffering and to the aged, whose increasing years bring them weakness, anxiety, distress, or loneliness. Grant that through him your Word and Spirit may heal, strengthen, and comfort them with the message of forgiveness of sins, life, and salvation; through Jesus Christ, your Son, our Lord, who lives and reigns with you and the Holy Spirit, one God, now and forever.** ⟨293⟩

Ⓒ Amen

OR

ℙ **O Lord, God of justice and mercy, your Son directed that in our works of mercy we also visit those in prison. Grant grace and power to ____name____ as he proclaims your Law to the impenitent and the comforting message of forgiveness to those who repent. Bless him with wisdom and discernment as he ministers to prisoners, giving them a right understanding of themselves and their lot as well as of your heavenly promises through Jesus Christ. May your servant ever comfort the distressed and give aid to the innocent. Grant that through his ministry they may, by the Holy Spirit, be set free from the bondage of sin and be brought to the glorious liberty of your children; through Jesus Christ, our Lord, who lives and reigns with you and the Holy Spirit, one God, now and forever.** ⟨294⟩

ᴄ Amen

MILITARY CHAPLAIN

ℙ **O Lord God of hosts, we thank you for calling your servant ____name____ for ministry in your name to the armed forces of our nation. Grant him grace and zeal that he may faithfully perform the work of an evangelist and pastor and set an example for all in speech, in life, in love, in faith, and in purity. Stretch forth your almighty arm to protect those who serve in the armed forces. Give them courage and loyalty, and keep them from temptation and harm; through Jesus Christ, your Son, our Lord, who lives and reigns with you and the Holy Spirit, one God, now and forever.** ⟨295⟩

ᴄ Amen

11. The service continues with the Prayer of the Church, or The Prayers. The newly installed missionary or chaplain may continue the service as the presiding minister.

PROPERS

INTROIT

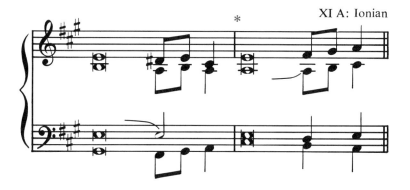

XI A: Ionian

"The Spirit of the Lord is on me,*
   because he has anointed me
   to preach good news to the poor.
He has sent me to proclaim freedom
for the prisoners*
   and recovery of sight for the blind,
to release the oppressed,*
   to proclaim the year of the Lord's
   favor."

The Lord is my light and my salvation—
whom shall I fear?*
   The Lord is the stronghold of my
   life—of whom shall I be afraid?
Though an army besiege me,
my heart will not fear;*
   though war break out against me,
   even then will I be confident.
In the day of trouble he will keep me
safe in his dwelling;*
   he will hide me in the shelter of his
   tabernacle and set me high upon a rock.

I am still confident of this:*
   I will see the goodness of the Lord
   in the land of the living.
Wait for the Lord;*
   be strong and take heart
   and wait for the Lord.

Glory be to the Father and to the Son*
   and to the Holy Spirit;
as it was in the beginning,*
   is now, and will be forever. Amen

"The Spirit of the Lord is on me,*
   because he has anointed me
   to preach good news to the poor.
He has sent me to proclaim freedom
for the prisoners*
   and recovery of sight for the blind,
to release the oppressed,*
   to proclaim the year of the Lord's
   favor."

*(Antiphon, Luke 4:18-19; Ps. 27:1, 3,
5, 13-14)*

COLLECT

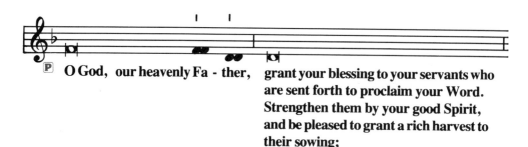

[P] O God, our heavenly Fa - ther, grant your blessing to your servants who
are sent forth to proclaim your Word.
Strengthen them by your good Spirit,
and be pleased to grant a rich harvest to
their sowing;

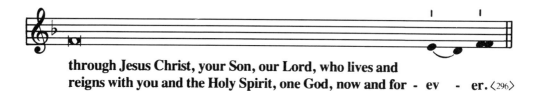

through Jesus Christ, your Son, our Lord, who lives and
reigns with you and the Holy Spirit, one God, now and for - ev - er. ⟨296⟩

READINGS

Psalm 48
Isaiah 52:7-10
1 Corinthians 1:18-31
Matthew 28:18-20

GRADUAL

XI A: Ionian

Praise the name of the Lord;*
    praise him, you servants of the Lord.
The Lord reigns, let the earth be glad;*
    let the distant shores rejoice. (*Ps. 135:1b; 97:1*)

VERSE

(Acts 2:47)

Al - le - lu - ia, al - le - lu - ia. The Lord adds

day by day those who are be - ing saved. Al - le - lu - ia.

PREFACE:Apostles and Evangelists

COLOR:red

NOTES

Preparation for the Rite

▶ *A chair is provided near the chancel for the seating of the one to be installed.*

ANNIVERSARY
OF AN ORDINATION

1. This rite immediately follows the Offertory in Divine Service I, the Creed in Divine Service II, or the Canticle in Matins or Morning Prayer, Vespers or Evening Prayer.

2. The Propers are those of the Sunday or festival on which the anniversary observance takes place.

3. A colleague who has played an important role in the life of the pastor to be honored may be invited to serve as the presiding minister. He, or another pastor, may preach the sermon.

4. Before the service begins, the presiding minister gathers all who will take part in it in some convenient place for the Word of God and prayer. Then all enter the church together, the pastor to be honored going before the assisting ministers, and the presiding minister last of all.

Sit

5. When the time for the observance has come, the pastor to be honored presents himself before the altar. The presiding minister addresses the congregation with these or similar words:

Ⓟ **With gratitude and joy we give thanks this day for _____name_____ , who _____number_____ year(s) ago was ordained and consecrated to the office of the public ministry in the one, holy, Christian, and apostolic Church. We thank God that he established this office in his Church through which "are imparted not bodily, but eternal things and gifts, namely, eternal righteousness, the Holy Spirit, and eternal life." We praise the Lord that he has permitted his servant _____name_____ to work in his Church these [many] years, that he has sustained and supported him and blessed his ministry [among us].**

238

Stand

P **Let us pray.**

Lord God, heavenly Father, you promised to send your servants the Holy Spirit and to give them power from on high. We give thanks that through your Word you also called _____name_____ **as your servant and entrusted him with the office of the public ministry. We praise your mercy and faithfulness and ask that you continue to keep him in faith and bless his work. Open everywhere the hearts of the faithful that your Word may be received and that laborers in your harvest will not be lacking. Cause your Church to grow up into him who is the head, Jesus Christ, who lives and reigns with you and the Holy Spirit, one God, now and forever.** ⟨297⟩

C Amen

6. The congregation sings "Lord Jesus Christ, Will You Not Stay," Hymn 344, or another appropriate hymn.

7. The honored pastor returns to his place.

8. The service continues with the prayers (or Litany) appropriate to the Divine Service, Matins or Morning Prayer, Vespers or Evening Prayer.

NOTES

General

▶ *The pastor to be honored may assist the presiding minister in the distribution of the Holy Communion.*

Preparation for the Rite

▶ *A chair is provided near the chancel for the seating of the pastor to be honored.*

The Service in Detail

8. ▶ Additional petitions for the honored pastor, and petitions for his family, may be included.

FAREWELL AND GODSPEED
TO A PASTOR

1. This rite is used to bid farewell and Godspeed to a pastor who according to the Church's usual order has accepted a call to a new field of service or who is retiring.

2. Another pastor of the congregation, a vacancy pastor, or an official of the Synod presides.

Sit

3. Immediately before the Benediction in the Divine Service the pastor who is leaving or retiring presents himself before the altar. The presiding minister addresses the congregation with these or similar words:

P **Dear brothers and sisters in Christ, Pastor ____name____ has accepted a call to a new field of service in the Church. At this time of farewell and Godspeed we look to the Word of our Lord for comfort, peace, and guidance.**

OR

P **Dear brothers and sisters in Christ, Pastor ____name____ is retiring from his pastorate at this congregation, and at this time of farewell and Godspeed we look to the Word of our Lord for comfort, peace, and guidance.**

Stand

4. The following selected portions of Psalmody are read responsively:

℗ **Glorify the Lord with me; let us exalt his name together. Know that the Lord is God.**

℃ It is he who made us, and we are his; we are his people, the sheep of his pasture.

℗ **Enter his gates with thanksgiving and his courts with praise; give thanks to him and praise his name.**

℃ For the Lord is good and his love endures forever; his faithfulness continues through all generations.

℗ **O Lord Almighty, blessed are those who dwell in your house.**

℃ O Lord Almighty, blessed is the man who trusts in you.

℗ **Blessed is the man who does not walk in the counsel of the wicked or stand in the way of sinners or sit in the seat of mockers.**

℃ But his delight is in the law of the Lord, and on his law he meditates day and night.

℗ **He is like a tree planted by streams of water, which yields its fruit in season and whose leaf does not wither. Whatever he does prospers.** (Ps. 34:3; 100:3-5; 84:1b, 4a, 12; 1:1-3)

℃ Glory be to the Father and to the Son and to the Holy Spirit; as it was in the beginning, is now, and will be forever. Amen

5. One of the following Prayers is said.

℗ **Let us pray.**

℗ **O Lord God, merciful and gracious Father, we give thanks for all the blessings you have bestowed on this congregation, its members, and the Church through the ministry of your servant ⎯⎯ name ⎯⎯ . By your Holy Spirit grant him grace in his new field of service, readiness and steadfastness in his ministry, patience, understanding, and great zeal. Support and strengthen him that by your Word your Church may be built and increased; through your Son, our great High Priest, Jesus Christ, our Lord.** ⟨298⟩

OR

242

℗ Lord God, heavenly Father, we give thanks for all the blessings you have bestowed on this congregation through the ministry of your servant ____name____ . By your Holy Spirit grant him grace that by his example of faithful devotion to your Word he may be a blessing to many. In your mercy support and strengthen him in his life, and grant him peace and blessedness, now and forever; through your Son, our great High Priest, Jesus Christ, our Lord. ⟨299⟩

℃ Amen

6. The minister turns to the pastor who is leaving or retiring and says:

℗ **Dear brother in Christ, the Lord will keep you from all harm—he will watch over your life; the Lord will watch over your coming and going both now and forevermore.** (Ps. 121:7-8)

℃ Amen

7. The pastor who is leaving or retiring concludes the service with the Benediction.

NOTES

Preparation for the Rite

▶ *A chair is provided near the chancel for the seating of the pastor who is leaving or retiring.*

FAREWELL AND GODSPEED TO A CANDIDATE FOR COMMISSIONING

1. This rite is used to bid farewell and Godspeed to the son or daughter of a congregation who has been declared a candidate for commissioning and has accepted his/her first call.

Sit

2. Immediately before the Prayer of the Church, or The Prayers, in the Divine Service, the candidate presents himself/herself before the altar. The pastor addresses the congregation with these or similar words:

P **People of God in Christ, ____name____ , a ___son/daughter___ of this congregation, who has been aided in ___his/her___ preparation for the teaching ministry by your encouragement, your gifts, and your prayers, has accepted a call according to the Church's usual order to ___his/her___ first field of service. At this time of farewell and Godspeed we look to the Word of our Lord for encouragement, strength, and guidance.**

Stand

3. The following selected portions of Psalmody are read responsively:

P **Sing to the Lord a new song; sing to the Lord, all the earth.**

C Sing for joy to the Lord; let us shout aloud to the Rock of our salvation.

P **I will open my mouth in parables, I will utter things hidden from of old—things that we have heard and known, things our fathers have told us.**

C We will not hide them from [our] children; we will tell the next generation the praiseworthy deeds of the Lord, his power, and the wonders he has done.

P **He decreed statutes for Jacob and established the law in Israel, which he commanded our forefathers to teach their children,**

C so the next generation would know them, even the children yet to be born, and they in turn would tell their children. Then they would put their trust in God and would not forget his deeds but would keep his commands.

P **Praise the Lord, O my soul; all my inmost being, praise his holy name.**

C Praise the Lord, O my soul, and forget not all his benefits.

P **God is our refuge and strength, an ever present help in trouble. The Lord Almighty is with us; the God of Jacob is our fortress. Delight yourself in the Lord and he will give you the desires of your heart.** (Ps. 96:1; 95:1; 78:2-7; 103:1-2; 46:1, 11; 37:4)

C Glory be to the Father and to the Son and to the Holy Spirit; as it was in the beginning, is now, and will be forever. Amen

4. The Prayer is said.

P **Let us pray.**

O Lord God, merciful and gracious Father, we give thanks for all the blessings you have bestowed on __name__ in __his/her__ preparation for the teaching ministry. By your Holy Spirit grant __him/her__ grace in __his/her__ first field of service, readiness to grow in wisdom, knowledge, and skill, steadfastness in ministering, patience, understanding, and great zeal. Support and strengthen __him/her__ that by your Word your Church may be built and increased; through your Son, our Lord and Savior Jesus Christ. ⟨300⟩

C Amen

5. The pastor dismisses and blesses the candidate.

P   **Go then in peace and joy. The almighty and most merciful God, the Father, the ✠ Son, and the Holy Spirit, go with you, bless and strengthen you for faithful service in his name.**

C   Amen

6. The candidate returns to his/her place.

Sit

7. The congregation sings "Take My Life, O Lord, Renew," Hymn 404, or "Let Children Hear the Mighty Deeds," Hymn 472, or "You Will I Love, My Strength," Hymn 375.

Stand

8. The service continues with the Prayer of the Church, or The Prayers.

NOTES

Preparation for the Rite
► *A chair is provided near the chancel for the seating of the candidate for commissioning.*

INSTALLATION OF A PROFESSOR OR INSTRUCTOR AT A COLLEGE OR SEMINARY

1. This rite is used by those so authorized to install professors or instructors at colleges or seminaries. The Seminary section is also appropriate for the installation of professors or instructors in the religion or theology departments of colleges.

2. The installation immediately follows the Offertory in Divine Service I, the Creed in Divine Service II, or the Canticle in Matins or Morning Prayer, Vespers or Evening Prayer.

3. The Propers are those of the Sunday or festival on which the installation takes place.

4. The president of the college or seminary or one whom he designates serves as the presiding minister. Other members of the faculty may serve as assisting ministers.

Sit

5. When the time has come for the installation, the one(s) to be installed present(s) himself/herself/themselves before the presiding minister.

P   **In the name of the Father and of the ✝ Son and of the Holy Spirit.**

R   Amen

COLLEGE

6. The minister turns to the assembly and says:

P   **Dear brothers and sisters in Christ, _____^{name(s)} has (have) been**

_____called/appointed to serve as _____title of position at this college. __He/She/They__ has (have) prepared __himself/herself/themselves__ for this service through advanced studies that qualifies (qualify) __him/her/them__ to instruct men and women who seek in a Christian environment such knowledge and skills as will equip them for responsible citizenship and chosen careers.

7. The minister addresses the called/appointed person(s):

℗   I now invite you to assure those present that you will do your utmost to carry out in a God-pleasing manner the tasks assigned to you. I therefore ask you: Do you solemnly promise to reflect the truths of the Word of God and the Holy Scriptures and to teach in conformity with the Lutheran Confessions as faithful expositions of those truths; to set an example for the students in speech, in life, in faith, in purity; to be concerned for and help the students develop their full potential for Christian service?

℞   I do.

8. The minister asks the assembly:

℗   You have heard the solemn promise of __him/her/them__ , __called/appointed__ to service at this college. Will you now receive __him/her/them__ , show __him/her/them__ fitting respect and honor, and pledge to cooperate with and support __him/her/them__ in __his/her/their__ work? If so, answer: We will with the help of God.

℞   We will with the help of God.

9. The minister addresses each called/appointed person:

℗   _____name , I install you as _____title of position at _____name of college , in the name of the Father and of the ✠ Son and of the Holy Spirit.

℞   Amen

Stand

10. The newly installed kneel(s) for prayer.

℗   Let us pray.

Gracious and bountiful Lord, we humbly pray that you will continue to make this college a center of godly learning and living. Give those who teach knowledge, patience, and a loving spirit and those who are taught a receptive heart and aptness to learn. Prosper the work of our instructors and students and all others who here assist them in their labors that your Church may be edified and your

holy name glorified; through Jesus Christ, your Son, our Lord. ⟨301⟩

℞ Amen

OR

SEMINARY

11. The minister turns to the assembly and says:

Ⓟ **Dear brothers and sisters in Christ, [the Reverend]** _____name(s)_____ **has (have) been** ____called/appointed____ **to be** ____professor/instructor____ **of** ___academic field___ **at this seminary. Hear now what the Word of God says concerning the office of the public ministry.**

12. The assisting ministers read one or more portions of Holy Scripture from each of the following sections.

THE INSTITUTION OF THE OFFICE OF THE PUBLIC MINISTRY

Ⓐ **[Jesus said,] "All authority in heaven and on earth has been given to me. Therefore go and make disciples of all nations, baptizing them in the name of the Father and of the Son and of the Holy Spirit, and teaching them to obey everything I have commanded you. And surely I will be with you always, to the very end of the age."** (Matt. 28:18-20)

When they had finished eating, Jesus said to Simon Peter, "Simon son of John, do you truly love me more than these?" "Yes, Lord," he said, "you know that I love you." Jesus said, "Feed my lambs." Again Jesus said, "Simon son of John, do you truly love me?" He answered, "Yes, Lord, you know that I love you." Jesus said, "Take care of my sheep." The third time he said to him, "Simon son of John, do you love me?" Peter was hurt because Jesus asked him the third time, "Do you love me?" He said, "Lord, you know all things; you know that I love you." Jesus said, "Feed my sheep." (John 21:15-17)

Again Jesus said, "Peace be with you! As the Father has sent me, I am sending you." And with that he breathed on them and said, "Receive the Holy Spirit. If you forgive anyone his sins, they are forgiven; if you do not forgive them, they are not forgiven." (John 20:21-23)

249

THE RESPONSIBILITIES OF THE OFFICE
OF THE PUBLIC MINISTRY

Ⓐ   We do not preach ourselves, but Jesus Christ as Lord, and ourselves as your servants for Jesus' sake. For God, who said, "Let light shine out of darkness," made his light shine in our hearts to give us the light of the knowledge of the glory of God in the face of Christ. (2 Cor. 4:5-6)

Do not neglect your gift, which was given you through a prophetic message when the body of elders laid their hands on you. Be diligent in these matters; give yourself wholly to them, so that everyone may see your progress. Watch your life and doctrine closely. Persevere in them, because if you do, you will save both yourself and your hearers. (1 Tim. 4:14-16)

Now if the ministry that brought death, which was engraved in letters on stone, came with glory, so that the Israelites could not look steadily at the face of Moses because of its glory, fading though it was, will not the ministry of the Spirit be even more glorious? (2 Cor. 3:7-8)

13. The minister addresses the called/appointed person(s):

Ⓟ   **Dear brother(s) in Christ, it is the aim of __name of seminary__ to prepare men for the office of the public ministry of Word and Sacrament in The Lutheran Church—Missouri Synod. To that end, the seminary seeks to equip the student with the knowledge, attitudes, and skills requisite for this ministry, leading him**

> **to display the gifts with which the Holy Spirit has endowed him, by reverence for God, by faithful use of Word and Sacrament, by diligent pursuit of opportunities for study and growth and for increase in the grace to edify his fellow Christians, by serving all people in their need, and by witnessing to all as a person of good reputation;**

> **to accept without reservation the Scripture of the Old and New Testaments as the written Word of God and the only rule and norm of faith and practice;**

> **to accept the Ecumenical Creeds and all the Symbolical Books of the Evangelical Lutheran Church contained in the *Book of Concord* as a true and unadulterated statement and exposition of the Word of God;**

> **to manifest an appreciation for and to have a comprehensive understanding of the theology of the Bible and the skill to interpret Holy Scripture on**

250

the basis of the original languages and in accordance with sound hermeneutical principles;

to exhibit an understanding of and appreciation for the Church's formulation of scriptural doctrine in the light of its varying needs and to have the skill to present such doctrine clearly;

to show an understanding of and appreciation for God's guidance in the history of the Church and to have the skill to investigate the Church's past and to interpret it to the present generation;

to give evidence of understanding the pastoral office as the ministry of proclaiming God's Word to human need within the discipline of worship, preaching, teaching, pastoral care and counseling for the edification of God's people, enabling them to carry on the mission of the Church; and

to indicate a complete dedication to the office of the public ministry and readiness to accept his first call.

Do you solemnly promise to instruct and guide the students at this seminary in accord with these aims?

℟ This is my solemn promise before God, who sees and knows all things, and I earnestly pray him graciously to strengthen and guide me in this my promise.

14. The minister asks the assembly:

℗ **You have heard the solemn promise of him** __called/appointed__ **to service and ministry at this seminary. Will you now receive him, show him fitting respect and honor, and pledge to cooperate with and support him in his work? If so, answer: We will with the help of God.**

℟ We will with the help of God.

15. The minister addresses each called/appointed person:

℗ _____name_____ **, I install you as** __title of position__ **, in the name of the Father and of the ✠ Son and of the Holy Spirit.**

℟ Amen

Stand

16. The newly installed kneel(s) for prayer.

℗ **Let us pray.**

O Lord, our God, by your Son the world has been redeemed and forgiven, and you want all to be saved and to come to the knowledge of the truth. Bless our seminary with teachers who are faithful to your Word, and with students who are eager to receive the wisdom that comes down from heaven. Fill those who study with a loving concern for your people and equip them with a competency to become able ministers of the New Testament, not of the letter but of the Spirit; through Jesus Christ, your Son, our Lord. ⟨302⟩

℟ Amen

℗ **Almighty and most gracious God, our heavenly Father, we give thanks that you send your people true and faithful servants. Grant that through their labors your Church may be nourished, sustained, and equipped for every good work and built up into him who is the head of his Church, Jesus Christ, our Lord, who lives and reigns with you and the Holy Spirit, one God, now and forever.** ⟨303⟩

17. The newly installed rise(s) and are (is) greeted in the Lord's Peace by his/her/their colleagues. The newly installed are (is) sent to his/her/their labor with these words:

℗ **Go then in peace and joy. The almighty and most merciful God, the Father, the ✝ Son, and the Holy Spirit, be with you, bless and strengthen you to your work in his name.**

℟ Amen

18. The service continues with the prayers (or Litany) appropriate to the Divine Service, Matins or Morning Prayer, Vespers or Evening Prayer.

NOTES

General

▶ *If the one to be installed is also to be ordained at this time, the minister who presides will first use pertinent sections in the rite of Ordination.*

▶ *If the one to be installed is also to be commissioned at this time, the minister who presides will first use pertinent sections of the rite of Commissioning and Installation of One Called to the Teaching Ministry. Rubric 11 of that rite will then be read:*

＿＿＿name＿＿＿ , **I commission you to the office of the teaching ministry, in the name of the Father and of the ⁜ Son and of the Holy Spirit.**

Thereafter the minister will continue with this installation rite.

Preparation for the Rite

▶ *A chair is provided near the chancel for the seating of the one to be installed.*

253

COMMISSIONING AND
INSTALLATION OF
ONE CALLED TO
THE TEACHING MINISTRY

1. This rite is administered by those so authorized to commission and install, according to the Church's usual order, such teacher candidates as have been certified by the Church to be ready and prepared for this ministry and who have received a regular call.

2. The rite is set within the Divine Service before the Prayer of the Church, or The Prayers. The Propers are those of the Sunday or festival on which the commissioning and installation take place.

3. Ordinarily the pastor of the congregation is the presiding minister. It is appropriate that other pastors and called teachers serve as assisting ministers, according to local custom and the direction of the presiding minister.

4. Before the service begins, the presiding minister gathers all who will take part in it in some convenient place for the Word of God and prayer. Then all enter the church together, the called teacher going before the assisting ministers, and the presiding minister last of all.

Sit

5. When the time for the commissioning and installation has come, the candidate presents himself/herself before the altar. The presiding minister, standing before the altar, says:

P   **In the name of the Father and of the ☩ Son and of the Holy Spirit.**

C   Amen

254

6. The minister addresses the congregation:

℗ Dear brothers and sisters in Christ, ____name____ has been called in the Church's usual order to the teaching ministry in the Church, a ministry established to strengthen and support the office of the public ministry and its work. __He/She__ has prepared __himself/herself__ for this ministry by prayer and study. __He/She__ has been examined and declared ready to undertake this sacred responsibility.

Hear the Word of God concerning this ministry.

7. One or more of the following portions of Holy Scripture are read.

Ⓐ Just as each of us has one body with many members, and these members do not all have the same function, so in Christ we who are many form one body, and each member belongs to all the others. We have different gifts, according to the grace given us. If a man's gift is prophesying, let him use it in proportion to his faith. If it is serving, let him serve; if it is teaching, let him teach; if it is encouraging, let him encourage; if it is contributing to the needs of others, let him give generously; if it is leadership, let him govern diligently; if it is showing mercy, let him do it cheerfully. (Rom. 12:4-8)

Above all, love each other deeply, because love covers over a multitude of sins. Offer hospitality to one another without grumbling. Each one should use whatever gift he has received to serve others, faithfully administering God's grace in its various forms. If anyone speaks, he should do it as one speaking the very words of God. If anyone serves, he should do it with the strength God provides, so that in all things God may be praised through Jesus Christ. To him be the glory and the power for ever and ever. Amen. (1 Peter 4:8-11)

Jesus called [the disciples] together and said, "You know that the rulers of the Gentiles lord it over them, and their high officials exercise authority over them. Not so with you. Instead, whoever wants to become great among you must be your servant, and whoever wants to be first must be your slave—just as the Son of Man did not come to be served, but to serve, and to give his life as a ransom for many." (Matt. 20:25-28)

Let the word of Christ dwell in you richly as you teach and admonish one another with all wisdom, and as you sing psalms, hymns and spiritual songs with gratitude in your hearts to God. And whatever you do, whether in word or deed, do it all in the name of the Lord Jesus, giving thanks to God the Father through him. (Col. 3:16-17)

8. The minister asks the candidate:

255

P Do you believe the canonical books of the Old and New Testaments to be the inspired Word of God and the only infallible rule of faith and practice?

R I do.

P Do you accept the three Ecumenical Creeds, namely, the Apostles', the Nicene, and the Athanasian Creeds, as faithful testimonies to the truth of the Holy Scriptures, and do you reject all errors which they condemn?

R I do.

P Do you believe that the Unaltered Augsburg Confession is a true exposition of the Word of God and a correct exhibition of the doctrine of the Evangelical Lutheran Church; that the Apology of the Augsburg Confession, the Small and Large Catechisms of Martin Luther, the Smalcald Articles, the Treatise on the Authority and Primacy of the Pope, and the Formula of Concord—as these are contained in the *Book of Concord*—are also in agreement with this one scriptural faith?

R I do.

P Do you solemnly promise faithfully to serve God's people in the teaching ministry in accordance with the Word of God, the Ecumenical Creeds, and the Confessions, or Symbols, of the Church?

R I do.

P Will you, trusting in God's care, seek to grow in love for those you serve, strive for excellence in your skills, and adorn the Gospel of Jesus Christ with a godly life?

R I will with the help of God.

9. *The minister addresses the congregation:*

P Brothers and sisters in Christ, you have heard the confession and solemn promise of __him/her__ called to the teaching ministry in the Church. I ask you now, in the presence of God: Will you receive __him/her__, show __him/her__ fitting love and honor, and support __him/her__ by your gifts and fervent prayer? If so, answer: We will with the help of God.

C We will with the help of God.

P The almighty and most merciful God strengthen and assist you always.

10. The minister asks the candidate:

ℙ **Are you ready and willing to assume the work of this ministry?**

ℝ I am.

11. The candidate kneels. The minister continues:

ℙ _____name_____ , **I commission you to the office of the teaching ministry and install you as (a) ____title of position____ in (at) ____place____ , in the name of the Father and of the ✠ Son and of the Holy Spirit.**

ℂ Amen

Stand

12. The following Prayers are said.

ℙ **Let us pray.**

Gracious and most merciful Lord, we thank you for providing faithful men and women in your Church to assist and support the office and work of the public ministry among us. Grant your blessing to those called to the teaching ministry that by their labors your people may be strengthened and sustained in the saving faith; through Jesus Christ, your Son, our Lord. ⟨304⟩

ℂ Amen

ℙ **Almighty God, the fountain and source of all wisdom, we thank you for hearing our prayers and leading ____name____ to accept our call. Grant to ___him/her___ your Holy Spirit and adorn ___him/her___ with wisdom and power from on high. Incline both young and old to godliness and obedience, and let them so profit by instruction in your holy Word that they may serve you all their days and finally obtain eternal life; through Jesus Christ, our Lord, who lives and reigns with you and the Holy Spirit, one God, now and forever.** ⟨305⟩

ℂ Amen

ℂ Our Father who art in heaven,	OR	ℂ Our Father in heaven,
hallowed be thy name,		hallowed be your name,
thy kingdom come,		your kingdom come,
thy will be done		your will be done
on earth as it is in heaven.		on earth as in heaven.

Give us this day our daily bread; and forgive us our trespasses as we forgive those who trespass against us; and lead us not into temptation, but deliver us from evil. For thine is the kingdom and the power and the glory forever and ever. Amen	Give us today our daily bread. Forgive us our sins as we forgive those who sin against us. Lead us not into temptation, but deliver us from evil. For the kingdom, the power, and the glory are yours now and forever. Amen

13. The minister dismisses and blesses the newly commissioned and installed.

P   **Go then in peace and joy. The almighty and most merciful God, the Father, the ☩ Son, and the Holy Spirit, go with you, bless and strengthen you for faithful service in his name.**

C   Amen

14. The newly commissioned and installed rises and is welcomed and greeted in the name of the Lord by the minister and fellow workers.

Peace be with you.   R   Peace be with you.

15. All return to their places. The service continues with the Prayer of the Church, or The Prayers.

NOTES

General

▶ *Commissioned men and women serve in one of the following positions: teacher in Lutheran elementary or secondary school, director of Christian education or minister of education in a congregation, District or synodical executive, professor in a synodical college.*

Preparation for the Rite

▶ *A chair is provided near the chancel for the seating of the one to be commissioned and installed.*

INSTALLATION OF ONE CALLED TO THE TEACHING MINISTRY

1. This rite is used by those so authorized to install such teachers as have been called according to the Church's usual order to a new field of service.

2. The installation is set within the Divine Service before the Prayer of the Church, or The Prayers. The Propers are those of the Sunday or festival on which the installation takes place.

3. Ordinarily the pastor of the congregation is the presiding minister. It is appropriate that other pastors and called teachers serve as assisting ministers, according to local custom and the direction of the presiding minister.

4. Before the service begins, the presiding minister gathers all who will take part in it in some convenient place for the Word of God and prayer. Then all enter the church together, the teacher-elect going before the assisting ministers, and the presiding minister last of all.

Sit

5. When the time for the installation has come, the teacher-elect presents himself/herself before the altar. The presiding minister, standing before the altar, says:

P **In the name of the Father and of the ✚ Son and of the Holy Spirit.**

C Amen

6. The minister addresses the congregation:

260

P Dear brothers and sisters in Christ, _____name_____ has been properly elected and called to serve as (a) _____title of position_____ in (at) _____place_____ . This ministry has been established to strengthen and support the office of the public ministry and its work.

Hear the Word of God concerning this ministry.

7. One or more of the following portions of Holy Scripture are read.

A Just as each of us has one body with many members, and these members do not all have the same function, so in Christ we who are many form one body, and each member belongs to all the others. We have different gifts, according to the grace given us. If a man's gift is prophesying, let him use it in proportion to his faith. If it is serving, let him serve; if it is teaching, let him teach; if it is encouraging, let him encourage; if it is contributing to the needs of others, let him give generously; if it is leadership, let him govern diligently; if it is showing mercy, let him do it cheerfully. (Rom. 12:4-8)

Above all, love each other deeply, because love covers over a multitude of sins. Offer hospitality to one another without grumbling. Each one should use whatever gift he has received to serve others, faithfully administering God's grace in its various forms. If anyone speaks, he should do it as one speaking the very words of God. If anyone serves, he should do it with the strength God provides, so that in all things God may be praised through Jesus Christ. To him be the glory and the power for ever and ever. Amen. (1 Peter 4:8-11)

Jesus called [the disciples] together and said, "You know that the rulers of the Gentiles lord it over them, and their high officials exercise authority over them. Not so with you. Instead, whoever wants to become great among you must be your servant, and whoever wants to be first must be your slave—just as the Son of Man did not come to be served, but to serve, and to give his life as a ransom for many." (Matt. 20:25-28)

Let the word of Christ dwell in you richly as you teach and admonish one another with all wisdom, and as you sing psalms, hymns and spiritual songs with gratitude in your hearts to God. And whatever you do, whether in word or deed, do it all in the name of the Lord Jesus, giving thanks to God the Father through him. (Col. 3:16-17)

8. The minister asks the teacher-elect:

P Do you believe the canonical books of the Old and New Testaments to be the inspired Word of God and the only infallible rule of faith and practice?

R I do.

P Do you accept the three Ecumenical Creeds, namely, the Apostles', the Nicene, and the Athanasian Creeds, as faithful testimonies to the truth of the Holy Scriptures, and do you reject all errors which they condemn?

R I do.

P Do you believe that the Unaltered Augsburg Confession is a true exposition of the Word of God and a correct exhibition of the doctrine of the Evangelical Lutheran Church; that the Apology of the Augsburg Confession, the Small and Large Catechisms of Martin Luther, the Smalcald Articles, the Treatise on the Authority and Primacy of the Pope, and the Formula of Concord—as these are contained in the *Book of Concord*—are also in agreement with this one scriptural faith?

R I do.

P Do you solemnly promise faithfully to serve God's people in the teaching ministry in accordance with the Word of God, the Ecumenical Creeds, and the Confessions, or Symbols, of the Church?

R I do.

P Will you, trusting in God's care, seek to grow in love for those you serve, strive for excellence in your skills, and adorn the Gospel of Jesus Christ with a godly life?

R I will with the help of God.

9. The minister addresses the congregation:

P Brothers and sisters in Christ, you have heard the confession and solemn promise of __him/her__ called to the teaching ministry in the Church. I ask you now, in the presence of God: Will you receive __him/her__ , show __him/her__ fitting love and honor, and support __him/her__ by your gifts and fervent prayer? If so, answer: We will with the help of God.

C We will with the help of God.

P The almighty and most merciful God strengthen and assist you always.

10. The minister asks the teacher-elect:

P Are you ready and willing to assume the work of this ministry?

R I am.

11. The teacher-elect kneels. The minister continues:

Ⓟ _____name_____ , I install you as (a) ___title of position___ in (at) ___place___ , in the name of the Father and of the ✠ Son and of the Holy Spirit.

Ⓒ Amen

Stand

12. The following Prayer is said.

Ⓟ **Let us pray.**

Almighty God, the fountain and source of all wisdom, we thank you for hearing our prayers and leading _____name_____ to accept our call. Grant to ___him/her___ your Holy Spirit and adorn ___him/her___ with wisdom and power from on high. Incline both young and old to godliness and obedience, and let them so profit by instruction in your holy Word that they may serve you all their days and finally obtain eternal life; through Jesus Christ, our Lord, who lives and reigns with you and the Holy Spirit, one God, now and forever. ⟨305⟩

Ⓒ Amen

13. The pastor dismisses and blesses the newly installed.

Ⓟ **Go then in peace and joy. The almighty and most merciful God, the Father, the ✠ Son, and the Holy Spirit, go with you, bless and strengthen you for faithful service in his name.**

Ⓒ Amen

14. The newly installed rises and is welcomed and greeted in the name of the Lord by the minister and fellow workers.

Peace be with you.   Ⓡ Peace be with you.

15. All return to their places. The service continues with the Prayer of the Church, or The Prayers.

NOTES

General

▶ *This rite is used to install commissioned men and women to serve in one of the following positions: teacher in Lutheran elementary or secondary school, director of Christian education or minister of education in a congregation.*

Preparation for the Rite

▶ *A chair is provided near the chancel for the seating of the one to be installed.*

ANNIVERSARY
OF A COMMISSIONING

1. This rite immediately follows the Offertory in Divine Service I, the Creed in Divine Service II, or the Canticle in Matins or Morning Prayer, Vespers or Evening Prayer.

2. The Propers are those of the Sunday or festival on which the anniversary observance takes place.

3. The local pastor or another pastor who has played an important role in the life of the one to be honored may serve as the presiding minister. One or the other may preach the sermon.

4. It is appropriate that other called teachers serve as assisting ministers, according to local custom and the direction of the pastor.

5. Before the service begins, the presiding minister gathers all who will take part in it in some convenient place for the Word of God and prayer. Then all enter the church together, the one to be honored going before the assisting ministers, and the presiding minister last of all.

Sit

6. When the time for the observance has come, the one to be honored presents himself/herself before the altar. The presiding minister addresses the congregation with these or similar words:

℗ **With gratitude and joy we give thanks this day for _____name_____ , who _____number_____ year(s) ago was commissioned to serve in the teaching ministry. We thank the Lord that this ministry has been established to assist and support the office of the public ministry among us, and that he has given his Church those who nourish Christ's people with the teaching of his Word. We praise him that he has** permitted his servant ___name___ to work these [many] years, that he has sustained and supported ___him/her___ and blessed ___his/her___ ministry [among us].

Stand

P **Let us pray.**

Lord God, heavenly Father, we give thanks that through your Word you called ___name___ to be a teacher in the Church. We praise your mercy and ask that you continue to keep ___him/her___ in faith and bless ___his/her___ work. Dispose your people to godliness and obedience and let them so profit by instruction in your holy Word that they may ever grow in faith, be preserved from all ungodliness, serve you all their days, and finally inherit eternal life; through Jesus Christ, your Son, our Lord, who lives and reigns with you and the Holy Spirit, one God, now and forever. ⟨306⟩

C Amen

7. The congregation sings "I Pray You, Dear Lord Jesus," Hymn 476, or another appropriate hymn.

8. The honored one returns to his/her place.

9. The service continues with the prayers (or Litany) appropriate to the Divine Service, Matins or Morning Prayer, Vespers or Evening Prayer.

NOTES

Preparation for the Rite

▶ *A chair is provided near the chancel for the seating of the one to be honored.*

The Service in Detail

9. ▶ *Additional petitions for the honored one, and petitions for his/her family, may be included in the prayers.*

FAREWELL AND GODSPEED TO A TEACHER

1. This rite is used to bid farewell and Godspeed to a teacher who according to the Church's usual order has accepted a call to a new field of service or who is retiring.

Sit

2. Immediately before the Benediction in the Divine Service the teacher who is leaving or retiring presents himself/herself before the altar. The pastor addresses the congregation with these or similar words:

P **People of God in Christ, _____name_____ has accepted a call to a new field of service in the Church. At this time of farewell and Godspeed we look to the Word of our Lord for comfort, peace, and guidance.**

OR

P **People of God in Christ, _____name_____ is retiring from the teaching ministry in our congregation, and at this time of farewell and Godspeed we look to the Word of our Lord for comfort, peace, and guidance.**

Stand

3. The following selected portions of Psalmody are read responsively:

P **Sing to the Lord a new song; sing to the Lord, all the earth.**

C Sing for joy to the Lord; let us shout aloud to the Rock of our salvation.

268

℗ I will open my mouth in parables, I will utter things hidden from of old—things that we have heard and known, things our fathers have told us.

℃ We will not hide them from [our] children; we will tell the next generation the praiseworthy deeds of the Lord, his power, and the wonders he has done.

℗ He decreed statutes for Jacob and established the law in Israel, which he commanded our forefathers to teach their children,

℃ so the next generation would know them, even the children yet to be born, and they in turn would tell their children. Then they would put their trust in God and would not forget his deeds but would keep his commands.

℗ Praise the Lord, O my soul; all my inmost being, praise his holy name.

℃ Praise the Lord, O my soul, and forget not all his benefits.

℗ God is our refuge and strength, an ever present help in trouble. The Lord Almighty is with us; the God of Jacob is our fortress. Delight yourself in the Lord and he will give you the desires of your heart. (Ps. 96:1; 95:1; 78:2-7; 103:1-2; 46:1, 11; 37:4)

℃ Glory be to the Father and to the Son and to the Holy Spirit; as it was in the beginning, is now, and will be forever. Amen

4. One of the following Prayers is said.

℗ Let us pray.

℗ O Lord God, merciful and gracious Father, we give thanks for all the blessings you have bestowed on this congregation, its members, and the Church through the ministry of your servant ⎯⎯ name ⎯⎯ . By your Holy Spirit grant ⎯⎯ him/her ⎯⎯ grace in ⎯⎯ his/her ⎯⎯ new field of service, readiness to continue to grow in wisdom, knowledge and skill, steadfastness in ministering, patience, understanding, and great zeal. Support and strengthen ⎯⎯ him/her ⎯⎯ that by your Word your Church may be built and increased; through your Son, our Lord and Savior Jesus Christ. ⟨307⟩

OR

℗ Lord God, heavenly Father, we give thanks for all the blessings you have bestowed on this congregation through the ministry of your servant ⎯⎯ name ⎯⎯ .

By your Holy Spirit grant ___him/her___ grace that by ___his/her___ example of faithful devotion to your Word ___he/she___ may be a blessing to many. In your mercy support and strengthen ___him/her___ in ___his/her___ life, and grant ___him/her___ peace and blessedness, now and forever; through your Son, our Lord and Savior Jesus Christ. ⟨308⟩

C Amen

5. The pastor turns to the teacher who is leaving or retiring and says:

P **Dear ___brother/sister___ in Christ, the Lord will keep you from all harm—he will watch over your life; the Lord will watch over your coming and going both now and forevermore.** (Ps. 121:7-8)

C Amen

6. The teacher returns to his/her place.

7. The service concludes with the Benediction.

NOTES

Preparation for the Rite

▶ *A chair is provided near the chancel for the seating of the teacher who is leaving or retiring.*

CONSECRATION AND INSTALLATION OF A CERTIFIED LAY CHURCH WORKER

1. This rite is administered by those so authorized to consecrate and install, according to the Church's usual order, such candidates as have been certified by the Church to be ready and prepared for full-time lay church work and who have received an appointment to such service.

2. The rite is set within the Divine Service before the Prayer of the Church, or The Prayers. The Propers are those of the Sunday or festival on which the consecration and installation take place.

3. The rite may be modified to fit the circumstances of the candidate and the particular kind of full-time service.

4. It is appropriate that other full-time servants serve as assisting ministers, according to local custom and the direction of the pastor.

5. Before the service begins, the pastor gathers all who will take part in it in some convenient place for the Word of God and prayer. Then all enter the church together, the candidate going before the assisting ministers, and the pastor last of all.

Sit

6. When the time for the consecration and installation has come, the candidate presents himself/herself before the altar. The pastor, standing before the altar, says:

P   In the name of the Father and of the ✝ Son and of the Holy Spirit.

C   Amen

7. The pastor addresses the congregation:

P   Dear brothers and sisters in Christ, ____name____ has been appointed in the Church's usual order as (a) ____title of position____ in the Church. This ministry has been established to strengthen and support the office of the public ministry and its work. ____He/She____ has prepared ____himself/herself____ for this ministry by prayer and study. ____He/She____ has been examined and declared ready to undertake this sacred responsibility.

Hear the Word of God concerning this ministry.

8. One or more of the following portions of Holy Scripture are read.

A   Just as each of us has one body with many members, and these members do not all have the same function, so in Christ we who are many form one body, and each member belongs to all the others. We have different gifts, according to the grace given us. If a man's gift is prophesying, let him use it in proportion to his faith. If it is serving, let him serve; if it is teaching, let him teach; if it is encouraging, let him encourage; if it is contributing to the needs of others, let him give generously; if it is leadership, let him govern diligently; if it is showing mercy, let him do it cheerfully. (Rom. 12:4-8)

Above all, love each other deeply, because love covers over a multitude of sins. Offer hospitality to one another without grumbling. Each one should use whatever gift he has received to serve others, faithfully administering God's grace in its various forms. If anyone speaks, he should do it as one speaking the very words of God. If anyone serves, he should do it with the strength God provides, so that in all things God may be praised through Jesus Christ. To him be the glory and the power for ever and ever. Amen. (1 Peter 4:8-11)

Jesus called [the disciples] together and said, "You know that the rulers of the Gentiles lord it over them, and their high officials exercise authority over them. Not so with you. Instead, whoever wants to become great among you must be your servant, and whoever wants to be first must be your slave—just as the Son of Man did not come to be served, but to serve, and to give his life as a ransom for many." (Matt. 20:25-28)

Let the word of Christ dwell in you richly as you teach and admonish one another with all wisdom, and as you sing psalms, hymns and spiritual songs with gratitude in your hearts to God. And whatever you do, whether in word or

deed, do it all in the name of the Lord Jesus, giving thanks to God the Father through him. (Col. 3:16-17)

9. The pastor asks the candidate:

P **Do you accept Holy Scripture to be the only rule and norm of all doctrine and life in the Church?**

R I do.

P **Do you accept the Confessions of the Evangelical Lutheran Church as contained in the *Book of Concord* to be a correct exposition of Holy Scripture?**

R I do.

P **Do you solemnly promise faithfully to serve God's people in accordance with the Word of God, the Ecumenical Creeds, and the Confessions of the Church?**

R I do.

P **Will you, trusting in God's care, seek to grow in love for those you serve, strive for excellence in your skills, and adorn the Gospel of Jesus Christ with a godly life?**

R I will with the help of God.

10. The pastor addresses the congregation:

P **Brothers and sisters in Christ, you have heard the confession and solemn promise of __him/her__ appointed to serve in the Church. I ask you now in the presence of God: Will you receive __him/her__ , show __him/her__ fitting love and honor, and support __him/her__ by your gifts and fervent prayer? If so, answer: We will with the help of God.**

R We will with the help of God.

P **The almighty and most merciful God strengthen and assist you always.**

11. The pastor asks the candidate:

P **Are you ready and willing to assume the work of this ministry?**

R I am.

12. The candidate kneels. The pastor continues:

P _____name_____ , **I consecrate you as a certified lay church worker and install you as (a)** ____title of position____ **in** ____name of congregation____ **, in the name of the Father and of the** ✠ **Son and of the Holy Spirit.**

C Amen

Stand

13. The following Prayers are said.

P **Let us pray.**

Gracious and most merciful Lord, by the Holy Spirit you have given your people diverse and singular gifts and raised up faithful men and women in your Church to assist and support the office and work of the public ministry. Grant your blessing to those who are appointed to service in your Church that by their labors the office of the public ministry may be strengthened to the glory of your name and the building up of your people; through Jesus Christ, your Son, our Lord, who lives and reigns with you and the Holy Spirit, one God, now and forever. ⟨309⟩

C Amen

P **Almighty and most gracious God, we give thanks that you send your people true and faithful servants. Grant to** ____name____ **, as** __he/she__ **now begins** __his/her__ **ministry in this place, the direction, aid, and counsel of your Holy Spirit that through** __his/her__ **labors your Church may be nourished, sustained, and equipped for every good work and built up into him who is the head, Jesus Christ, our Lord.** ⟨310⟩

C Amen

| **C** Our Father who art in heaven,
    hallowed be thy name,
    thy kingdom come,
    thy will be done
        on earth as it is in heaven.
Give us this day our daily bread;
and forgive us our trespasses
    as we forgive those
        who trespass against us;
and lead us not into temptation,
    but deliver us from evil.
For thine is the kingdom
    and the power and the glory
    forever and ever. Amen | OR | **C** Our Father in heaven,
    hallowed be your name,
    your kingdom come,
    your will be done
        on earth as in heaven.
Give us today our daily bread.
Forgive us our sins
    as we forgive those
        who sin against us.
Lead us not into temptation,
    but deliver us from evil.
For the kingdom, the power,
    and the glory are yours
    now and forever. Amen |

14. The pastor dismisses and blesses the newly consecrated and installed.

P **Go then in peace and joy. The almighty and most merciful God, the Father, the ⊹Son, and the Holy Spirit, go with you, bless and strengthen you to your work in his name.**

C Amen

15. The newly consecrated and installed rises and is welcomed and greeted in the name of the Lord by the pastor and fellow workers.

Peace be with you.   **R** Peace be with you.

16. All return to their places. The service continues with the Prayer of the Church, or The Prayers.

NOTES

General

▶ *The men and women in this category serve in one of the following positions: deaconess, lay minister, parish worker, parish assistant, and director of evangelism. Included are also persons who otherwise qualify for minister of religion classification but who choose not to apply.*

Preparation for the Rite

▶ *A chair is provided near the chancel for the seating of the one to be consecrated and installed.*

INSTALLATION
OF A CERTIFIED
LAY CHURCH WORKER

1. This rite is used by those so authorized to install certified lay church workers who have received an appointment according to the Church's usual order to a new field of service.

2. The rite is set within the Divine Service before the Prayer of the Church, or The Prayers. The Propers are those of the Sunday or festival on which the installation takes place.

3. The rite may be modified to fit the circumstances of the one to be installed and the particular kind of full-time service.

4. It is appropriate that other full-time servants serve as assisting ministers, according to local custom and the direction of the pastor.

5. Before the service begins, the pastor gathers all who will take part in it in some convenient place for the Word of God and prayer. Then all enter the church together, the one to be installed going before the assisting ministers, and the pastor last of all.

Sit

6. When the time for the installation has come, the one to be installed presents himself/herself before the altar. The pastor, standing before the altar, says:

Ⓟ **In the name of the Father and of the ✠ Son and of the Holy Spirit.**

Ⓒ Amen

276

7. The pastor addresses the congregation:

P   Dear brothers and sisters in Christ, ____name____ has been properly elected and appointed to serve as (a) ____title of position____ in (at) ____place____ . This ministry has been established to strengthen and support the office of the public ministry and its work.

Hear the Word of God concerning this ministry.

8. One or more of the following portions of Holy Scripture are read.

A   Just as each of us has one body with many members, and these members do not all have the same function, so in Christ we who are many form one body, and each member belongs to all the others. We have different gifts, according to the grace given us. If a man's gift is prophesying, let him use it in proportion to his faith. If it is serving, let him serve; if it is teaching, let him teach; if it is encouraging, let him encourage; if it is contributing to the needs of others, let him give generously; if it is leadership, let him govern diligently; if it is showing mercy, let him do it cheerfully. (Rom. 12:4-8)

Above all, love each other deeply, because love covers over a multitude of sins. Offer hospitality to one another without grumbling. Each one should use whatever gift he has received to serve others, faithfully administering God's grace in its various forms. If anyone speaks, he should do it as one speaking the very words of God. If anyone serves, he should do it with the strength God provides, so that in all things God may be praised through Jesus Christ. To him be the glory and the power for ever and ever. Amen. (1 Peter 4:8-11)

Jesus called [the disciples] together and said, "You know that the rulers of the Gentiles lord it over them, and their high officials exercise authority over them. Not so with you. Instead, whoever wants to become great among you must be your servant, and whoever wants to be first must be your slave—just as the Son of Man did not come to be served, but to serve, and to give his life as a ransom for many." (Matt. 20:25-28)

Let the word of Christ dwell in you richly as you teach and admonish one another with all wisdom, and as you sing psalms, hymns and spiritual songs with gratitude in your hearts to God. And whatever you do, whether in word or deed, do it all in the name of the Lord Jesus, giving thanks to God the Father through him. (Col. 3:16-17)

9. The pastor asks the one to be installed:

P **Do you accept Holy Scripture to be the only rule and norm of all doctrine and life in the Church?**

R I do.

P **Do you accept the Confessions of the Evangelical Lutheran Church as contained in the *Book of Concord* to be a correct exposition of Holy Scripture?**

R I do.

P **Do you solemnly promise faithfully to serve God's people in accordance with the Word of God, the Ecumenical Creeds, and the Confessions of the Church?**

R I do.

P **Will you, trusting in God's care, seek to grow in love for those you serve, strive for excellence in your skills, and adorn the Gospel of Jesus Christ with a godly life?**

R I will with the help of God.

10. The pastor addresses the congregation:

P **Brothers and sisters in Christ, you have heard the confession and solemn promise of __him/her__ appointed to serve in the Church. I ask you now, in the presence of God: Will you receive __him/her__ , show __him/her__ fitting love and honor, and support __him/her__ by your gifts and fervent prayer? If so, answer: We will with the help of God.**

R We will with the help of God.

P **The almighty and most merciful God strengthen and assist you always.**

11. The pastor asks the one to be installed:

P **Are you ready and willing to assume the work of this ministry?**

R I am.

12. The one to be installed kneels. The pastor continues:

P **__name__ , I install you as (a) __title of position__ in __name of congregation__ , in the name of the Father and of the ✠ Son and of the Holy Spirit.**

C Amen

278

Stand

13. The following Prayer is said.

P̄ **Let us pray.**

Almighty and most gracious God, we give thanks that you send your people true and faithful servants. Grant to _____name_____ **, as** ____he/she____ **now begins** ___his/her___ **ministry in this place, the direction, aid, and counsel of your Holy Spirit that through** ___his/her___ **labors your Church may be nourished, sustained, and equipped for every good work and built up into him who is the head, Jesus Christ, our Lord.** ⟨310⟩

C̄ Amen

14. The pastor dismisses and blesses the newly installed.

P̄ **Go then in peace and joy. The almighty and most merciful God, the Father, the ✠ Son, and the Holy Spirit, go with you, bless and strengthen you for faithful service in his name.**

C̄ Amen

15. The newly installed rises and is welcomed and greeted in the name of the Lord by the pastor and fellow workers.

Peace be with you.   R̄ Peace be with you.

16. All return to their places. The service continues with the Prayer of the Church, or The Prayers.

NOTES

General

▶ *The men and women in this category serve in one of the following positions: deaconess, lay minister, parish worker, parish assistant, and director of evangelism. Included are also persons who otherwise qualify for minister of religion classification but who choose not to apply.*

Preparation for the Rite

▶ *A chair is provided near the chancel for the seating of the one to be installed.*

PLACING IN OFFICE
OF THE CHURCH COUNCIL

Sit

1. Before the Prayer of the Church, or The Prayers, those who have been elected or otherwise selected to hold office in the congregation present themselves before the altar. The pastor announces the names and offices in which they are to serve. He then continues:

℗ **Dear brothers and sisters in Christ, Holy Scripture tells us that the Twelve gathered all the disciples together and said, "It would not be right for us to neglect the ministry of the word of God in order to wait on tables. Brothers, choose seven men from among you who are known to be full of the Spirit and wisdom. We will turn this responsibility over to them and will give our attention to prayer and the ministry of the word." (Acts 6:2-4)**

You have been chosen to fill specific positions of responsibility in the congregation. As such, you are to work with me (us), the minister(s) of Word and Sacrament, that our life together in Christ may be orderly and pleasing in his sight.

You are to see that the services of God's house are held at the proper times, in accordance with the order of our Church, that the Word of God is purely preached and taught according to the Lutheran Confessions, that the sacraments of Christ are administered according to his institution, that provision is made for the Christian instruction of young and old, that the erring are admonished, and that discipline is maintained.

You are to see that the temporal affairs of the congregation are properly administered and that proper support is provided for the workers of this congregation. You are to assist in caring for the poor and the sick, in cultivating harmony among the members, in promoting the general welfare of the congregation, and in furthering the kingdom of Christ here and throughout the world.

While holiness of life and work is the way of all who trust in Christ, it is especially important that you, as office-bearers in his Church, show yourselves, by word and example, to be patterns of good works and Christian devotion.

In the presence of God and of this congregation I therefore ask you: Do you accept the offices entrusted to you, and do you promise faithfully to carry out your duties, trusting in the Lord and conforming yourself to his Word in accordance with the faith of the Evangelical Lutheran Church? If so, answer: I do.

℟   I do.

℗   _____names_____ , I place you as _____officers/members_____ of the church council of _____name of congregation_____ , in the name of the Father and of the ☩ Son and of the Holy Spirit.

🅲   Amen

℗   The almighty and most merciful God, our heavenly Father, enlighten and strengthen you in your office that you may be good and faithful stewards to the glory of his name and the good of his people.

🅲   Amen

Stand

2. The pastor addresses the congregation:

℗   **Let us pray.**

Lord God, heavenly Father, we give thanks that you have raised up these servants for work among your people. We humbly implore you to grant them, by your Holy Spirit, those gifts which they will need for the faithful carrying out of their tasks, most especially wisdom, strength, and willing hearts. Let your blessing rest on this congregation; strengthen the faith, quicken the love, and enkindle the zeal of its members that your name may be glorified and that here and in all places under heaven the kingdom of your Son may be advanced. We remember with thanksgiving those who have faithfully served your people, who now retire from their time of service, and we pray that in the end of days we, with all your faithful people, may hear the voice of Christ, saying: "Come, you who are blessed by my Father; take your inheritance, the kingdom prepared for you since the creation of the world"; through Jesus Christ, your Son, our Lord, who lives and reigns with you and the Holy Spirit, one God, now and forever. ⟨311⟩

C Amen

3. The pastor dismisses and blesses those who have been placed.

P Go then in the name of the Lord. Be steadfast, unmovable, always abounding in the work of the Lord, for your labor in the Lord is not in vain. The almighty and most merciful God, the Father, the ☩ Son, and the Holy Spirit, bless and preserve you.

C Amen

4. All return to their places.

5. The service continues with the Prayer of the Church, or The Prayers.

PLACING OF SUNDAY AND OTHER CHURCH SCHOOL OFFICERS AND TEACHERS

Sit

1. Before the Prayer of the Church, or The Prayers, the church school officers and teachers who are to be placed present themselves before the altar. The pastor announces the names and offices in which they are to serve. He then continues:

℗ Dear brothers and sisters in Christ, you have come to be placed as ___officers/teachers___ in the ___Sunday school/church school___ of this congregation, a work in which our Father in heaven has great joy.

You are to assist the ministry of the Word and sacraments by instructing God's children according to his holy Word. You are to prepare yourselves for this work by your individual and corporate study of the Word of God and the faith drawn from it as it has been delivered to us in the Creeds and Confessions of the Evangelical Lutheran Church.

While holiness of life and work is the way of all who trust in Christ, it is especially important that you show yourselves, by word and example, to be patterns of good works and Christian devotion.

In the presence of God and of this congregation I therefore ask you: Do you accept the offices entrusted to you, and do you promise faithfully to carry out your duties, trusting in him and conforming yourself to his Word in accordance with the faith of the Evangelical Lutheran Church? If so, answer: I do.

℞ I do.

284

Ⓟ ___names___ , **I place you as** ___officers/teachers___ **of** ___name of congregation___ **, in the name of the Father and of the ✝ Son and of the Holy Spirit.**

Ⓒ Amen

Ⓟ **The almighty and most merciful God, our heavenly Father, enlighten and strengthen you in your office that you may be good and faithful** ___officers/teachers___ **, to the glory of his name and the salvation of his people.**

Ⓒ Amen

Stand

2. The pastor addresses the congregation:

Ⓟ **Let us pray.**

Grant, O Lord, to these your people the gifts of wisdom and discretion, kindness and faithfulness so that they may effectively teach and guide; and grant to all your people a ready willingness to learn. Let the knowledge of your Word be preserved and extended among us that all may know you and, from the least to the greatest, praise you now and forever; through Jesus Christ, your Son, our Lord, who lives and reigns with you and the Holy Spirit, one God, now and forever. ⟨312⟩

Ⓒ Amen

3. The pastor dismisses and blesses those who have been placed.

Ⓟ **Go in the peace of the Lord. The almighty and most merciful God, the Father, the ✝ Son, and the Holy Spirit, bless and preserve you.**

Ⓒ Amen

4. All return to their places.

5. The service continues with the Prayer of the Church, or The Prayers.

PLACING OF SERVANTS
OF THE CONGREGATION

Sit

1. Before the Prayer of the Church, or The Prayers, those to be placed present themselves before the altar. The pastor announces the work in which they are to serve. He then continues:

℗ **Dear friend(s) in Christ, you have been chosen to serve our Lord in this congregation. Hear what the apostle Paul says:**

Each one should test his own actions. Then he can take pride in himself, without comparing himself to somebody else, for each one should carry his own load. Anyone who receives instruction in the word must share all good things with his instructor. Let us not become weary in doing good, for at the proper time we will reap a harvest if we do not give up. Therefore, as we have opportunity, let us do good to all people, especially to those who belong to the family of believers. (Gal. 6:4-5, 9-10)

In the presence of God and of this congregation I therefore ask you: Do you accept the responsibilities entrusted to you, and do you promise reverently and faithfully to carry out your duties, trusting in the Lord and conforming yourself to his Word in accordance with the faith of the Evangelical Lutheran Church? If so, answer: I do.

℟ I do.

℗ ____name(s)____ **, I place you as** ____title of position____ **in** ____name of congregation____ **, in the name of the Father and of the** ✙ **Son and of the Holy Spirit.**

ℂ Amen

286

ℙ **The almighty and most merciful God, our heavenly Father, enlighten and strengthen you that you may be (a) good and faithful servant(s), to the glory of his name and the good of his people.**

ℂ Amen

Stand

2. The pastor addresses the congregation:

ℙ **Let us pray.**

VICAR

3. The vicar kneels, and the pastor places his hands on his head and prays:

ℙ **Almighty God, our Father, through your dear Son you commanded us to pray that you send laborers into the harvest. Bless, we pray you, and send your Holy Spirit upon _____ name _____ that through his service as vicar in this congregation your Word may be proclaimed and taught in joyfulness and your Church built upon the one foundation which you yourself have laid, Jesus Christ, who lives and reigns with you and the Holy Spirit, one God, now and forever.** ⟨313⟩

ℂ Amen

TEACHER-INTERN

ℙ **Almighty God, the fountain and source of all wisdom, grant _____ name _____ your blessing. Sanctify by your truth, and enrich with the gifts of your gracious Spirit _____ his/her _____ life that the seed of the Word sown by _____ him/her _____ in many hearts may spring up unto eternal life. May those who are taught be strengthened for every duty and enabled to render to you and all people true and acceptable service; through Jesus Christ, our Lord, who lives and reigns with you and the Holy Spirit, one God, now and forever.** ⟨314⟩

ℂ Amen

EVANGELISM WORKERS

ℙ **Almighty God, our Father, through your dear Son you made us all your witnesses. You commanded us to pray that you send laborers into the harvest. Enlighten by your Holy Spirit all who speak to others the message of salvation through Jesus' blood and merit. Grant this blessing upon _____ name(s) _____ so that your Word may reach out and bear much fruit for the growth of your Church, built upon** the one foundation which you yourself have laid, Jesus Christ, who lives and reigns with you and the Holy Spirit, one God, now and forever. ⟨315⟩

C Amen

ACOLYTES, READERS, ALTAR AND COMMUNION ASSISTANTS

P **God of all grace and mercy, bless those who serve as** _____ acolytes/readers/ altar and Communion assistants _____ **that they may be faithful in serving at your altar. Grant them steadfast devotion and strong faith that through their holy service your Church may be built up in faith to the honor of your most holy name; through Jesus Christ, who lives and reigns with you and the Holy Spirit, one God, now and forever.** ⟨316⟩

C Amen

DIRECTORS OF MUSIC, ORGANISTS, MUSICIANS, AND SINGERS

P **God of all grace and mercy, bless those who seek by music to enrich your people's praise and worship. Grant that through their service your Church may be built up in faith to the honor of your most holy name; through Jesus Christ, who lives and reigns with you and the Holy Spirit, one God, now and forever.** ⟨317⟩

C Amen

ALTAR GUILD MEMBERS

P **God of all grace and mercy, bless those who serve as members of the altar guild that they may be faithful in their service. Grant them steadfast devotion and strong faith. By their loving service to your house of prayer and your altar of worship may your Church be built up to the praise and honor of your most holy name; through Jesus Christ, who lives and reigns with you and the Holy Spirit, one God, now and forever.** ⟨318⟩

C Amen

4. The pastor dismisses and blesses those who have been placed.

℗ **Go then in the name of the Lord. Be steadfast, unmovable, always abounding in the work of the Lord, for your labor in the Lord is not in vain. The almighty and most merciful God, the Father, the ✠ Son, and the Holy Spirit, bless and preserve you.**

☉ Amen

5. All return to their places.

6. The service continues with the Prayer of the Church, or The Prayers.

RECOGNITION OF OFFICERS OF CONGREGATIONAL AUXILIARIES

1. This rite is used to recognize officers of auxiliaries, youth groups, men's and women's organizations.

Sit

2. Before the Prayer of the Church, or The Prayers, those to be recognized present themselves before the altar. The pastor announces the names and offices in which they are to serve. He then continues:

℗ Dear brothers and sisters in Christ, you have been elected to fill positions of responsibility in auxiliaries of this congregation. Hear what the apostle Paul says:

There are different kinds of gifts, but the same Spirit. There are different kinds of service, but the same Lord. There are different kinds of working, but the same God works all of them in all men. Now to each one the manifestation of the Spirit is given for the common good. (1 Cor. 12:4-7)

℗ In the presence of God and of this congregation I therefore ask you: Do you accept the office(s) entrusted to you, and do you promise faithfully to carry out your duties, trusting in the Lord and conforming yourself to his Word in accordance with the faith of the Evangelical Lutheran Church? If so, answer: I do.

℟ I do.

℗ The almighty and most merciful God, our heavenly Father, enlighten and

290

strengthen you in your office that you may be good and faithful stewards to the glory of his name and the good of his people.

C Amen

Stand

3. The pastor addresses the congregation:

P **Let us pray.**

O Lord God, visit, we pray, this congregation and these new officers with your love and favor. Enlighten their minds with the light of your Gospel. Place in their hearts a love of the truth and increase in them true faith. Nourish them with your goodness, and of your great mercy keep them in your love; through Jesus Christ, your Son, our Lord, who lives and reigns with you and the Holy Spirit, one God, now and forever. ⟨319⟩

C Amen

4. The pastor dismisses and blesses those who have been recognized.

P **Go in the peace of the Lord. The almighty and most merciful God, the Father, the ✠ Son, and the Holy Spirit, bless and preserve you.**

C Amen

5. All return to their places.

6. The service continues with the Prayer of the Church, or The Prayers.

GROUND BREAKING

1. The pastor of the congregation or an official of the Synod serves as the presiding minister.

2. The Propers are those of the Sunday or festival on which the ground breaking takes place or those appointed on pages 294—96.

3. When the place of worship is near the site of the ground breaking, the congregation and ministers may go in procession to the site, singing a hymn of invocation of the Holy Spirit.

4. It is appropriate that the procession be led by a crucifix or cross. The order of procession is crucifer and torchbearers, choir, officers of the congregation or the Synod, and ministers leading the congregation.

5. The ground breaking follows the Sermon in the Divine Service, Vespers, or Evening Prayer.

6. At the site the presiding minister says:

[P] **The Lord be with you.**

[C] And with your spirit.

[P] **Let us pray.**

Almighty and gracious Lord, let your blessing rest upon this place which we now consecrate to the glory of your holy name, that here we may offer you the

292

praise of grateful hearts and faithful service; through Jesus Christ, your Son, our Lord, who lives and reigns with you and the Holy Spirit, one God, now and forever. ⟨320⟩

C Amen

7. The minister takes a spade and turns a spadeful of earth as he names each person of the Holy Trinity.

CHURCH

P **With this spade I now break ground that the building here to be constructed be set apart for the invocation and adoration of God's most holy name. In the name of the Father and of the Son and of the Holy Spirit.**

C Amen

P **May the Gospel be preached, the sacraments administered, and prayers and praises be offered here from generation to generation.**

C Amen

SCHOOL, PARISH HALL, HOSPITAL, HOME FOR THE AGED, OR OTHER FACILITY

P **With this spade I now break ground that the building here to be constructed be set apart for the invocation and adoration of God's most holy name. In the name of the Father and of the Son and of the Holy Spirit.**

C Amen

8. Assisting ministers, members of the building committee, and members of the congregation may each turn over three spadesful of earth, saying:

In the name of the Father and of the Son and of the Holy Spirit.

9. The minister continues:

P **Taught by our Lord, we are bold to pray:**

C Our Father who art in heaven,	OR	**C** Our Father in heaven,
hallowed be thy name,		hallowed be your name,
thy kingdom come,		your kingdom come,
thy will be done		your will be done
on earth as it is in heaven.		on earth as in heaven.

Give us this day our daily bread;
and forgive us our trespasses
 as we forgive those
  who trespass against us;
and lead us not into temptation,
 but deliver us from evil.
For thine is the kingdom
 and the power and the glory
 forever and ever. Amen

Give us today our daily bread.
Forgive us our sins
 as we forgive those
  who sin against us.
Lead us not into temptation,
 but deliver us from evil.
For the kingdom, the power,
 and the glory are yours
 now and forever. Amen

10. *The service is concluded in the place of worship or at the site.*

PROPERS

INTROIT

XI B♭: Ionian

How lovely is your dwelling place, *
 O Lord Almighty!

God is our refuge and strength, *
 an ever present help in trouble.
Therefore we will not fear, though the
earth give way *
 and the mountains fall into the heart
 of the sea,
though its waters roar and foam *
 and the mountains quake with their
 surging.
There is a river whose streams make glad
the city of God, *

the holy place where the Most High
dwells.
God is within her, she will not fall; *
 God will help her at break of day.
Nations are in uproar, kingdoms fall; *
 he lifts his voice, the earth melts.
The Lord Almighty is with us; *
 The God of Jacob is our fortress.
Come and see the works of the Lord, *
 the desolations he has brought on the
 earth.
He makes wars cease to the ends of the
earth; *
 he breaks the bow and shatters the
 spear, he burns the shields with fire.

294

"Be still, and know that I am God; *
   I will be exalted among the nations,
   I will be exalted in the earth."
The Lord Almighty is with us; *
   the God of Jacob is our fortress.

Glory be to the Father and to the Son *

and to the Holy Spirit;
as it was in the beginning, *
   is now, and will be forever. Amen

How lovely is your dwelling place, *
   O Lord Almighty!

(Antiphon, Ps. 84:1; Ps. 46)

COLLECT

Almighty and e - ter - nal God, **we bless your name for having led us to undertake the building of a house to your glory and honor.**

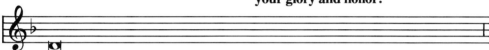

Grant that what we have begun this day to the praise of your most holy name may be successfully completed to the good of your people;

through Jesus Christ, your Son, our Lord, who lives and reigns with you and the Holy Spirit, one God, now and for - ev - er. ⟨321⟩

READINGS

Psalm 127
Exodus 3:1-6
Hebrews 11:8-10
Luke 6:47-49

GRADUAL

I lift up my eyes to the hills— *
   where does my help come from?

My help comes from the Lord, *
   the Maker of heaven and earth.
(Ps. 121:1-2)

VERSE

(Ps. 127:1)

Al - le - lu - ia, al - le - lu - ia. Unless the Lord builds the

house, its builders la - bor in vain. Unless the Lord watches over the cit - y,

the watchmen stand guard in vain. Al - le - lu - ia.

NOTES

General

▶ *Because of the solemn character of Holy Week, it is inappropriate to schedule this rite in that period.*

▶ *The rite of Ground Breaking may be used in a separate service at the site. The service might be arranged thus: Hymn, Invocation, Scripture Reading(s), Address, (rite of) Ground Breaking, Hymn, Prayer, and Blessing.*

Preparation for the Service

▶ *Stakes, white lime, or cord may be used to outline the proposed building. A new spade should be provided.*

Propers

Additional Psalms and Readings

Psalm 42
Psalm 87
Psalm 100

1 Corinthians 3:10-14
Ephesians 2:19-22

LAYING OF
A CORNERSTONE

1. The pastor of the congregation or an official of the Synod serves as the presiding minister.

2. The Propers are those of the Sunday or festival on which the cornerstone laying takes place or those appointed on pages 300—302.

3. When the place of worship is near the site of the cornerstone laying, the congregation may go in procession to the site, singing a hymn of invocation of the Holy Spirit.

4. It is appropriate that the procession be led by a crucifix or cross. The order of procession is crucifer and torchbearers, choir, officers of the congregation or the Synod, and ministers leading the congregation.

5. The cornerstone laying follows the Sermon in the Divine Service, Vespers, or Evening Prayer.

6. At the site, the stone having been set in place by the builder, the presiding minister takes a hammer or trowel and says:

℗ **Our help is in the name of the Lord,**

℃ who made heaven and earth.

℗ **Unless the Lord builds the house,**

℃ its builders labor in vain.

℗ **The stone the builders rejected**

℃ has become the head of the corner.

298

7. The presiding minister strikes the stone as he names each person of the Holy Trinity.

CHURCH

℗ **I lay this cornerstone that here the only living and true God may be worshiped, his Gospel proclaimed, and his holy sacraments administered, in the name of the Father and of the Son and of the Holy Spirit.**

℘ Amen

SCHOOL, PARISH HALL, HOSPITAL, HOME FOR THE AGED, OR OTHER FACILITY

℗ **I lay this cornerstone that here the honor of the only true God may dwell, in the name of the Father and of the Son and of the Holy Spirit.**

℘ Amen

8. The presiding minister continues:

℗ **Other foundation can no one lay than that which is laid, which is Jesus Christ.**

℘ Amen

℗ **Lord God, as you have made us living stones built into your holy temple, bless and prosper the building of this __type of building__ to the honor and glory of your most holy name; through Jesus Christ, your Son, our Lord, who lives and reigns with you and the Holy Spirit, one God, now and forever.** ⟨322⟩

℘ Amen

9. The service is concluded in the place of worship or at the site.

PROPERS

INTROIT

XI B♭: Ionian

The Lord loves the gates of Zion*
    more than all the dwellings of Jacob.

How lovely is your dwelling place,*
    O Lord Almighty!
My soul yearns, even faints for the
courts of the Lord;*
    my heart and my flesh cry out for
    the living God.
Even the sparrow has found a home,*
    and the swallow a nest for herself,
    where she may have her young—
a place near your altar,*
    O Lord Almighty, my King and my
    God.
Blessed are those who dwell in your
house;*
    they are ever praising you.
Blessed are those whose strength is in
you,*
    who have set their hearts on
    pilgrimage.
As they pass through the Valley of
Baca, they make it a place of springs;*
    the autumn rains also cover it with
    pools.
They go from strength to strength*
    till each appears before God in Zion.

Hear my prayer,
O Lord God Almighty;*
    listen to me, O God of Jacob.
Look upon our shield, O God;*
    look with favor on your anointed one.
Better is one day in your courts than a
thousand elsewhere;*
    I would rather be a doorkeeper in the
    house of my God than dwell in the
    tents of the wicked.
For the Lord God is a sun and shield;*
    the Lord bestows favor and honor;
no good thing does he withhold*
    from those whose walk is blameless.
O Lord Almighty,*
    blessed is the man who trusts in you.

Glory be to the Father and to the Son*
    and to the Holy Spirit;
as it was in the beginning,*
    is now, and will be forever. Amen

The Lord loves the gates of Zion*
    more than all the dwellings of Jacob.

(Antiphon, Ps. 87:2; Ps. 84)

COLLECT

P Almighty and e - ter - nal God, whose the heavens cannot contain but whose will it is to gather people for your service,

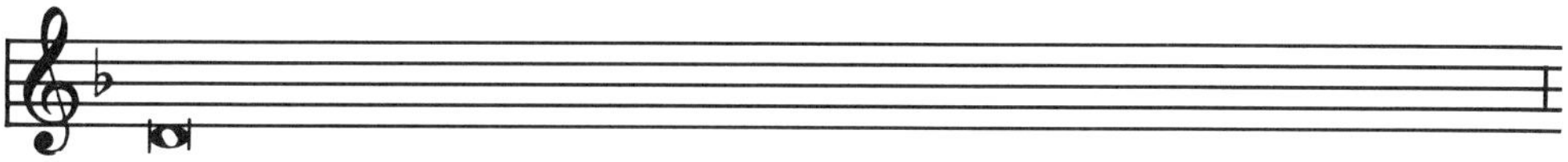

bless and prosper the work that we have here begun in your name that your will may be done, your name magnified, and your kingdom extended;

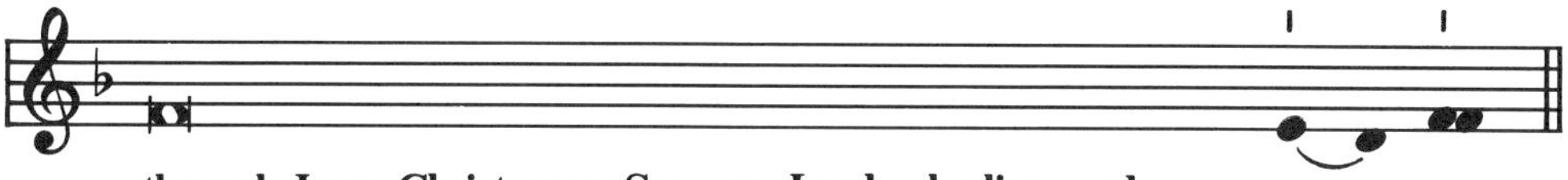

through Jesus Christ, your Son, our Lord, who lives and reigns with you and the Holy Spirit, one God, now and for - ev - er. <323>

READINGS

Psalm 118:19-29
Genesis 28:10-22
Ephesians 2:19-22
Matthew 16:13-19

GRADUAL

XI B♭: Ionian

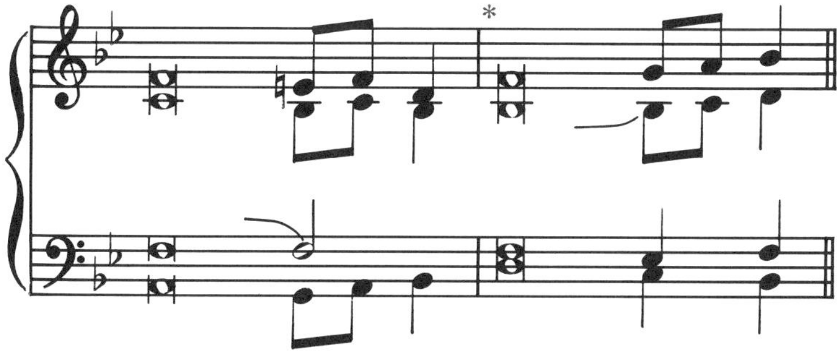

Great is the Lord, and most worthy of praise, *
in the city of our God, his holy mountain.
It is beautiful in its loftiness, *
the joy of the whole earth.
Like the utmost heights of Zaphon is Mount Zion, *
the city of the Great King. *(Ps. 48:1-2)*

VERSE

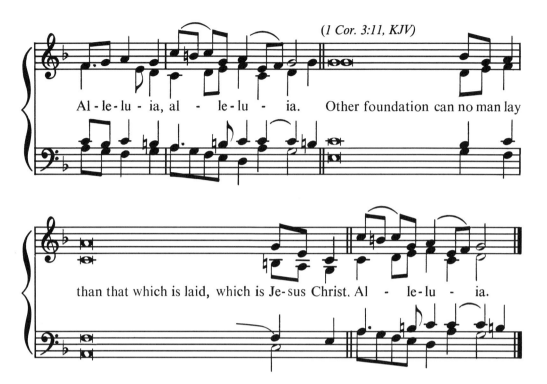

(1 Cor. 3:11, KJV)

Al - le - lu - ia, al - le - lu - ia. Other foundation can no man lay

than that which is laid, which is Je - sus Christ. Al - le - lu - ia.

NOTES

General

▶ *Because of the solemn character of Holy Week, it is inappropriate to schedule this rite in that period.*

Preparation for the Service

▶ *The contents of the cornerstone will vary with the purpose of the building. For a church, the contents may include: a Bible, the* Book of Concord *(1580), a hymnal, a catechism, the constitution and history of the congregation; a list containing the names of the pastors, teachers, and officers and members of the congregation; the names of the building committee, architect, and builder; and other memorabilia.*

Propers

Additional Psalms and Readings

Psalm 42
Psalm 87
Psalm 100

1 Corinthians 3:10-14

DEDICATION OF A CHURCH BUILDING

---

1. This rite is intended to be set within the Divine Service. The pastor of the congregation presides. Neighboring pastors may be invited to serve as assisting ministers.

2. The congregation and ministers gather at a suitable place and go in procession to the door of the new church building.

3. It is appropriate that the procession be led by a crucifix or cross. The order of procession is crucifer and torchbearers, choir, architect, builders and artists, officers of the congregation bearing the Bible and the sacramental vessels, assisting ministers, and the pastor leading the congregation.

4. A hymn of invocation of the Holy Spirit may be sung in procession.

5. The Propers are those appointed on pages 307—9.

6. At the door of the church the pastor says:

P   **In the name of the Father and of the ✠ Son and of the Holy Spirit let the doors be opened.**

C   Amen

7. The builder gives the keys to an officer of the congregation, and the door is unlocked and opened. The pastor, using the base of the processional crucifix or cross, marks the threshold with the sign of the cross as he says:

P   ✠ **Peace be to this house and to all who enter here.**

C Amen

P **Our help is in the name of the Lord,**

C who made heaven and earth.

P **I open the doors of this church for the preaching of the saving Word of God, for the celebration of his holy sacraments, and for offering God's glorious majesty the sacrifice of praise and thanksgiving, in the name of the Father and of the ✚ Son and of the Holy Spirit.**

C Amen

8. As the procession moves into the church, the Introit or the appointed Psalm is sung. The officers of the congregation, carrying the Bible and sacramental vessels, come to the entrance of the chancel and give them to the pastor, who puts them in their proper places. The pastor and the assisting ministers take their places, and the Divine Service continues with the Kyrie.

9. After the Prayer of the Church, or The Prayers, the pastor says:

P **Almighty and most merciful God, your glory fills the whole earth. You cannot be contained in houses built by men. And yet we pray that you will be pleased to be with us here and to make known to us your glory so that through your Word and holy sacraments your name may be hallowed and we may be fed and nourished; through Jesus Christ, your Son, our Lord, who lives and reigns with you and the Holy Spirit, one God, now and forever.** ⟨324⟩

C Amen

P **Our prayers rise to the throne of God our Father through the intercession of Jesus Christ, our Lord, in the power of the Holy Spirit. We set apart and dedicate this Evangelical Lutheran Church of _____name_____ [and all that is in it] to the glory, honor, and worship of God, in the name of the Father and of the ✚ Son and of the Holy Spirit.**

C Amen

10. The pastor goes to the baptismal font and says:

P **Almighty and most merciful God, your dear Son, our Savior, commanded that all should be baptized and receive through this washing the forgiveness of sins, membership in his body, the gift of the Holy Spirit, and the sure promise of eternal life. Grant that we who have been baptized into the death and resurrection of Christ** and have put on Christ may daily walk by faith in newness of life. Gather those who are here given new birth by water and the Spirit, together with all your people, to rejoice at the last in the final fulfillment of all your promises; through Jesus Christ, our Lord, who lives and reigns with you and the Holy Spirit, one God, now and forever. ⟨325⟩

℄ Amen

℗ We set apart and dedicate this baptismal font to the glory of God, in the name of the Father and of the ☩ Son and of the Holy Spirit.

℄ Amen

11. The pastor goes to the altar and says:

℗ O God, you delighted in the praises of your faithful servants Abel, Noah, and Abraham and accepted the sacrifices offered on their altars. Look upon us and graciously accept this altar and our sacrifice of praise and thanksgiving. Grant that the body and blood of Christ Jesus, once offered on the altar of the cross as the full and only atoning sacrifice for the sins of the whole world and given us here to eat and drink, will nourish and strengthen us until at last we gather about the heavenly banquet to feast with the Lamb and all his saints; through Jesus Christ, your Son, our Lord, who lives and reigns with you and the Holy Spirit, one God, now and forever. ⟨326⟩

℄ Amen

℗ We set apart and dedicate this altar to the honor and glory of God, in the name of the Father and of the ☩ Son and of the Holy Spirit.

℄ Amen

12. The pastor goes to the pulpit and says:

℗ Lord Jesus Christ, you stepped into Simon Peter's boat and, making it your pulpit, taught the crowds. Richly bless us with your favor that from this place your saving and merciful Word may be proclaimed. As you blessed Peter with the draught of fish and called him to be a fisher of men, bless your Word here read and proclaimed that many may be brought to eternal salvation; for you live and reign with the Father and the Holy Spirit, one God, now and forever. ⟨327⟩

℄ Amen

℗ We set apart and dedicate this pulpit to the glory of God and the reading and

preaching of his holy Word, in the name of the Father and of the ☩ Son and of the Holy Spirit.

C Amen

13. If sacramental vessels, bells, altar linens and paraments, vestments, altar or processional crucifixes or crosses, windows, and other items are to be dedicated, consult Dedication of Sacramental Vessels, Furnishings, and Ornaments.

14. The Divine Service continues with the Preface (23) in Divine Service I, with the Offering (19) in Divine Service II.

PROPERS

INTROIT

I will speak of your statutes
before kings, [O Lord,] *
  and will not be put to shame.

God is our refuge and strength, *
  an ever present help in trouble.
Therefore we will not fear, though
the earth give way *
  and the mountains fall into the
  heart of the sea,
though its waters roar and foam *
  and the mountains quake with
  their surging.

The Lord Almighty is with us; *
  the God of Jacob is our fortress.

Glory be to the Father and to the
Son *
  and to the Holy Spirit;
as it was in the beginning, *
  is now, and will be forever. Amen

I will speak of your statutes
before kings, [O Lord,] *
  and will not be put to shame.

(Antiphon, Ps. 119:46; Ps. 46:1-3, 7)

COLLECT

P Lord God, heavenly Fa - ther, the unfailing giver of every good gift,

we implore you to dwell continually among us with your holy Word and sacraments,
so that by grace we poor sinners may be turned to you and saved eternally;

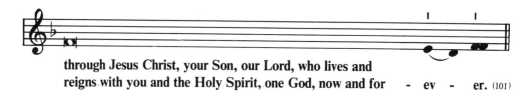

through Jesus Christ, your Son, our Lord, who lives and
reigns with you and the Holy Spirit, one God, now and for - ev - er. (101)

READINGS

Psalm 84:1-7
or 1 Kings 8:22-30
Revelation 21:1-5
Luke 19:1-10

GRADUAL

I rejoiced with those who said
to me,*
    "Let us go to the house of the
    Lord."
That is where the tribes go up,
the tribes of the Lord,*
    to praise the name of the Lord
    according to the
    statute given to Israel. *(Ps. 122:1, 4)*

VERSE

(Ps. 84:1-2a)

Al - le - lu - ia, al - le - lu - ia. How lovely is your dwelling place, O Lord Al - might - y! My soul yearns, even faints for the courts of the Lord. Al - le - lu - ia.

NOTES

General

▶ *Because of the solemn character of Holy Week, it is inappropriate to schedule this rite in that period.*

▶ *This rite may be adapted to serve in dedicating a remodeled or reclaimed church building.*

▶ *Custom has it that a congregation observe the festival day of its patron or title, for example, St. John on December 27, St. Mark on April 25, Trinity on Trinity Sunday. When the name is less obviously related to the Church's year, a day considered appropriate may be chosen for the congregation's patronal or titular festival.*

▶ *If the organ is to be dedicated at the time of the dedication of the church, the rite for the Dedication of an Organ, rubrics 3 to 5, follows immediately after rubric 7 in this rite.*

The Rite in Detail

8. ▶ If the organ is to be dedicated at the time of the dedication of the church, the procession moves in silence into the church, and the participants proceed to their places. Rubrics 4 to 6 in the rite for the Dedication of an Organ follow the placing of the Bible and the sacramental vessels. After the Introit, the appointed Psalm, or an Entrance Hymn, the Divine Service continues with the Kyrie.

9. ▶ The phrase [and all that is in it] is not said if the appointments and vessels are dedicated separately.

10. ▶ Crucifer and torchbearers, if desired, may accompany the pastor(s) and the assisting ministers to the font ⟨10⟩, the altar ⟨11⟩, and the pulpit ⟨12⟩.

DEDICATION OF SACRAMENTAL VESSELS, FURNISHINGS, AND ORNAMENTS

1. This rite may be set within the Prayer of the Church, or The Prayers, in the Divine Service. It may also be used as part of the Dedication of a Church Building, pages 304—9.

2. As convenient, the vessels, vestments, crucifix, and other appointments are placed on a credence or other table in the chancel. At the dedication such appointments may be brought to the altar and handed to the presiding minister.

SACRAMENTAL VESSELS

℗ **Most gracious God and Father, whose only-begotten Son instituted the Blessed Sacrament of the Altar, grant that all who eat and drink the body and the blood of our Lord Jesus Christ from these vessels may rejoice in the forgiveness, life, and salvation thus given them; through Jesus Christ, our Lord, who lives and reigns with you and the Holy Spirit, one God, now and forever.** ⟨328⟩

Ⓒ Amen

℗ **We set apart and dedicate this** ___paten/chalice/ciborium/cruet___ **for service at the altar of God, in the name of the Father and of the ☩ Son and of the Holy Spirit.**

Ⓒ Amen

BELLS

℗ **O God, you have told us that everything is sanctified by your Word and prayer. Accept our offering of** ___this bell/these bells___ **which we dedicate this day that** ___its/their___ **song of praise may call your people to joyful worship both now and** in generations to come; through Jesus Christ, your Son, our Lord, who lives and reigns with you and the Holy Spirit, one God, now and forever. ⟨329⟩

C Amen

3. *The bell(s) is/are briefly sounded as the minister names each person of the Holy Trinity.*

P We set apart and dedicate this bell, in the name of the Father and of the ☩ Son and of the Holy Spirit.

C Amen

4. *The bell(s) may now be sounded in praise of God.*

ALTAR LINENS AND PARAMENTS

P O God, you are clothed in majesty and splendor and your bountiful works proclaim your wondrous deeds and gifts. From your gifts of thread and skill we offer these ___linens/paraments/hangings___ for the vesting of your altar and praise of your holy name; through Jesus Christ, your Son, our Lord, who lives and reigns with you and the Holy Spirit, one God, now and forever. ⟨330⟩

C Amen

P We set apart and dedicate these ___paraments/linens/hangings___ for service at the altar of God, in the name of the Father and of the ☩ Son and of the Holy Spirit.

C Amen

VESTMENTS

P O God, you revealed your only-begotten Son clothed in majesty and glory, and your saints in light serve you clothed in white robes washed in the blood of the Lamb. Accept now these vestments which we bring before you, and grant that your ministers who serve at this altar may be clothed in righteousness to the praise and honor of your holy name; through Jesus Christ, our Lord, who lives and reigns with you and the Holy Spirit, one God, now and forever. ⟨331⟩

C Amen

P We set apart and dedicate these vestments for service at the altar of God, in the name of the Father and of the ☩ Son and of the Holy Spirit.

C Amen

ALTAR OR PROCESSIONAL CRUCIFIX OR CROSS

℗ **Lord Jesus Christ, through the cross you brought forgiveness, life, and immortality to light so that all who believe in you might have eternal life. Grant that we who behold this cross may be drawn closer to you as we praise and glorify your name; for you live and reign with the Father and the Holy Spirit, one God, now and forever.** ⟨332⟩

ᴄ Amen

℗ **We set apart and dedicate this** ____altar/processional____ ____crucifix/cross____ **for service at the altar of God, in the name of the Father and of the ☩ Son and of the Holy Spirit.**

ᴄ Amen

WINDOWS

℗ **O God, you sent your Son to be the light of the world and commanded light to shine out of darkness. Accept, we implore you,** ____this window/these windows____ **that** ____its/their____ **light may shine forth in beauty to the honor and praise of your holy name; through Jesus Christ, our Lord, who lives and reigns with you and the Holy Spirit, one God, now and forever.** ⟨333⟩

ᴄ Amen

℗ **We set apart and dedicate** ____this window/these windows____ **to the glory of the eternal Trinity, the Father, the ☩ Son, and the Holy Spirit.**

ᴄ Amen

ANY CHURCH ORNAMENT

℗ **O God, you have directed us to bring offerings for your glory. Be pleased to accept** ____name of item(s)____ **which we bring before you to be put to your service. Grant that** ____it/they____ **may reflect our love for you, benefit your Church, and bring joy to those who use** ____it/them____ **; through Jesus Christ, your Son, our Lord, who lives and reigns with you and the Holy Spirit, one God, now and forever.** ⟨334⟩

ᴄ Amen

℗ **We set apart and dedicate** ____name of item(s)____ **for service in your house, in the name of the Father and of the ☩ Son and of the Holy Spirit.**

ᴄ Amen

LONGER RITE OF DEDICATION

1. Should a longer rite be desired, it is set within the Divine Service before the Prayer of the Church, or The Prayers.

2. If the item is a gift, it may be presented before the altar by the donor or the minister with these or similar words:

_____I/We_____ present this __name of item__ to be set apart by the Word of God and prayer for service in the house of God.

P **Our help is in the name of the Lord,**

C who made heaven and earth.

P **Honor and majesty are before him;**

C strength and beauty are in his sanctuary.

P **The Lord be with you.**

C And with your spirit.

P **O God, we thank you for leading your people to bring offerings for your service. We know that such gifts of love are pleasing and acceptable in your sight. Look with favor upon us as we now present for dedication this __name of item__ for your praise and glory [and in __memory/honor__ of ___name___]; through Jesus Christ, our Lord.** ⟨335⟩

C Amen

3. The dedication for the respective item follows (see pages 311—13).

NOTES

General

▶ *Prayers for the dedication of a baptismal font, altar, and pulpit are included in the rite for Dedication of a Church Building, pages 305—6.*

▶ *When the object to be dedicated is fixed, it is appropriate that there be a procession to that place.*

DEDICATION OF AN ORGAN

1. This rite is to be used with and immediately prior to the Divine Service, Vespers, or Evening Prayer.

2. The pastor of the congregation or an official of the Synod serves as the presiding minister.

3. The ministers and the choir proceed into the nave and go to their places in silence, without instrumental music.

Stand

4. The presiding minister says:

℗ **In the name of the Father and of the ☩ Son and of the Holy Spirit.**

© Amen

℗ **Sing to the Lord, bless his name;**

© tell of his salvation from day to day.

℗ **Praise him with the sounding of the trumpet,**

© praise him with the strings and pipe.

P Let everything that has breath praise the Lord.

C Praise the Lord.

P **Let us pray.**

Almighty and everlasting God, you dwell in the heavens surrounded by angels and archangels and all the company of heaven as they offer their worship and say: Holy, holy, holy Lord, God of Sabaoth. We thank you that we may also join in their unending hymn of praise. Of your goodness you have blessed us with this organ to enliven our offerings of psalms and hymns and spiritual songs. Accept our sacrifice of praise and thanksgiving as we with heart and voice glorify your holy name; through Jesus Christ, your Son, our Lord, who lives and reigns with you and the Holy Spirit, one God, now and forever. ⟨336⟩

C Amen

5. The minister extends his hand toward the organ and says:

P **We set apart and dedicate this organ to the worship, honor, praise, and glory of God and to the edification of his holy people, in the name of the Father and of the ✠ Son and of the Holy Spirit.**

C Amen

6. The organ sounds for the first time, leading the congregation in singing the Introit, the appointed Psalm, or an Entrance Hymn in the Divine Service. If the dedication is set within Vespers or Evening Prayer, the service continues with the opening sentences.

7. The Propers are those of the Sunday or festival on which the dedication takes place or those here appointed.

PROPERS

INTROIT

VII F : Mixolydian

Make music to the Lord with the harp,*
  with the harp and the sound of
  singing.

Praise the Lord. Praise God in his
sanctuary;*
  praise him in his mighty heavens.

Praise him for his acts of power;*
  praise him for his surpassing
  greatness.

Praise him with the sounding of the
trumpet,*
  praise him with the harp and lyre,
praise him with tambourine and
dancing,*

praise him with the strings and
flute,
praise him with the clash of cymbals,*
  praise him with resounding cymbals.
Let everything that has breath praise
the Lord.*
  Oh, praise the Lord.

Glory be to the Father and to the Son*
  and to the Holy Spirit;
as it was in the beginning,*
  is now, and will be forever. Amen

Make music to the Lord with the harp,*
  with the harp and the sound of
  singing. *(Antiphon, Ps. 98:5; Ps. 150)*

COLLECT

P O God,   before whose throne trumpets sound and saints and angels sing
        the songs of Moses and the Lamb,

grant that we may make music to you and proclaim your name all the days of our
lives and finally join the saints before your throne in unending praise;

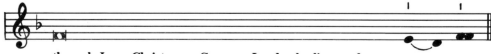

through Jesus Christ, your Son, our Lord, who lives and
reigns with you and the Holy Spirit, one God, now and   for- ev - er. ⟨337⟩

READINGS

Psalm 47
2 Chronicles 29:25-31
Ephesians 5:19-20
or Revelation 5:9-14
Matthew 21:9-11

GRADUAL

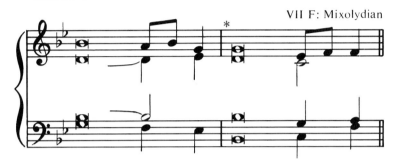

Sing to the Lord a new song, *
    for he has done marvelous things.
Shout for joy to the Lord, all the earth, *
    burst into jubilant song with music.   *(Ps. 98:1a, 4)*

VERSE

NOTES

General

▶ *Because of the solemn character of Holy Week, it is inappropriate to schedule this rite in that period.*

▶ *This rite may be used to precede a dedicatory organ concert.*

▶ *When the organ is dedicated at the time of the dedication of a church, consult the notes on the Dedication of a Church Building.*

DEDICATION OF A SCHOOL, PARISH HALL, HOSPITAL, HOME FOR THE AGED, OR OTHER FACILITY

1. The pastor of the congregation or an official of the Synod serves as the presiding minister.

2. The Propers are those of the Sunday or festival on which the dedication takes place or those appointed on pages 324—26.

3. When it is appropriate to schedule the dedicatory service in the building to be dedicated, the congregation assembles in some convenient place, and this rite, beginning at rubric 6, precedes the Introit of the Day, the appointed Psalm, or an Entrance Hymn in the Divine Service (3 or 4) or the opening sentences in Vespers or Evening Prayer (2 or 1).

4. When the dedicatory service is held in the church, after the Sermon in the Divine Service, Vespers, or Evening Prayer the congregation and ministers go in procession to the building to be dedicated.

5. It is appropriate that the procession be led by a crucifix or cross. The order of the procession is crucifer and torchbearers, choir, architect, builders and artists, officers of the congregation or the Synod, and ministers leading the congregation.

6. When the congregation has assembled at the building to be dedicated, the builder or one of the officers of the congregation hands the keys to the presiding minister, who unlocks the doors. As the doors are opened, the presiding minister says:

℗ **Let the doors be opened in the name of the Father and of the ☩ Son and of the Holy Spirit.**

☐ Amen

7. The congregation enters and assembles in the building or facility.

8. A hymn of praise may be sung.

9. The minister says:

SCHOOL, CHRISTIAN EDUCATION BUILDING, OR PARISH HALL

℗ **Let this building be a place of nourishment in the Word of God that all who come here may grow in the knowledge and wisdom of the only true and saving God.**

☉ Amen

℗ **Let us pray.**

O almighty and eternal God, you have granted us grace to build this house to your praise and glory. We give to you what is your own that it may be consecrated to your name. Come, Lord, take possession of this house that it may be a workshop of your Spirit so that, being instructed in your Word, we may be made wise to salvation; through Jesus Christ, your Son, our Lord, who lives and reigns with you and the Holy Spirit, one God, now and forever. ⟨338⟩

☉ Amen

HOSPITAL OR PLACE OF HEALING

℗ **Let this building be a place of love and healing where the honor of God dwells that all who come here may praise and magnify the only true and saving God.**

☉ Amen

℗ **Let us pray.**

O God, your Son comes among us as the great Physician to heal and restore. Look in mercy on all who come to this place. Bless all who minister here that they may be instruments of healing in your hands; through Jesus Christ, our Lord, who lives and reigns with you and the Holy Spirit, one God, now and forever. ⟨339⟩

☉ Amen

HOME FOR THE AGED

[P] **Let this building be a place of love and respect where the honor of God dwells that all who come here may praise and magnify the only true and saving God.**

[C] Amen

[P] **Let us pray.**

Lord Jesus Christ, the same yesterday, today, and forever, your coming was welcomed and praised by Simeon and Anna in their old age. Keep all who dwell here in your grace and strength that they may worthily praise your holy name all their days; for you live and reign with the Father and the Holy Spirit, one God, now and forever. ⟨340⟩

[C] Amen

OTHER FACILITY

[P] **Let this be a place where the Lord's will is done and his name is glorified.**

[C] Amen

[P] **Let us pray.**

Almighty God, heavenly Father, without whom no word or work of ours avails, grant your blessing to all who use this _____ type of facility _____ . Help them to grow day by day in the knowledge of your will and in the grace to perform it, to the honor and praise of your name and the good of all people; through Jesus Christ, your Son, our Lord, who lives and reigns with you and the Holy Spirit, one God, now and forever. ⟨341⟩

[C] Amen

10. The minister continues:

[P] **We set apart and dedicate this _____ type of building or facility _____ to the glory and honor of God, the Father, the ☩ Son, and the Holy Spirit.**

[C] Amen

11. The service is concluded in the newly dedicated building or facility, or the ministers and congregation return to the church for the remainder of the service.

323

PROPERS

INTROIT

IX b: Aeolian

Enter his gates with thanksgiving
and his courts with praise;*
   give thanks to him and praise
   his name.

Blessed is the man who does not
walk in the counsel of the wicked*
   or stand in the way of sinners
   or sit in the seat of mockers.
But his delight is in the law of
the Lord,*
   and on his law he meditates day
   and night.
He is like a tree planted by
streams of water,
which yields its fruit in season
and whose leaf does not wither.*
   Whatever he does prospers.
Not so the wicked!*
   They are like chaff that the wind
   blows away.

Therefore the wicked will not stand
in the judgment,*
   nor sinners in the assembly of the
   righteous.
For the Lord watches over the way
of the righteous,*
   but the way of the wicked
   will perish.

Glory be to the Father
and to the Son*
   and to the Holy Spirit;
as it was in the beginning,*
   is now and will be forever. Amen

Enter his gates with thanksgiving
and his courts with praise;*
   give thanks to him and praise
   his name.

(Antiphon, Ps. 100:4; Ps. 1)

COLLECT

P Lord God, heavenly Fa - ther, the unfailing giver of every good gift,

we implore you to dwell continually among us with your holy Word and sacraments,
so that by grace we poor sinners may be turned to you and saved eternally;

**through Jesus Christ, your Son, our Lord, who lives and
reigns with you and the Holy Spirit, one God, now and for - ev - er.** (101)

READINGS

1 Samuel 3:1-10
or Deuteronomy 6:4-9
2 Timothy 2:1-15
or Ephesians 2:13-22
Luke 2:40-52
or Luke 19:1-10
or John 5:1-9

GRADUAL

The Lord is good and his love
endures forever; *
   his faithfulness continues
   through all generations. *(Ps. 100:5)*

VERSE

Al - le - lu - ia, al - le - lu - ia.

How lovely is your
dwelling place, O Lord Al-

325

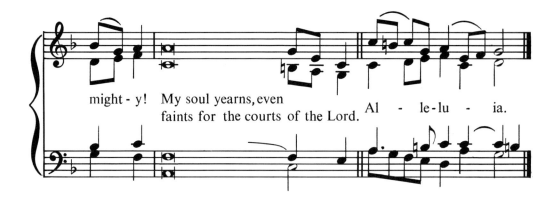

might - y! My soul yearns, even
faints for the courts of the Lord. Al - le - lu - ia.

NOTES

General

► *Because of the solemn character of Holy Week, it is inappropriate to schedule this rite in that period.*

The Rite in Detail

9. ► The section Other Facility may be used for the dedication of a gymnasium, youth center, retreat center, camp, or a similar church facility.

DEDICATION
OF A CEMETERY

1. If the cemetery is located near the place of worship, this rite may be set within the Divine Service, Vespers, or Evening Prayer, with the congregation going in procession to the site after the Sermon.

2. The rite may also be used in a separate service at the site.

3. The pastor of the congregation or an official of the Synod serves as the presiding minister.

4. The Propers are those of the Sunday or festival on which the dedication takes place or those appointed on pages 330—32.

5. It is appropriate that the procession be led by a crucifix or cross. The order of procession is crucifer and torchbearers, choir, officers of the congregation or the Synod, and ministers leading the congregation.

RITE OF DEDICATION

6. The Sermon ended, the congregation and ministers proceed to the site.

7. An appropriate hymn may be sung.

8. The presiding minister says:

ℙ   **Christ has indeed been raised from the dead, the firstfruits of those who have fallen asleep. The body that is sown is perishable, it is raised imperishable; it is sown in dishonor, it is raised in glory; it is sown in weakness, it is raised in power.** (1 Cor. 15:20, 42b-43)

P **Let us pray.**

Almighty God, Lord of the living and the dead, we give you thanks that your Son, our Lord Jesus Christ, through his death and resurrection took away the sting of death and gave us victory over the grave so that all who die in him will rise and stand before him in new life. Spread now your protecting hand over this ground that it may be a peaceful resting place for the bodies of your saints until you awaken and clothe them with incorruption and immortality. Strengthen our faith that at the appointed time we may peacefully fall asleep in you and be gathered with all your saints in light; through Jesus Christ, our Lord, who lives and reigns with you and the Holy Spirit, one God, now and forever. ⟨342⟩

C Amen

P **We set apart and dedicate this ground for the Christian burial of our dead, in the name of the Father and of the ✠ Son and of the Holy Spirit.**

C Amen

9. The ministers and congregation return to the church for the remainder of the service.

SERVICE OF DEDICATION

1. The Rite of Dedication may be used in a separate service at the site.

2. A hymn of invocation may be sung.

3. The presiding minister says:

P **In the name of the Father and of the ✠ Son and of the Holy Spirit.**

C Amen

P **Let us pray.**

Almighty God, heavenly Father, by the death of your Son Jesus Christ you destroyed the devil who held the power of death, by his rest in the tomb you sanctified the graves of all who die in him, and by his resurrection you gained the victory over death. We implore you to raise us up at the last from death and the grave and give to us, together with all your saints, eternal life in heaven, where we shall praise and glorify you with the Son and the Holy Spirit, one God, now and forever. ⟨343⟩

C Amen

4. One or more of the appointed Readings are used. The Holy Gospel is always read. After the Holy Gospel the minister says:

℗ **This is the Gospel of the Lord.**

5. The Sermon follows.

6. The minister says:

℗ **Christ has indeed been raised from the dead, the firstfruits of those who have fallen asleep. The body that is sown is perishable, it is raised imperishable; it is sown in dishonor, it is raised in glory; it is sown in weakness, it is raised in power. (1 Cor. 15:20, 42b-43)**

℗ **Let us pray.**

Almighty God, Lord of the living and the dead, we give you thanks that your Son, our Lord Jesus Christ, through his death and resurrection took away the sting of death and gave us victory over the grave so that all who die in him will rise and stand before him in new life. Spread now your protecting hand over this ground that it may be a peaceful resting place for the bodies of your saints until you awaken and clothe them with incorruption and immortality. Strengthen our faith that at the appointed time we may peacefully fall asleep in you and be gathered with all your saints in light; through Jesus Christ, our Lord, who lives and reigns with you and the Holy Spirit, one God, now and forever. ⟨342⟩

ⓒ Amen

℗ **We set apart and dedicate this ground for the Christian burial of our dead, in the name of the Father and of the ✠ Son and of the Holy Spirit.**

ⓒ Amen

℗ **Taught by our Lord, we are bold to pray:**

ⓒ Our Father who art in heaven,
hallowed be thy name,
thy kingdom come,
thy will be done
on earth as it is in heaven.
Give us this day our daily bread;
and forgive us our trespasses
as we forgive those
who trespass against us;

OR

ⓒ Our Father in heaven,
hallowed be your name,
your kingdom come,
your will be done
on earth as in heaven.
Give us today our daily bread.
Forgive us our sins
as we forgive those
who sin against us.

and lead us not into temptation,
    but deliver us from evil.
For thine is the kingdom
    and the power and the glory
    forever and ever. Amen
	Lead us not into temptation,
	    but deliver us from evil.
	For the kingdom, the power,
	    and the glory are yours
	    now and forever. Amen

7. The minister blesses the congregation.

P **The grace of our Lord Jesus Christ and the love of God and the communion of the Holy Spirit ✠ be with you all.**

C Amen

PROPERS

INTROIT

XI C: Ionian

No harm will befall you,*
    no disaster will come hear your
    tent.

Lord, you have been our dwelling
place*
    throughout all generations.
Before the mountains were born or you
brought forth the earth and the world,*
    from everlasting to everlasting you are
    God.
You turn men back to dust, saying,*
    "Return to dust, O sons of men."
For a thousand years in your sight are like

a day that has just gone by,*
    or like a watch in the night.
You sweep men away in the sleep of
death;*
    they are like the new grass of the
    morning—
though in the morning it springs up
new,*
    by evening it is dry and withered.
We are consumed by your anger*
    and terrified by your indignation.
You have set our iniquities before you,*
    our secret sins in the light of your
    presence.

All our days pass away under your wrath;*
  we finish our years with a moan.
The length of our days is seventy
years—or eighty, if we have the strength;*
  yet their span is but trouble and
  sorrow, for they quickly pass, and we
  fly away.
Who knows the power of your anger?*
  For your wrath is as great as the fear
  that is due you.
Teach us to number our days aright,*
  that we may gain a heart of wisdom.
Relent, O Lord! How long will it be?*
  Have compassion on your servants.
Satisfy us in the morning with your
unfailing love,*
  that we may sing for joy and be glad
  all our days.
Make us glad for as many days as you
have afflicted us,*
  for as many years as we have seen
  trouble.
May your deeds be shown to your
servants,*
  your splendor to their children.
May the favor of the Lord our God rest
upon us;*
  establish the work of our hands for us
  —yes, establish the work of our hands.

Glory be to the Father and to the Son*
  and to the Holy Spirit;
as it was in the beginning,*
  is now, and will be forever. Amen

No harm will befall you,*
  no disaster will come near
  your tent.

(Antiphon, Ps. 91:10; Ps. 90)

COLLECT

P Almighty God, heavenly Fa - ther, by the death of your Son Jesus Christ you destroyed the devil who held the power of death, by his rest in the tomb you sanctified the graves of all who die in him, and by his resurrection you gained the victory over death.

We implore you to raise us up at the last from death and the grave and give to us, together with all your saints, eternal life in heaven,

where we shall praise and glorify you with the Son and the Holy Spirit, one God, now and for - ev - er. ⟨343⟩

READINGS

Psalm 142
Genesis 23:1-20
1 Corinthians 15:35-58
John 11:5-27

GRADUAL

He who dwells in the shelter of the Most
High
   will rest in the shadow of the
   Almighty.
I will say of the Lord, "He is my refuge
and my fortress,
   my God, in whom I trust." *(Ps. 91:1-2)*

VERSE

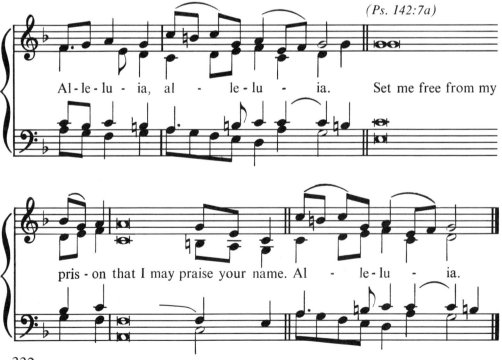

NOTES

General

▶ *Prior to the service a cross may be erected at the site. The ministers and congregation may assemble at the cross.*

▶ *This rite may be adapted to serve in dedicating a mausoleum.*

DEDICATION
OF A PARSONAGE
OR TEACHERAGE

1. If the parsonage or teacherage is located near the place of worship, this rite may be set within the Divine Service, Vespers, or Evening Prayer, with the congregation going in procession to the site after the Sermon.

2. The rite may also be used in a separate service at the site.

3. It is appropriate that the procession be led by a crucifix or cross. The order of procession is crucifer and torchbearers, choir, architect or builder, officers of the congregation, and pastor leading the congregation.

4. The Propers are those of the Sunday or festival on which the dedication takes place.

RITE OF DEDICATION

5. The Sermon ended, the pastor and congregation proceed to the parsonage or teacherage.

6. The pastor says:

℗ **In the name of the Father and of the ✝ Son and of the Holy Spirit.**

☉ Amen

℗ **Our help is in the name of the Lord,**

☉ who made heaven and earth.

℗ **Since all things are sanctified by the Word of God and prayer, let us pray.**

O Lord, almighty God, you have enabled us to build this house. We ask you now to enter and abide here that all who live in this house may hallow your name and give you glory and honor; through Jesus Christ, your Son, our Lord. ⟨344⟩

G Amen

P **We implore you, Father, to visit this dwelling place. Drive far from it the evil one. Let your holy angels encamp around it night and day. Defend it from all danger, from fire and every evil. Hold your protecting hand over them who are to dwell here. May this house be a place where your name is praised forevermore; through Jesus Christ, your Son, our Lord, who lives and reigns with you and the Holy Spirit, one God, now and forever.** ⟨345⟩

G Amen

P **We set apart and dedicate this** __parsonage/teacherage__ **, in the name of the Father and of the ☩ Son and of the Holy Spirit.**

G Amen

7. The congregation may sing, "Oh, Blest the House," Hymn 467, or another appropriate hymn.

8. The pastor and congregation return to the church for the remainder of the service.

SERVICE OF DEDICATION

1. The Rite of Dedication may be used in a separate service at the parsonage or teacherage.

2. A hymn of invocation may be sung.

3. The pastor says:

P **In the name of the Father and of the ☩ Son and of the Holy Spirit.**

G Amen

P **Our help is in the name of the Lord,**

G who made heaven and earth.

4. The Reading from Holy Scripture is announced and read. Other appropriate portions of Scripture may be read instead.

P   **Hear the Word of God from the eighteenth chapter of the Book of Acts.**

Then Paul left the synagogue and went next door to the house of Titius Justus, a worshiper of God. Crispus, the synagogue ruler, and his entire household believed in the Lord; and many of the Corinthians who heard him believed and were baptized. One night the Lord spoke to Paul in a vision: "Do not be afraid; keep on speaking, do not be silent. For I am with you and no one is going to attack and harm you, because I have many people in this city." So Paul stayed for a year and a half, teaching them the word of God. (Acts 18:7-11)

P   **This is the Word of the Lord.**

5. The Prayers and dedication follow.

P   **Since all things are sanctified by the Word of God and prayer, let us pray.**

O Lord, almighty God, you have enabled us to build this house. We ask you now to enter and abide here that all who live in this house may hallow your name and give you glory and honor; through Jesus Christ, your Son, our Lord. ⟨344⟩

C   Amen

P   **We implore you, Father, to visit this dwelling place. Drive far from it the evil one. Let your holy angels encamp around it night and day. Defend it from all danger, from fire and every evil. Hold your protecting hand over them who are to dwell here. May this house be a place where your name is praised forevermore; through Jesus Christ, your Son, our Lord, who lives and reigns with you and the Holy Spirit, one God, now and forever.** ⟨345⟩

C   Amen

P   **We set apart and dedicate this __parsonage/teacherage__ , in the name of the Father and of the ✠ Son and of the Holy Spirit.**

C   Amen

6. The congregation may sing, "Oh, Blest the House," Hymn 467, or another appropriate hymn.

[P] **Taught by our Lord, we are bold to pray:**

[C] Our Father who art in heaven,
    hallowed be thy name,
    thy kingdom come,
    thy will be done
       on earth as it is in heaven.
Give us this day our daily bread;
and forgive us our trespasses
    as we forgive those
       who trespass against us;
and lead us not into temptation,
    but deliver us from evil.
For thine is the kingdom
    and the power and the glory
    forever and ever. Amen

OR

[C] Our Father in heaven,
    hallowed be your name,
    your kingdom come,
    your will be done
       on earth as in heaven.
Give us today our daily bread.
Forgive us our sins
    as we forgive those
       who sin against us.
Lead us not into temptation,
    but deliver us from evil.
For the kingdom, the power,
    and the glory are yours
    now and forever. Amen

7. The pastor blesses the people.

[P] **The grace of our Lord Jesus Christ and the love of God and the communion of the Holy Spirit ✠ be with you all.**

[C] Amen

DEDICATION OF A DWELLING

1. It is appropriate that homes of Christians be consecrated by the Word of God and prayer. The rite of dedication may be used when a new home is occupied, when the family moves to another home, or at another appropriate time.

2. The family, relatives, and friends gather in a convenient place in the home, and the pastor says:

℗ **Peace be to this house and all who dwell here.**

℟ Amen

℗ **Our help is in the name of the Lord,**

℟ who made heaven and earth.

3. The pastor announces and reads one or more of the following portions of Holy Scripture.

℗ **[Jesus said:] "Everyone who hears these words of mine and puts them into practice is like a wise man who built his house on the rock. The rain came down, the streams rose, and the winds blew and beat against that house; yet it did not fall, because it had its foundation on the rock. But everyone who hears these words of mine and does not put them into practice is like a foolish man who built his house on sand. The rain came down, the streams rose, and the winds blew and beat against that house, and it fell with a great crash." When Jesus had finished saying these things, the crowds were amazed at his teaching, because he taught as one who had authority, and not as their teachers of the law. (Matt. 7:24-29)**

338

As Jesus and his disciples were on their way, he came to a village where a woman named Martha opened her home to him. She had a sister called Mary, who sat at the Lord's feet listening to what he said. But Martha was distracted by all the preparations that had to be made. She came to him and asked, "Lord, don't you care that my sister has left me to do the work by myself? Tell her to help me!" "Martha, Martha," the Lord answered, "you are worried and upset about many things, but only one thing is needed. Mary has chosen what is better, and it will not be taken away from her." (Luke 10:38-42)

Jesus entered Jericho and was passing through. A man was there by the name of Zacchaeus; he was a chief tax collector and was wealthy. He wanted to see who Jesus was, but being a short man he could not, because of the crowd. So he ran ahead and climbed a sycamore-fig tree to see him, since Jesus was coming that way. When Jesus reached the spot, he looked up and said to him, "Zacchaeus, come down immediately. I must stay at your house today." So he came down at once and welcomed him gladly. All the people saw this and began to mutter, "He has gone to be the guest of a 'sinner.'" But Zacchaeus stood up and said to the Lord, "Look, Lord! Here and now I give half of my possessions to the poor, and if I have cheated anybody out of anything, I will pay back four times the amount." Jesus said to him, "Today salvation has come to this house, because this man, too, is a son of Abraham. For the Son of Man came to seek and to save what was lost." (Luke 19:1-10)

℗ This is the Word of the Lord.

4. *The Prayers and dedication follow.*

℗ Let us pray.

Visit this house, O Lord. Drive far from it the evil one and let your holy angel descend to dwell here. Preserve the people of this house that they may dwell in safety all the days of their lives and at the end enter your heavenly home; through Jesus Christ, your Son, our Lord, who lives and reigns with you and the Holy Spirit, one God, now and forever. ⟨346⟩

℟ Amen

℗ We set apart and dedicate this dwelling, in the name of the Father and of the ✠ Son and of the Holy Spirit.

℟ Amen

℗ Taught by our Lord, we are bold to pray:

All Our Father who art in heaven,
 hallowed be thy name,
 thy kingdom come,
 thy will be done
  on earth as it is in heaven.
Give us this day our daily bread;
and forgive us our trespasses
 as we forgive those
  who trespass against us;
and lead us not into temptation,
 but deliver us from evil.
For thine is the kingdom
 and the power and the glory
 forever and ever. Amen

OR

All Our Father in heaven,
 hallowed be your name,
 your kingdom come,
 your will be done
  on earth as in heaven.
Give us today our daily bread.
Forgive us our sins
 as we forgive those
  who sin against us.
Lead us not into temptation,
 but deliver us from evil.
For the kingdom, the power,
 and the glory are yours
 now and forever. Amen

5. *The pastor blesses the people.*

P **The Lord watch over your coming and going both now and forevermore.**

R Amen

THANKSGIVING AT
THE RETIREMENT OF A DEBT

1. This rite may be used when a congregation has paid off a mortgage, retired a debt, or fulfilled some special financial obligation.

2. When set within the Divine Service, it may be used before the Prayer of the Church, or The Prayers.

Sit

3. A representative of the congregation may step forward and present a completed debt agreement [cancelled mortgage] to the president of the congregation. The president addresses the congregation with these or similar words:

It is with joy and gratitude that we announce the completion of a major venture of this congregation: _____ name of specific obligation fulfilled _____ .

Stand

4. The Prayers are said.

P **Let us pray.**

Lord God, heavenly Father, we give thanks that you have guided us in wisdom and given us the courage and resources for fulfilling ___ name of obligation ___ **. With gratitude we remember our years of planning and working. Continue to grant us unity of counsel, purity of intention, and the holy purpose to nurture your people by Word and Sacrament and to extend your Church for the salvation of the world through Jesus Christ, your Son, our Lord.** ⟨347⟩

C Amen

P **Direct us, O Lord, in all our actions by your gracious favor, and further us with your continual help that in all our works, begun, continued, and ended in your name, we may glorify your holy name and finally by your mercy receive eternal life; through Jesus Christ, your Son, our Lord, who lives and reigns with you and the Holy Spirit, one God, now and forever.** (8)

C Amen

5. *A hymn of thanksgiving may be sung.*

6. *All return to their places.*

7. *The service continues with the Prayer of the Church, or The Prayers.*

NOTES

The Rite in Detail

3. ▶ If desired, a fire may be built in a large brazier, and a photocopy of the completed debt agreement burned. (The original should be placed in the congregation's archives.) While the photocopy is burning, the president may say these or similar words:

We now with joy and gratitude transform the completed debt agreement [cancelled mortgage] into the incense of praise, symbolic of our completed task.

342

DISPOSITION
OF A CHURCH BUILDING

1. This rite is used when a congregation vacates a church building and moves to another building.

2. When set within the Divine Service, this rite follows the Post-Communion Collect, or Post-Communion Prayer, and concludes the service.

Sit

3. The pastor addresses the congregation with these or similar words:

℗ Dear brothers and sisters in Christ, let us be grateful for the use of this building, which was set apart and dedicated to the glory, honor, and worship of God and for the ministry of God's holy Word and Sacrament, even though it will no longer be used for this purpose.

This building holds cherished memories, and we will feel a sense of loss. However, we can be comforted in the revelation that God may choose various places or structures for the proclamation of his Word and the administration of his holy sacraments.

That we may be comforted, let us hear the Word of the Lord.

4. The following or another appropriate portion of Holy Scripture is read.

℗ Moses said to [the Lord], "If your Presence does not go with us, do not send us up from here. How will anyone know that you are pleased with me and with your people unless you go with us?" The Lord replied, "My Presence will go with you, and I will give you rest." (Ex. 33:15, 14)

343

Stand

5. *The Prayers are said. Other appropriate prayers may be used instead.*

P **Let us pray.**

Lord God, we give thanks for revealing your presence in Word and Sacrament and for the blessings bestowed on your people in this place of worship. As we leave this house, continue your many mercies that we may ever be conscious of your unchanging love, grow in faith, and finally be united with you in the glorious company of your saints; through Jesus Christ, our Lord. ⟨348⟩

C Amen

P **O God, you make the minds of your faithful to be of one will; therefore grant to your people that they may love what you command and desire what you promise, that among the manifold changes of this age our hearts may ever be fixed where true joys are to be found; through Jesus Christ, your Son, our Lord, who lives and reigns with you and the Holy Spirit, one God, now and forever.** (39)

C Amen

6. *The pastor blesses the congregation.*

P **The Lord bless you and keep you.**
The Lord make his face shine on you and be gracious to you.
The Lord look upon you with favor and ✠ give you peace.

C Amen

A **Let us go forth in peace**

C in the name of the Lord.

7. *Designated persons come forth to receive the furnishings and sacramental vessels and to prepare to join the procession.*

8. *The ministers lead those carrying the furnishings and sacramental vessels, followed by the congregation.*

9. *An appropriate hymn is sung as the procession moves out of the building.*

NOTES

General

▶ *The cornerstone or its contents may be removed prior to this service. The latter may be carried in the procession out of the building. Care should be exercised in removing the contents, for they will likely be quite fragile. They should be handed over to the congregation's archivist for preservation as soon as possible.*

The Rite in Detail

2. ▶ When this rite concludes another service, it replaces the Benedicamus and Blessing.

OPENING OF
THE CONVENTIONS OF THE
SYNOD AND ITS DISTRICTS

1. Time and circumstances will determine whether the conventions of the Synod and its Districts are opened with the Divine Service, Matins or Morning Prayer, Vespers or Evening Prayer. The president of the Synod or District presides.

2. If the first session is held immediately after one of the aforementioned services, the president of the Synod or District calls the assembly to order and asks for the report of the registration committee. Thereafter the president says:

℗ **A quorum having been established, I now declare this convention to be in session, in the name of the Father and of the ✠ Son and of the Holy Spirit.**

℟ Amen

3. The president may then give his presidential address and report.

OR

4. If the first session is held at another time, the opening devotion may begin with a hymn of invocation of the Holy Spirit followed by the president's address.

Stand

℗ **Let us pray.**

5. One or more of the following Prayers are said. Other appropriate prayers may be used instead.

P O God, you once taught the hearts of your faithful people by sending them the light of your Holy Spirit. Grant us in our day by the same Spirit to have a right understanding in all things and evermore to rejoice in his holy consolation; through Jesus Christ, your Son, our Lord. (43)

R Amen

OR

P Almighty God, heavenly Father, by your Son, Jesus Christ, you promised to be with your Church to the end of the world and that the gates of hell should not overcome it. Graciously make your strength perfect in our weakness and, according to your promise, be present with us, your unworthy servants, and grant us your merciful help; through Jesus Christ, our Lord. ⟨349⟩

R Amen

OR

P Direct us, O Lord, in all our actions by your gracious favor, and further us with your continual help that in all our works, begun, continued, and ended in your name, we may glorify your holy name and finally by your mercy receive eternal life; through Jesus Christ, your Son, our Lord, who lives and reigns with you and the Holy Spirit, one God, now and forever. (8)

R Amen

Sit

6. The president of the Synod or District calls the assembly to order and asks for the report of the registration committee. The president says:

A quorum having been established, I now declare this convention to be in session, in the name of the Father and of the ✠ Son and of the Holy Spirit.

R Amen

7. One of the earliest items of business is the president's report.

CLOSING OF
THE CONVENTIONS
OF THE SYNOD
AND ITS DISTRICTS

1. Time and circumstances will determine whether the conventions of the Synod and its Districts are closed with the Divine Service, Vespers, or Evening Prayer. It is appropriate that in the service commemoration be made of pastors and teachers who have died in the Lord since the last convention.

2. The president of the Synod or District presides.

3. A hymn of praise or thanksgiving may be sung.

4. The president or one whom he designates may give a brief address.

5. The installation of District officers and elected board members may take place at this time (see pages 351—61).

Stand

P **Let us pray.**

6. One or both of the following Prayers are said. Other appropriate prayers may be used instead.

P **Almighty and everlasting God, send down upon your pastors and upon the congregations committed to their charge the healthful Spirit of your grace and that they may truly please you, pour upon them the continual dew of your blessing; through Jesus Christ, your Son, our Lord.** (109)

R Amen

OR

P Almighty God, grant to your Church your Holy Spirit and the wisdom which comes down from heaven that your Word may not be bound but have free course and be preached to the joy and edifying of Christ's holy people, that in steadfast faith we may serve you and in the confession of your name may abide to the end; through Jesus Christ, your Son, our Lord, who lives and reigns with you and the Holy Spirit, one God, now and forever. (166)

R Amen

7. The president continues:

P Lord God our Father, you kept Abraham and Sarah in safety throughout the days of their pilgrimage, you led the children of Israel through the midst of the sea, and by a star you led the Wise Men to the infant Jesus. Protect and guide us now in this time as we set out to travel, make our ways safe and our homecomings joyful, and bring us at last to our heavenly home, where you dwell in glory with your Son and the Holy Spirit, God forever. (191)

R Amen

8. The president says:

P I now declare this convention closed, in the name of the Father and of the ✠ Son and of the Holy Spirit.

R Amen

9. The service concludes:

P The Lord watch over your coming and going both now and forevermore. The grace of our Lord Jesus Christ and the love of God and the communion of the Holy Spirit ✠ be with you all.

R Amen

NOTES

General

▶ *If opportunity presents itself, the Synod's representative may install the District president in a service during the convention; the District president may install the other elected District officers and board and commission members immediately before the closing of the convention.*

▶ *If such opportunity does not present itself, the synodical representative installs the District president and all other District officers and board members immediately before the closing.*

▶ *Officers of the Synod are installed in a special service as determined in the Synod's Bylaws.*

INSTALLATION OF THE PRESIDENT OF THE SYNOD OR OF A DISTRICT

1. This rite is used by those so authorized to install the president of the Synod or of a District of the Synod.

2. The installation takes place, when possible, in the Divine Service before the Prayer of the Church, or The Prayers. The Propers are those appointed for the Sunday or festival on which the installation takes place.

3. Before the service begins, the presiding minister gathers all who will take part in it in some convenient place for the Word of God and prayer. Then all enter the church together, the president-elect preceded by any others to be installed, then the assisting ministers, and the presiding minister last of all.

Sit

4. When the time for the installation has come, the president-elect presents himself before the altar. The presiding minister, standing before the altar, says:

℗ **In the name of the Father and of the** ☩ **Son and of the Holy Spirit.**

℅ Amen

5. The minister addresses the president-elect:

℗ **Dear brother in Christ, you have been properly elected to serve as president of [the _____name_____ District of] The Lutheran Church—Missouri Synod.**

Hear the words of Holy Scripture.

6. The assisting ministers read the following portions of Holy Scripture. Other appropriate portions of Scripture may be added.

Ⓐ The grace of God that brings salvation has appeared to all men. It teaches us to say "No" to ungodliness and worldly passions, and to live self-controlled, upright and godly lives in this present age, while we wait for the blessed hope—the glorious appearing of our great God and Savior, Jesus Christ, who gave himself for us to redeem us from all wickedness and to purify for himself a people that are his very own, eager to do what is good. (Titus 2:11-14)

What you heard from me, keep as the pattern of sound teaching, with faith and love in Christ Jesus. Guard the good deposit that was entrusted to you—guard it with the help of the Holy Spirit who lives in us. (2 Tim. 1:13-14)

As for you, continue in what you have learned and have become convinced of, because you know those from whom you learned it. (2 Tim. 3:14)

Be strong in the grace that is in Christ Jesus. (2 Tim. 2:1)

Do your best to present yourself to God as one approved, a workman who does not need to be ashamed and who correctly handles the word of truth. (2 Tim. 2:15)

Preach the Word; be prepared in season and out of season; correct, rebuke and encourage—with great patience and careful instruction. (2 Tim. 4:2)

Set an example for the believers in speech, in life, in love, in faith and in purity. (1 Tim. 4:12b)

7. The minister addresses the president-elect:

Ⓟ Dear brother, receive and keep these words in your heart that you may be strengthened and encouraged in your labors. Read and take God's Word to heart at all times, calling upon him to uphold you in the ministry which is committed to you.

I ask you now in the presence of God and of this assembly:

Do you accept this office in the Church to which you have been elected?

Ⓡ I do.

[P] Do you believe the canonical books of the Old and New Testaments to be the inspired Word of God and the only infallible rule of faith and practice?

[R] I do.

[P] Do you accept the statement and exposition of that Word of God in the Ecumenical Creeds, namely, the Apostles', Nicene, and Athanasian Creeds, and in the Confessions of the Evangelical Lutheran Church, namely, the Augsburg Confession and its Apology, the Small Catechism, the Large Catechism, the Smalcald Articles, the Treatise on the Authority and Primacy of the Pope, and the Formula of Concord, as these are contained in the *Book of Concord* ?

[R] I do.

[P] Do you solemnly promise that you will perform the duties of your office in accordance with these Confessions, or Symbols, and in accordance with the Constitution and Bylaws of the Lutheran Church—Missouri Synod [and the Bylaws of this District] to the glory of Christ, our Lord, and in service to his holy Church?

[R] I do.

[P] Finally, will you adorn the Gospel of Jesus Christ with a godly life?

[R] I will with the help of God.

8. The minister takes the right hand of the president-elect and says:

[P] _____name_____ , I install you as president of [the ____name____ District of] The Lutheran Church—Missouri Synod, in the name of the Father and of the ✠ Son and of the Holy Spirit.

9. For the installation of the president of the Synod the minister may vest the newly installed president with a pectoral cross, saying:

[P] Receive this cross as the emblem of the office to which you have been called and as a reminder of him whom you serve.

10. For the installation of the president of the Synod the minister may present the newly installed president with the books whereby he is to administer the Church.

As he presents the Bible, he says:

353

℗ Receive the Holy Scriptures of the Old and New Testaments, the Word of God, according to which all doctrine taught in the Church of Jesus Christ is to be judged.

As he presents the Book of Concord, *he says:*

℗ Receive the *Book of Concord,* the Confessions of the Evangelical Lutheran Church, our Church's witness to the world of the teachings of Holy Scripture.

As he presents the Handbook *of The Lutheran Church—Missouri Synod, he says:*

℗ Receive the *Handbook* of The Lutheran Church—Missouri Synod, containing the Constitution and Bylaws by which this Church is governed.

Stand

11. The newly installed kneels for prayer.

℗ Let us pray.

Almighty God, heavenly Father, grant to your servant _____name_____ your Holy Spirit that he may faithfully perform the duties of his office to the glory of your name and the well-being of your people; through Jesus Christ, your Son, our Lord, who lives and reigns with you and the Holy Spirit, one God, now and forever. ⟨350⟩

℃ Amen

12. The minister dismisses and blesses the newly installed president.

℗ Go then in peace and joy. The almighty and most merciful God, the Father, the ✠ Son, and the Holy Spirit, go with you, bless and strengthen you to your work in his name.

℃ Amen

13. If the service continues with the installation of the vice-presidents, other officers and members of the Board of Directors, and members of boards and commissions, the newly installed president serves as the presiding minister. Otherwise the service continues with the Prayer of the Church, or The Prayers.

NOTES

General

▶ *If opportunity presents itself, the Synod's representative may install the District president in a service during the convention; the District president may install the other elected District officers and board and commission members immediately before the closing of the convention.*

▶ *If such opportunity does not present itself, the synodical representative installs the District president and all other District officers and board members immediately before the closing.*

▶ *Officers of the Synod are installed in a special service as determined in the Synod's Bylaws.*

INSTALLATION OF VICE-PRESIDENTS, OTHER OFFICERS AND MEMBERS OF THE BOARD OF DIRECTORS, AND MEMBERS OF BOARDS AND COMMISSIONS OF THE SYNOD OR OF A DISTRICT

1. This rite is used and administered according to the Church's usual order by the president of the Synod to install the vice-presidents, other elected officers and members of the Board of Directors, and elected members of boards and commissions. As far as possible, this procedure is also followed for District installations.

2. The installation takes place, when possible, in the Divine Service before the Prayer of the Church, or The Prayers. The Propers are those appointed for the Sunday or festival on which the installation takes place.

3. When circumstances dictate that this installation occur in the same service as the installation of the president of the Synod or of a District, this rite follows it, beginning with the address to the newly elected vice-presidents ⟨6⟩ .

4. When this rite is used separately, the president, as presiding minister, before the service begins, gathers all together for the Word of God and prayer. Then all enter the church together, the newly elected officers and members of boards and commissions going before the assisting ministers, and the presiding minister last of all.

5. When the time for the installation has come, the newly elected present themselves before the altar, lined up in groups, the vice-presidents first, other officers and members of the Board of Directors second, elected members of boards and commissions third. The president, as presiding minister, standing before the altar, says:

P   **In the name of the Father and of the ☩ Son and of the Holy Spirit.**

C   Amen

6. The minister addresses the newly elected vice-presidents:

P   **Dear brothers in Christ, you have been properly elected to serve as vice-presidents of [the _____name_____ District of] The Lutheran Church—Missouri Synod.**

7. If the newly elected vice-presidents are being installed in a service separate from that of the president, the minister continues:

P   **Hear the words of Holy Scripture.**

A   **The grace of God that brings salvation has appeared to all men. It teaches us to say "No" to ungodliness and worldly passions, and to live self-controlled upright and godly lives in this present age, while we wait for the blessed hope—the glorious appearing of our great God and Savior, Jesus Christ, who gave himself for us to redeem us from all wickedness and to purify for himself a people that are his very own, eager to do what is good.** (Titus 2:11-14)

What you heard from me, keep as the pattern of sound teaching, with faith and love in Christ Jesus. Guard the good deposit that was entrusted to you—guard it with the help of the Holy Spirit who lives in us. (2 Tim. 1:13-14)

As for you, continue in what you have learned and have become convinced of, because you know those from whom you learned it. (2 Tim. 3:14)

Be strong in the grace that is in Christ Jesus. (2 Tim. 2:1)

Do your best to present yourself to God as one approved, a workman who does not need to be ashamed and who correctly handles the word of truth. (2 Tim. 2:15)

Preach the Word; be prepared in season and out of season; correct, rebuke and encourage—with great patience and careful instruction. (2 Tim. 4:2)

Set an example for the believers in speech, in life, in love, in faith and in purity. (1 Tim. 4:12b)

OR

8. If the newly elected vice-presidents are being installed in the same service as that of the president, the minister says:

P You have heard the words of Holy Scripture addressed to the president of [the ____name____ District of] The Lutheran Church—Missouri Synod. Your acceptance of the office of vice-president obligates you to serve the ____Synod/District____ not only in the duties laid down by its Constitution and Bylaws but also by promoting and preserving among its congregations the unity of the Spirit in the bond of peace, by maintaining to the best of your ability its truly Christian and Lutheran character, and by doing your utmost that it will continue uncompromisingly to adhere to God's Word and in no point swerve from the scriptural position clearly stated and defined in the Confessions of the Evangelical Lutheran Church.

9. The minister continues:

P I ask you now in the presence of God and of this assembly:

Are you willing and ready to assume the office to which you have been elected?

R I am.

P Will you endeavor faithfully to perform all the duties of your office as stipulated in the Constitution and Bylaws of [the ____name____ District of] The Lutheran Church—Missouri Synod [and of this District] and in accordance with the doctrines of Holy Scripture as set forth in the Confessions of the Evangelical Lutheran Church, and will you adorn the Gospel of Jesus Christ with a godly life?

R I will with the help of God.

10. The minister takes the right hand of each in turn and says:

P ____names____ , I install you as vice-presidents of [the ____name____ District of] The Lutheran Church—Missouri Synod, in the name of the Father and of the ✠ Son and of the Holy Spirit.

11. The newly installed vice-presidents step to the rear of the group. The other

358

elected officers (and counselors, when appropriate) and members of the Board of Directors step forward. The minister says:

P You have been properly elected to the offices of secretary and of treasurer and for positions on the Board of Directors of [the ____name____ District of] The Lutheran Church—Missouri Synod.

Hear the words of Holy Scripture.

A There are different kinds of gifts, but the same Spirit. There are different kinds of service, but the same Lord. There are different kinds of working, but the same God works all of them in all men. Now to each one the manifestation of the Spirit is given for the common good. To one there is given through the Spirit the message of wisdom, to another the message of knowledge by means of the same Spirit, to another faith by the same Spirit. All these are the work of one and the same Spirit, and he gives them to each man, just as he determines. (1 Cor. 12:4-9a, 11)

P I ask you now in the presence of God and of this assembly: Are you ready to assume and faithfully to carry out the duties of the offices to which you have been elected?

R Yes, with the help of God.

12. The minister takes the right hand of each in turn and says:

P ____name____ , I install you as secretary, you, ____name____ , as treasurer, and you, ____names____ , as members of the Board of Directors of [the ____name____ District of] The Lutheran Church—Missouri Synod, in the name of the Father and of the ☩ Son and of the Holy Spirit.

13. The newly installed officers and board members step to the rear of the group. The newly elected members of boards and commissions step forward. The minister says:

P You have heard the words of Holy Scripture directed to the officers of [the ____name____ District of] The Lutheran Church—Missouri Synod. They also apply to you who have been elected to serve on ____titles of boards/commissions____ .

I ask you now in the presence of God and of this assembly: Are you ready to assume

359

and faithfully to carry out the duties of the board or commission to which you have been elected?

℞ Yes, with the help of God.

℗ **Upon your solemn promises, I install you as members of the board or commission to which you have been elected, in the name of the Father and of the ☩ Son and of the Holy Spirit.**

Stand

℗ **Let us pray.**

Almighty and gracious God, our heavenly Father, we give thanks that you send faithful laborers into your vineyard. Grant that through the labors of these your servants your Church may be nourished, enriched, guided, and sustained in the Word of God and built up into him who is the head of the Church, Jesus Christ, our Lord, who lives and reigns with you and the Holy Spirit, one God, now and forever. ⟨351⟩

ⓒ Amen

14. The minister dismisses and blesses the newly installed.

℗ **Go then in peace and joy. The almighty and most merciful God, the Father, the ☩ Son, and the Holy Spirit, go with you, bless and strengthen you to your work in his name.**

ⓒ Amen

15. The newly installed return to their places. The service continues with the Prayer of the Church, or The Prayers.

NOTES

General

▶ *Consult the notes on Installation of the President of the Synod or of a District, page 355.*

INSTALLATION
OF AN EXECUTIVE
OF THE SYNOD
OR OF A DISTRICT

1. This rite is used by those so authorized to install an executive of the Synod or District who according to the Church's usual order has been called or appointed to such service.

2. The rite may follow the Offertory in Divine Service I, the Creed in Divine Service II, the Canticle in Matins or Morning Prayer, Vespers or Evening Prayer, or immediately precede Responsive Prayer 1 or 2.

3. Ordinarily the president of the Synod or District presides, or the chairman of the respective board or commission may be authorized by the president of the District to serve in that capacity.

Sit

4. When the time for the installation has come, the one to be installed presents himself/herself before the altar. The presiding minister, standing before the altar, says:

P **In the name of the Father and of the ✠ Son and of the Holy Spirit.**

C Amen

5. The minister addresses the congregation:

P **Dear brothers and sisters in Christ, _____name_____ has been properly elected and ____called/appointed____ by ___name of board/commission___ to serve as ____title of position____ .**

6. The minister may describe the duties of the position. He continues:

P **Hear the Word of God concerning this ministry.**

362

7. One or both of the following portions of Holy Scripture are read.

Ⓐ   **Just as each of us has one body with many members, and these members do not all have the same function, so in Christ we who are many form one body, and each member belongs to all the others. We have different gifts, according to the grace given us. If a man's gift is prophesying, let him use it in proportion to his faith. If it is serving, let him serve; if it is teaching, let him teach; if it is encouraging, let him encourage; if it is contributing to the needs of others, let him give generously; if it is leadership, let him govern diligently; if it is showing mercy, let him do it cheerfully.** (Rom. 12:4-8)

Above all, love each other deeply, because love covers over a multitude of sins. Offer hospitality to one another without grumbling. Each one should use whatever gift he has received to serve others, faithfully administering God's grace in its various forms. If anyone speaks, he should do it as one speaking the very words of God. If anyone serves, he should do it with the strength God provides, so that in all things God may be praised through Jesus Christ. To him be the glory and the power for ever and ever. Amen. (1 Peter 4:8-11)

8. The one to be installed kneels, and the minister asks:

Ⓟ   **_____ name _____ , do you solemnly promise to carry out the responsibilities of your office in conformity with Holy Scripture as the infallible Word of God and in keeping with the Confessions, or Symbols, of the Evangelical Lutheran Church as a true exposition of the Scriptures?**

Ⓡ   I do.

Ⓟ   **Do you solemnly promise to perform the duties of your office to the best of your ability and in accordance with the policies of the _____ Synod/District _____ and the directives of the _____ board/commission _____ ?**

Ⓡ   I do.

9. The members of the respective board/commission rise. The minister addresses them:

Ⓟ   **Members of the _____ board/commission _____ , you have heard the solemn promises of _____ him/her _____ whom you have _____ called/appointed _____ to serve the _____ Synod/District _____ . Will you support and pray for _____ name _____ in this work? If so, answer: We will.**

Ⓡ   We will.

10. The minister asks the one to be installed:

℗ **Are you ready and willing to assume your work?**

℟ I am.

11. The minister continues:

℗ _____name_____ **, I install you as** ____title of position____ **of** ___name of board/commission___ **of [the** _____name_____ **District of] The Lutheran Church—Missouri Synod, in the name of the Father and of the ☩ Son and of the Holy Spirit.**

© Amen

Stand

12. The Prayer is said.

℗ **Let us pray.**

Almighty and most gracious God, we give thanks that you send your people true and faithful servants. Grant to _____name_____ **, as** ___he/she___ **now begins** ___his/her___ **service in this position, the direction, aid, and counsel of your Holy Spirit that through** ___his/her___ **labors your Church may be nourished, sustained, and equipped for every good work and built up into him who is the head, Jesus Christ, our Lord.** ⟨310⟩

© Amen

13. The minister dismisses and blesses the newly installed.

℗ **Go then in peace and joy. Remember to keep alive the gifts God has given you, and use them in accordance with the grace that he supplies. The almighty and most merciful God, the Father, the ☩ Son, and the Holy Spirit, go with you, bless and strengthen you for faithful service in his name.**

© Amen

14. The newly installed returns to his/her place.

15. The service continues with the prayers appropriate to the Divine Service, Matins or Morning Prayer, Vespers or Evening Prayer, or with Responsive Prayer 1 or 2.

NOTES

General

▶ *If the one to be installed is also to be ordained at this time, the minister who presides will first use pertinent sections in the rite of Ordination.*

▶ *If the one to be installed is also to be commissioned at this time, the minister who presides will first use pertinent sections of the rite of Commissioning and Installation of One Called to the Teaching Ministry. Rubric 11 of that rite will then read:*

_____name_____ , **I commission you to the office of the teaching ministry, in the name of the Father and of the ✠ Son and of the Holy Spirit.**

Thereafter the minister will continue with this installation rite.

Preparation for the Rite

▶ *A chair is provided near the chancel for the seating of the one to be installed.*

COLLECTS AND PRAYERS

AT HOLY BAPTISM

O merciful Father, through Holy Baptism you called us to be your own possession; clothe us, we humbly pray, with love, joy, peace, patience, kindness, goodness, faithfulness, gentleness, and self-control according to the image of your only-begotten Son, Jesus Christ, our Savior. (248)

Almighty, everlasting God, mercifully behold your servants whom you have made your children through Holy Baptism and, according to your grace, grant that your promises may be fulfilled in us through Christ, our Lord. (249)

ANNIVERSARY OF A BAPTISM

Gracious Lord, we give thanks that in Holy Baptism we receive forgiveness of sins, deliverance from death and the devil, and eternal salvation. We ask you to bless ____name____ continually with your Word and Spirit on this anniversary of __his/her__ Baptism that __he/she__ may faithfully keep the covenant into which __he/she__ has been called, boldly confess __his/her__ Savior, and finally share with all your saints the joys of eternal life; through Jesus Christ, our Lord. ⟨352⟩

FOR THE CATECHUMENS

Lord God, heavenly Father, in Holy Baptism you began your good work in these catechumens, and you have blessed their instruction and training in your Word. We implore you to pour out your Holy Spirit on their hearts and minds so that they will truly love and revere you, confess their faith with joy and boldness, endeavor to live according to your commandments, and praise and glorify you as their faithful God and Lord, for the sake of Jesus Christ, your Son, our Lord. (205)

AT CONFIRMATION

Almighty God, grant that we, who have been redeemed from the old life of sin through our Baptism into the death and resurrection of your Son Jesus Christ, may be renewed in your Holy Spirit and live in righteousness and true holiness; through Jesus Christ, our Lord. ⟨353⟩

ANNIVERSARY OF A MARRIAGE

Your mercies are new every morning, O Lord Jesus. We give thanks for another year of life together for _____name_____ and _____name_____ . We ask you to keep them open to receive always more of your love that their love for each other may never grow weary but deepen and grow through every joy and sorrow shared; for you live and reign with the Father and the Holy Spirit, one God, now and forever. (155)

FOR THE ESTRANGED AND DIVORCED

Regard in mercy, O Lord, your servants for whom the bond of wedded love and faithfulness has been broken, and grant that, repenting their part in their condition and confessing before you, they may have the assurance of your compassion and the knowledge of your healing power; through Jesus Christ, our Lord. (149)

FOR THE SICK

O Father of mercies and God of all comfort, our only help in time of need, look with favor upon your servant(s) _____name(s)_____ . Assure _____him/her/them_____ of your mercy, comfort _____him/her/them_____ with the awareness of your goodness, preserve _____him/her/them_____ from the temptations of the evil one, and give _____him/her/them_____ patience in _____his/her/their_____ tribulation. If it please you, restore _____him/her/them_____ to health or give _____him/her/them_____ grace to accept this affliction; through Jesus Christ, our Lord. (214)

O Lord, you are the great Physician of soul and body; you chasten and you heal. We beg you to show mercy to your servant(s) _____name(s)_____ . Spare _____his/her/their_____ life (lives), we pray, and restore _____his/her/their_____ strength. Because you gave your Son to bear our infirmities and sicknesses, deal compassionately with your servant(s), and bless _____him/her/them_____ with your healing power. We commit _____him/her/them_____ to your gracious mercy and protection; through Jesus Christ, our Lord. (215)

O Lord God, by the example of your blessed Son, grant us grace to take joyfully the sufferings of the present time in full assurance of the glory that shall be revealed to us; through Jesus Christ, our Lord. ⟨354⟩

O Lord of heavenly might, you rule over the bodies and souls of men, and in your Son, our Savior Jesus Christ, you healed all manner of infirmities and cured all manner of diseases. Mercifully help your servant _____name_____ in body and soul and, if it be your will, free _____him/her_____ from _____his/her_____ sickness that, restored to health, _____he/she_____ may with a thankful heart bless your holy name; through Jesus Christ, our Lord. ⟨355⟩

FOR A SICK CHILD

O almighty God, our Father in heaven, take pity on _____name_____ , now afflicted with sickness. Mercifully spare, we pray, the life you have given and, as the only Help of the helpless, relieve the pains of this child. Direct the ministry of healing for _____his/her_____ recovery, and revive _____his/her_____ spirit that the frailty of the body may pass away. Renew _____his/her_____ strength, and grant to _____him/her_____ many years of life to serve you faithfully. Yet, O Father, whatever your will may be concerning this child, we trust that _____he/she_____ is in your keeping, and we pray that _____his/her_____ soul may be yours now and forever; through Jesus Christ, our Lord. (211)

FOR THOSE WHO WILL UNDERGO SURGERY

Lord Jesus Christ, in your ministry you healed many with frail and diseased bodies. Be present with your servant(s) _____name(s)_____ as _____he/she/they_____ undergoes (undergo) surgery. Bless _____him/her/them_____ with faith in your loving-kindness and protection. Endow the surgeon(s) and the medical team(s) with alertness and skill so that, if it be your will, this surgery may help your servant(s) to a speedy restoration of health and strength. We pray this in your name as you live and reign with the Father and the Holy Spirit, one God, forever and ever. (216)

FOR THOSE WHO HAVE UNDERGONE SURGERY

Lord Jesus Christ, we thank and praise you for hearing our prayers on behalf of your servant(s) ____name(s)____ , who has (have) successfully undergone surgery, and for giving to the surgeon(s) and the medical team(s) special skills which have been effectually administered. May it please you to restore ____him/her/them____ fully to health and strength, in your time and according to your good and gracious will; for you live and reign with the Father and the Holy Spirit, one God, forever and ever. (217)

FOR THOSE SUFFERING FROM ADDICTION

O blessed Jesus, since you minister to all who are afflicted, look with compassion on those who through addiction have lost their health and freedom. Restore to them the assurance of your unfailing mercy, remove the fears that attack them, strengthen them in the recovery of their self-possession and health, and give skill, patience, and understanding love to those who provide care for them; for your own mercy's sake. (125)

FOR THOSE WHO MINISTER TO THE SICK

Lord God, be with the doctors and nurses and all others who will be ministering to the bodily needs of your servant ____name____ , that blessed by you their tender care may serve to the healing of ____his/her____ sickness and an early return to health; through Jesus Christ, our Lord. ⟨356⟩

DURING AN EPIDEMIC

Almighty God, heavenly Father, you are justly displeased because of our sins, but as we see you in Christ, your Son, we are assured that even when you discipline and chasten you are acting in love. In that faith give us grace to trust you also in this time of distress. In mercy put an end to the epidemic afflicting us. Grant relief to those who suffer, and comfort all that mourn. Give hope to all, and cause your people ever to serve you in righteousness and holiness; through Jesus Christ, our Lord. ⟨357⟩

FOR THE MENTALLY SICK

O Lord, merciful Father, sustain and comfort your servants who have lost the natural faculties of reason and self-control. Do not allow the evil one to trouble them, but provide them with people who in wisdom and sympathy will minister to them in their need. Strengthen them and their families in the knowledge of your redeeming love so that they may evermore look to you for rescue and help. Deliver them from the darkness of the world to recognize always the glory of your healing and saving presence; through Jesus Christ, our Lord. ⟨358⟩

THANKSGIVING FOR THE RECOVERY OF A SICK CHILD

Gracious God, our Father, we thank and praise you for blessing ____name____ with recovery from sickness and pain. Continue to strengthen ____him/her____ in body, mind, and soul; grant ____him/her____ an increase and continuance of well-being; and bless ____him/her____ with all things necessary to grow and to maintain the health you give. Grant this for the sake of Jesus Christ, our Lord. (212)

THANKSGIVING FOR THE RECOVERY OF A SICK ADULT

God, the Giver of life, of health, of safety, and of strength, we bless you for having granted to your servant(s) ____name(s)____ recovery from ____his/her/their____ bodily sickness. Fill ____his/her/their____ heart(s) with daily remembrance of your great goodness that ____he/she/they____ may serve you with a holy and obedient life; through Jesus Christ, our Lord. (218)

Almighty and gracious God, we give thanks that you have restored the health of your servant _____name_____ , on whose behalf we praise your name. Grant that _____he/she_____ may continue the mission you have given _____him/her_____ in this world and also share in eternal glory at the appearing of your Son, Jesus Christ, our Lord. (126)

FOR THOSE WHO ARE DEAF

O Lord Jesus Christ, your compassion encompassed every infirmity of body and soul, and you touched and opened the ears of one who was deaf. Let your grace rest on all who suffer the loss of hearing. Grant that, although they cannot hear the spoken word, their hearts may ever know your loving voice, be joyous with your praise, and be attentive to your Spirit. May they find the harmony with you that will give them happiness in this life and joy in the life to come; for you live and reign with the Father and the Holy Spirit, one God, now and forever. ⟨359⟩

FOR THOSE WHO ARE BLIND

O God, you sent your Son to be the true Light of the world. Grant that those who cannot see the things of the world may be more fully enlightened and comforted by your presence. Reveal yourself to those who do not know you, and enliven those who know you by faith to an ever deeper understanding of your love. Grant them steadfast faith in this life and strengthen them in your service that in the life to come they may behold you as you are and awake to the full revelation of your glory; through Jesus Christ, our Lord. ⟨360⟩

FOR THOSE WHO ARE DISABLED

Lord God, heavenly Father, we thank you for the gift of life and everything in your creation that enriches life, especially the forgiveness of sins and the gift of new life in your Son Jesus Christ. Help us ever to attribute proper worth to all whom you have created and whom your Son has redeemed. Forgive our frequent lack of understanding and insensitivity toward those who are physically, mentally, or emotionally disabled. Help us, disabled as well as able, to recognize and use the gifts you have given us for our mutual growth in Christ and for the extension of your kingdom; through Jesus Christ, our Lord. ⟨361⟩

FOR THE AGED

Almighty God and gracious Father, in your mercy look on all whose increasing years bring them weakness, anxiety, distress, or loneliness. Provide them with homes where love and respect, concern and understanding are shown. Grant them willing hearts to accept help and, as their strength wanes, increase their faith and the assurance of your love through Jesus Christ, their Savior. (247)

AT RETIREMENT

Eternal God, you continually call your people to new tasks and set before them new opportunities. We give thanks for your servant _____name_____ and for _____his/her_____ years of service. By your Spirit prosper those deeds done according to your will and so continue _____his/her_____ work even as _____he/she_____ retires from it. Grant that _____name_____ may be open to the new opportunities which you now permit _____him/her_____ to enjoy; through Jesus Christ, our Lord. ⟨362⟩

FOR THE LONELY

Almighty God, merciful Father, by Word and Sacrament you have created your Church in this world to be a godly communion and family. Grant your blessing to those who dwell in loneliness that they may find a place of solace and pleasant fellowship among people faithful to you; through Jesus Christ, our Lord. (159)

FOR THOSE WHO LIVE ALONE

Almighty God, grant that those who live alone may not be lonely but find fulfillment in loving you and their neighbors as they follow in the footsteps of Jesus Christ, our Lord. ⟨363⟩

FOR THOSE IN DISTRESS

Keep in remembrance, O Lord, the tempted, the distressed, and the erring; gently guide them and by your great goodness bring them into the way of peace and truth. Let the light of your truth shine on those who do not know you that they may be turned toward you and so find peace. Graciously regard all who are in trouble, danger, temptation, and bondage of sin and those to whom death draws near. In your mercy draw them to yourself; for the sake of Jesus Christ, our Lord. (140)

Almighty and everlasting God, the consolation of the sorrowful and the strength of the weak, may the prayers of those who in any tribulation or distress cry to you graciously come before you, so that in all their necessities they may mark and receive your manifold help and comfort; through Jesus Christ, our Lord. (118)

FOR THE UNEMPLOYED

Heavenly Father, we remember before you those who suffer want and anxiety from lack of work. Lead us so to use the wealth and resources of this rich land that all persons may find suitable and fulfilling employment and receive just payment for their labor; through your Son, Jesus Christ, our Lord. (124)

FOR ONE NEAR DEATH

Eternal Father, you alone make the decisions about life and death. We ask you to show mercy to your servant ___name___ , whose departure seems near. If it be your gracious will, restore ___him/her___ and lengthen ___his/her___ earthly life; if not, O Father, keep ___him/her___ in ___his/her___ baptismal grace and prepare ___him/her___ to commit ___himself/herself___ to your eternal care and keeping. Give ___him/her___ a truly repentant heart, firm faith, and lively hope. Let not the pain or fear of death cause ___him/her___ to waver in confidence and trust. Grant ___him/her___ a peaceful departure and a joyous entrance into everlasting life with the glorious company of all your saints; through Jesus Christ, our Savior. (219)

AT BURIAL

General

Lord, you know the secrets of our hearts; shut not your ears to our prayers, but spare us, Lord most holy, O God most mighty, O holy and merciful Savior, O most worthy Judge eternal. Do not let the pains of death turn us away from you at our last hour. But keep us in everlasting fellowship with the Church Triumphant, and let us rest together in your presence from our labors; through Jesus Christ, our Lord. ⟨364⟩

O God, whose days are without end and whose mercies cannot be numbered, we implore you to make us deeply aware of the shortness and uncertainty of life. Let your Holy Spirit lead us in faith, in holiness, and in righteousness all our days that, when we have served you in our generation, we may be gathered unto our fathers; through Jesus Christ, our Lord. ⟨365⟩

Almighty and everlasting God, we give you hearty thanks for the good examples of all your servants who, having finished their course in faith, now rest from their labors. And we implore your mercy that we, together with all who have departed in the saving faith, may have our perfect consummation and bliss, in both body and soul, in your eternal and everlasting glory; through Jesus Christ, our Lord. (89)

For an Adult

O God of grace and glory, we remember before you this day our ___brother/sister___ ___name___ . We thank you for giving ___him/her___ to us, to know and to love as a companion on our earthly pilgrimage. In your boundless compassion console us who mourn. Give us ever the faith to see in death the gate of eternal life so that in quiet confidence we may continue our course on earth until by your call we are reunited with those who in saving faith have gone before us; through Jesus Christ, our Lord. ⟨366⟩

Almighty God, heavenly Father, we thank and praise you that you called ___name___ to the knowledge of your dear Son, kept ___him/her___ in the true faith, and granted ___him/her___ a blessed end. We implore you, help us by your Holy Spirit rightly to know and lament our sins and to be so strengthened in our faith in Christ that in all things we may grow up into him who is our Head, evermore praising you in newness of life and cheerfully awaiting the glorious appearance of our Savior Jesus Christ, who lives and reigns with you and the Holy Spirit, one God, now and forever. ⟨367⟩

For a Husband and Father or a Wife and Mother

Eternal God, merciful Father, look graciously upon us, who sorrow at the loss of a Christian ___brother/sister___ , a beloved ___husband and father/wife and mother___ . Teach us, O Lord, ever to remember that your thoughts are higher than our thoughts and your ways higher than our ways and that in all things you work for the good of those who love you. Help us call to mind the many mercies which from ___his/her___ youth you bestowed on our departed ___brother/sister___ by receiving ___him/her___ as your own dear child in Holy Baptism, comforting ___him/her___ with the forgiveness of sins in Christ Jesus, guiding ___his/her___ feet in the paths of righteousness, and finally calling ___him/her___ to the unending joy of heaven. Comfort us with the assurance that you will raise in power and glory the body here sown in weakness and that we shall see ___him/her___ again with you in everlasting life. Comfort with your holy Word the hearts of those sorely afflicted by this death, the ___wife/husband___ and children of our beloved ___brother/sister___ . Shed light in the darkness of their grief, and finally bring them, together with the ___father/mother___ for whom they mourn, to a joyous and blessed reunion in heaven. Teach us all to number our days that we may gain a heart of wisdom and, when our last hour comes, be with us and grant us a blessed end; through Jesus Christ, our Lord. ⟨368⟩

At a Sudden Death

O Lord God, by this sudden death of our ___brother/sister___ ___name___ you have shown that your thoughts are not our thoughts nor your ways our ways. We give thanks for the blessings of body and soul which you bestowed on the departed. We pray that you would comfort the members of ___his/her___ family, who mourn ___his/her___ death, and remind all of us ever to prepare for your final summons when we will depart and be with Christ in blessedness and glory; through Jesus Christ, our only Mediator and Redeemer. (221)

For Families of the Departed

Lord God, the Maker of heaven and earth, the Giver of life, we give thanks for all the mercies you granted to our ___brother(s)/sister(s)___ ___name(s)___ during ___his/her/their___ earthly life (lives), especially for calling ___him/her/them___ to faith in Jesus Christ. Comfort the survivors who mourn ___his/her/their___ death(s) with the hope of the glorious resurrection and a happy reunion in heaven. Lead all of us to remember that we are mortal so that we will ever prepare our hearts to fall asleep in faith and finally receive the glory promised to all who trust in your beloved Son, Jesus Christ, our Lord. (220)

For Parents of a Departed Child

Almighty and everlasting God, you give and you take away according to your wisdom and grace. We give thanks for all the mercies granted to this child, ___name___ , during ___his/her___ short life on earth and for taking ___him/her___ to yourself. Enable ___his/her___ parents to accept your holy will that they may be comforted with the assurance that through the power of Holy Baptism their beloved child was delivered from sin and has been received among the saints in glory. Keep all of us in your grace that when our last hour comes we may depart in peace; through Jesus Christ, your Son, our Lord and Savior. (213)

For Parents of a Stillborn Child

O Lord God, your ways are often hidden, unsearchable, and beyond our understanding. For reasons beyond our knowing you have turned the hopes of these parents from joy to sadness, and now you desire that in humble faith we bow before your ordering of these events. You are the Lord. You do what you know to be good. In their hour of sorrow, comfort them with your life-giving Word, for the sake of Jesus Christ, your Son, our Lord. (210)

At the Burial of a Suicide

When the circumstances are such as to make it possible for a Christian minister to officiate

Merciful Father, how mysterious are your judgments and your will beyond understanding. We are troubled but not crushed; sometimes in doubt but never in despair; dejected but not destroyed. Your grace is all we need, for your power is greatest when we are weak. In these dark hours we ask you to help us make diligent use of your holy Word and Sacrament so that our faith may be able to resist the evil foe who seeks to destroy our souls and minds and bodies. Take into your care those whose hearts are heavy with sorrow and grief, and lead them to look to you for confidence and strength as they face the future. Sustain them with your right hand, and finally receive them and us into glory, for the sake of Jesus Christ, our only Mediator and Redeemer. (224)

For Those Who Mourn

Almighty God, Father of mercies and Giver of all comfort, deal graciously, we implore you, with all those who mourn that, casting every care on you, they may know the consolation of your love; through Jesus Christ, our Lord. ⟨369⟩

AT AN ORDINATION

O God, you led your holy apostles to ordain pastors in every place. Grant that your Church, under the guidance of your Holy Spirit, may choose suitable men for the ministry of Word and Sacrament and may uphold them in their work for the extension of your kingdom; through him who is the chief Shepherd of our souls, Jesus Christ, our Lord. ⟨370⟩

ANNIVERSARY OF AN ORDINATION

Almighty and gracious God, we give thanks for feeding us with the holy food of the body and blood of your Son Jesus Christ and for uniting us through him in the fellowship of your Holy Spirit. We thank you for raising·up among us faithful servants for the ministry of your Word and Sacrament, especially for _____name_____ , and we pray that he may continue to follow in word and deed the example of your Son. Grant that we, with him, may serve you now in the Church on earth and evermore praise you in the kingdom of heaven; through Jesus Christ, our Lord. ⟨371⟩

FOR THE INCREASE OF THE MINISTRY

Almighty and gracious Lord, look mercifully upon the world which you redeemed by the blood of your dear Son. Incline the hearts of many to prepare and dedicate themselves to the pastoral and teaching ministry of your Church; through Jesus Christ, our Lord. ⟨372⟩

FOR THE MISSION OF THE CHURCH

Almighty and gracious God, you want all men to be saved and to come to the knowledge of the truth. Magnify the power of the Gospel in our hearts that it may be to us the sacred truth for the blessing of all people. Enable your Church to spread the good news of salvation. Protect, encourage, and bless all missionaries of the cross so that Christ, being lifted up, may draw all people to himself, and the kingdoms of the world may become the kingdom of our Lord. ⟨373⟩

FOR SEMINARIES AND CHURCH COLLEGES

O God, Source of all abiding knowledge, through Word and Spirit you both enlighten the minds and sanctify the lives of those whom you draw to your service. Therefore look with favor on the seminaries and colleges of the Church, blessing those who teach and those who learn that they may apply themselves with ready diligence to your will and faithfully fulfill their service according to your purpose; through Jesus Christ, our Lord. (151)

FOR EDUCATION

Almighty God, the fountain of all wisdom, enlighten by your Holy Spirit those who teach and those who learn that, rejoicing in the knowledge of your truth, they may worship you and serve you from generation to generation; through Jesus Christ, our Lord. ⟨374⟩

AT A COMMISSIONING

Gracious Father, through your holy apostle you direct each person to use the gift __he/she__ has received and to serve others with the strength you provide. Fill _____name_____ , whom you have called to be __title__ , with wisdom and patience, with love and faithfulness to your Word that with gladness __he/she__ may teach, comfort, counsel, and guide your people on the way to life everlasting; through Jesus Christ, your Son, our Lord. ⟨375⟩

AT THE CONSECRATION OF CERTIFIED LAY CHURCH WORKERS

General

Almighty God, heavenly Father, as you chose workers for varied tasks, both in the world and in your Church, so you have chosen _____name_____ for special service in the Church. Grant __him/her__ much joy and a spirit of bold trust that __his/her__ work may stir up each of us to a life of faith and fruitful service to you and our fellow Christians; through Jesus Christ, your Son, our Lord. ⟨376⟩

For a Deaconess

Almighty and most merciful God, as you chose Phoebe, Dorcas, and others to assist in the work of the apostles and to serve in works of love, so you have chosen _____name_____ . Grant her grace and strength that in her labors of love and her good example she may serve you faithfully, to the glory of your name, to the help of those in need, and to the everlasting benefit of your Church; through Jesus Christ, your Son, our Lord. ⟨377⟩

Eternal God, Father of our Lord Jesus Christ, Creator of man and woman, you anointed with the Holy Spirit the prophetesses Miriam, Deborah, Hannah, and Huldah. You chose the virgin Mary to be the mother of your only Son, and you set apart women for service in your holy temple. Bless your servant _____ name _____ , who has been chosen for the work of deaconess. Protect her, and grant that in singleness of purpose she may accomplish the work committed to her to your honor and the praise of Christ, to whom be glory with you and the Holy Spirit forever and ever. ⟨378⟩

FOR THOSE WHO HAVE PARTICULAR RESPONSIBILITY IN THE CHURCH

Lord and Shepherd, in all the many things that need to be done for your Church, grant to those entrusted with special responsibilities zeal and faithfulness to perform their tasks to the upbuilding of your Church and the glory of your saving name; for you live and reign with the Father and the Holy Spirit, one God, now and forever. (153)

FOR MEN'S ORGANIZATIONS

Almighty and gracious God, in every age you have inspired men to labor, with hearts united, in your kingdom. Continue, we implore you, to grant men the insight to recognize and seize the opportunities to use their talents unselfishly. Let them ever discover the deep joy and satisfaction that comes in serving you as they, together with us all, respond to your redeeming love in Christ Jesus by yielding their lives to you, devoting themselves to the seeking and doing of your holy will and following in the footsteps of our Lord Jesus Christ. In his name we pray. ⟨379⟩

FOR WOMEN'S ORGANIZATIONS

Lord Jesus, in your earthly ministry you were loved and served by devoted women. You were friend of Mary and Martha; you enjoyed rest and refreshment in their home. Give us grace to recognize and accept the varied and singular gifts you bestow on women that your kingdom may be extended, your Church enriched, and your gracious will be done to the glory of your holy name; as you live and reign with the Father and the Holy Spirit, one God, now and forever. ⟨380⟩

FOR YOUTH ORGANIZATIONS

Almighty God, gracious Father, whose years know no end and before whom the generations come and go, teach our youth to number their days and to apply their hearts to eternal wisdom. By your Word and Spirit increase their faith. Lead them to choose and ever to strive for holiness of living, to the end that they may faithfully serve you and finally obtain the heavenly inheritance; through Jesus Christ, our Lord. ⟨381⟩

TO OPEN A CHURCH CONVENTION

Almighty and gracious God, send your Holy Spirit to bless, with his grace and presence, the pastors, teachers, and laity here [soon to be] assembled in your name that your Church, being preserved in true faith and godly discipline, may fulfill the mind of him who loved her and gave himself for her, your Son, Jesus Christ, our Savior; who lives and reigns with you and the Holy Spirit, one God, now and forever. ⟨382⟩

TO OPEN A CONGREGATIONAL MEETING

Almighty God and Lord, as you have called us to labor in your vineyard, so grant us now your presence. Enlighten and guide us by your Word that in all matters of deliberation we may always consider the best interests of your Church. Let your Holy Spirit rule and direct our hearts that, in the spirit of Christian love, we may peaceably present and discuss matters and be kindly disposed to one another, to the end that all we say and do may please you; through Jesus Christ, your Son, our Lord. ⟨383⟩

O God, you taught the hearts of your faithful people by sending them the light of your Holy Spirit. Grant us by the same Spirit to have a right understanding in all things and evermore to rejoice in his holy consolation; through Jesus Christ, your Son, our Lord. (43)

TO OPEN A CHURCH COUNCIL MEETING

Almighty God, direct and guide us by your Holy Spirit both to plan and to do those things that will benefit your Church and glorify your name; through Jesus Christ, your Son, our Lord. ⟨384⟩

Direct us, O Lord, in all our actions by your most gracious favor, and further us with your continual help that in all our works, begun, continued, and ended in your name, we may glorify your holy name and finally by your mercy receive eternal life; through Jesus Christ, your Son, our Lord. (8)

TO OPEN A COMMITTEE MEETING

Almighty God, we give thanks that through the varied gifts of the members of this ___committee/task force/group___ you provide for the work of your Church. Cause us to recognize and to act on every opportunity for fruitful service. Send your Holy Spirit to blend our diverse gifts into a oneness that everything we think, say, and do may be for the common good of your Church and the glory of your name; through Jesus Christ, your Son, our Lord. ⟨385⟩

PRAYER OF THE CHURCH

Almighty God, we give thanks for all your goodness. We bless you for the love that sustains us from day to day. We praise you for the gift of your Son, our Savior, in whom we have redemption, the forgiveness of sins. We thank you for the Holy Spirit, the Comforter; for your holy Church, for the means of grace, for the lives of all faithful and good people, and for the hope of the life to come. Help us to treasure in our hearts all that our Lord has done for us, and enable us to show our thankfulness by lives that are wholly given to your service. Lord, in your mercy,

C hear our prayer.

Save and defend your whole Church, purchased with the precious blood of Christ. Give her pastors and ministers filled with your Spirit, and strengthen her through the Word and the holy sacraments. Make her perfect in love and in all good works, and establish her in the faith delivered to the saints. Lord, in your mercy,

C hear our prayer.

Give your wisdom and heavenly grace to all pastors and to those who hold office in your Church that, by their faithful service, faith may abound and your kingdom increase. Lord, in your mercy,

C hear our prayer.

Send the light of your truth into all the earth. Raise up faithful servants of Christ to advance the Gospel both at home and in distant lands. Lord, in your mercy,

C hear our prayer.

In your mercy strengthen the newly established churches, and support them in times of trial. Make them steadfast, abounding in the work of the Lord, and let their faith and zeal for the Gospel refresh and renew the witness of your people everywhere. Lord, in your mercy,

C hear our prayer.

Preserve our nation in justice and honor that we may lead a peaceable life of integrity. Grant health and favor to all who bear office in our land,

(USA) especially the President and Congress of the United States, the Governor of this State (Commonwealth), and all those who make, administer, and judge our laws,

(Canada) especially Her (His) Gracious Majesty, the Queen (King); the Governor General; the Prime Minister and the Parliament; the Governments of this Province; and all who have authority over us,

and help them to serve this people according to your holy will. Lord, in your mercy,

C hear our prayer.

Take from us all hatred and prejudice, give us the spirit of love, and dispose our days in your peace. Prosper the labor of those who take counsel for the nations of the world that mutual understanding and common endeavor may be increased among all peoples. Lord, in your mercy,

C hear our prayer.

Bless the schools of the Church and all colleges, universities, and centers of research and those who teach in them. Grant your wisdom in such measure that people may serve you in church and state and that our common life may be conformed to the ways of your truth and justice. Lord, in your mercy,

C hear our prayer.

Sanctify our homes with your presence and joy. Keep our children in the covenant of their Baptism, and enable their parents to bring them up in a life of faith and devotion. By the spirit of affection and service unite the members of all families that they may show your praise in our land and in all the world. Lord, in your mercy,

C hear our prayer.

Let your blessing rest upon the seedtime and harvest, the commerce and industry, the leisure and rest, the arts and culture of our people. Take under your special protection those whose work is difficult or dangerous, and be with all who put their hands to any useful task. Give them just rewards for their labor and the knowledge that their work is good in your sight. Lord, in your mercy,

C hear our prayer.

Here special supplications, intercessions, and prayers may be made.

Comfort by your Word and Holy Spirit all who are in sorrow or need, sickness or adversity. Remember those who suffer persecution for the faith. Have mercy on those to whom death draws near. Bring consolation to those in sorrow or mourning. And to all grant a measure of your love, taking them into your tender care. Lord, in your mercy,

C hear our prayer.

We remember with thanksgiving those who have loved and served you in your Church on earth, who now rest from their labors (especially those most dear to us, whom we name in our hearts before you). Keep us in fellowship with all your saints, and bring us at last to the joy of your heavenly kingdom. Lord, in your mercy,

C hear our prayer.

All these things and whatever else you see that we need, grant us, Father, for the sake of him who died and rose again and now lives and reigns with you and the Holy Spirit, one God forever. ⟨386⟩

C Amen

ACKNOWLEDGMENTS

Material from the following sources is acknowledged:

Holy Bible: *New International Version*, copyright © 1978 by the International Bible Society. Used by permission of Zondervan Bible Publishers: Psalms and Scripture readings.

International Consultation on English Texts: liturgical texts "Lamb of God," and "Lord, now you let your servant go in peace" (in Commendation of the Dying and Good Friday at Noonday).

The Contemporary Worship series, copyright © by Lutheran Church in America, The American Lutheran Church, The Evangelical Lutheran Church of Canada, and The Lutheran Church—Missouri Synod: Contemporary Worship 10: prayer 282 (in Burial of the Dead).

Lutheran Worship ("Pew Edition"), copyright © 1982 by Concordia Publishing House: Holy Baptism, Confirmation, Service of Corporate Confession and Absolution, Individual Confession and Absolution; hymn "All Glory, Laud, and Honor," setting copyright 1976 by Concordia Publishing House; hymn "Lord, You I Love with All My Heart," st. 3, text copyright © 1982 by Concordia Publishing House; prayers 1-204.

Lutheran Worship Altar Book, copyright © 1982 by Concordia Publishing House: prayers 205-249.

Lutheran Book of Worship, copyright © 1978 by Lutheran Church in America, The American Lutheran Church, The Evangelical Lutheran Church of Canada, The Lutheran Church—Missouri Synod: prayer 363, adapted.

The Occasional Services from the Service Book and Hymnal, together with Additional Orders and Offices, for the use of the Lutheran Churches cooperating in The Commission on the Liturgy and Hymnal (Minneapolis: Augsburg Publishing House, 1962). Copyright 1962 by The American Evangelical Lutheran Church, The American Lutheran Church, The Augustana Evangelical Lutheran Church, The Finnish Evangelical Lutheran Church in America, The United Lutheran Church in America: prayers 354 and 355, adapted.

Occasional Services, a companion to Lutheran Book of Worship (Minneapolis: Augsburg Publishing House, 1982). Copyright 1982 by Association of Evangelical Lutheran Churches, Lutheran Church in America, The American Lutheran Church, and The Evangelical Lutheran Church of Canada: prayers 362, 371, 376, 378, and 385, adapted.

The Book of Common Prayer (1928). Adapted: prayer 372, adapted.

The Book of Common Prayer (1979) : prayers 353 and 374.

The Book of Common Prayer (1979). Adapted: prayers 364, 365, 366, 367, 369, 370, and 382, adapted.

Collects and Prayers for Use in Church, prepared by the Common Service Book Committee (Philadelphia: The Board of Publication of the United Lutheran Church in America, 1935). Copyright 1935 by the Board of Publication of the United Lutheran Church in America: prayers 356, 357, 358, 359, 361, 373, and 381, adapted.

Additional sources consulted:

The Alternative Service Book 1980 (London: The Society for Promoting Christian Knowledge, 1980) copyright © 1980 by The Central Board of Finance of the Church of England.

The Lutheran Agenda, copyright © 1948 by Concordia Publishing House.

The Book of Occasional Services, The Church Hymnal Corp., copyright © 1979 by The Church Pension Fund.

Composers/arrangers of liturgical music are acknowledged: Paul G. Bunjes, b. 1914—psalm tones, their harmonizations, and pointing system; "Come, Holy Spirit" (Ordination); Verses (Ground Breaking, Laying of a Cornerstone, Dedication of a Church Building, Dedication of an Organ, Dedication of a School, etc., Dedication of a Cemetery); Reproaches (Good Friday I and II); Easter Proclamation (Vigil of Easter). M. Alfred Bichsel, b. 1909—pointing of psalms, introits, and graduals in collaboration with Paul G. Bunjes.

The Commission on Worship of The Lutheran Church—Missouri Synod: Paul G. Bunjes, Charles J. Evanson (secretary), Alfred Fremder, Norman E. Nagel, Roger D. Pittelko (chairman), Robert C. Sauer (advisory). **Church staff:** Fred L. Precht, executive secretary, Commission on Worship; Kay Cogswell, office secretary.

Music composition and typesetting: Chapman Associates, Burlington, Vermont

INDEXES

COMPREHENSIVE INDEX OF COLLECTS AND PRAYERS

	Prayer Number	Page Number		
		Pew Edition	Altar Book	Agenda
Acolytes	⟨316⟩	—	—	288
Addiction				
See Healing, For those suffering from addiction				
Adoption				
Of children	(158)	132	145	—
Spiritual	(19)	31	180	—
	(32)	46	195	87
	(194)	276	110	49, 66
Adoration	(48)	66	215	—
	(246)	—	154	—
	⟨336⟩	—	—	317
See also Praise; Worship				
Affliction				
See Comfort and Rest, For those in affliction or distress; Healing; Trial				
Aged	(247)	—	154	369
	⟨268⟩	—	—	135
	⟨340⟩	—	—	323
Birthdays of	(152)	131	144	—
Those who minister to	⟨293⟩	—	—	217, 233
See also Retirement, Of a pastor; Retirement, Of a teacher				
Agriculture	(143)	130	143	—
	(199)	278	112	51, 67
See also Harvest; Weather				
Altar Guild	⟨318⟩	—	—	288

Prayers having seasonal emphases (such as the coming of Christ in Advent) and emphases related to various occasions (such as a national holiday) may be found in the appropriate propers in Lutheran Worship *("Pew Edition") and* Lutheran Worship Altar Book.

When prayers begin on one page and continue to the next, only the page number on which the prayer begins is cited for each book.

	Prayer Number	Page Number		
		Pew Edition	Altar Book	Agenda
Angels	(96)	114	263	—
	(141)	129	142	—
	(184)	267	101	—
	(187)	272	106	—
	(190)	275	109	—
	(245)	—	154	—
	⟨336⟩	—	—	317
	⟨346⟩	—	—	339
Anniversary				
Of a commissioning	⟨306⟩	—	—	266
Of a congregation	(101)	118	268	308, 324
Of an ordination	⟨297⟩	—	—	239
Of Holy Baptism	⟨352⟩	—	—	366
Of marriage	(155)	131	144	366
	⟨268⟩	—	—	135
	⟨269⟩	—	—	135
	⟨270⟩	—	—	135
Armed Forces	(145)	130	143	—
For those who minister in	(146)	130	143	—
	⟨295⟩	—	—	218, 234
Ascension	(41)	55	204	—
	(161)	144	282	—

Assurance
See Faith; Guidance; Trust

Baptism
See Holy Baptism

Belief
See Faith

Bereavement
See Comfort and Rest, For those in Bereavement; Faithful Departed, the

Bible
See Scriptures; Word of God

Blessing
See Dedication of Ground; Thanksgiving

Blind
See Disabled, Blind

Burial
See Comfort and Rest, For those in bereavement; Death; Faithful Departed, the; Hope, Christian; Life Everlasting; Resurrection; Suicide, Burial of

	Prayer Number	Pew Edition	Altar Book	Agenda
Calling				
Church Workers	(156)	131	144	—
	(235)	—	152	—
	(237)	—	152	—'
Pastors	(148)	130	143	—
	(233)	—	151	—
	(234)	—	151	—
	(235)	—	152	—
	(237)	—	152	—
	⟨290⟩	—	—	215, 226
	⟨370⟩	—	—	372
Teachers	(156)	131	144	—
	(235)	—	152	—
	(236)	—	152	—
	(237)	—	152	—
	⟨305⟩	—	—	257, 263

	Prayer Number	Pew Edition	Altar Book	Agenda
Calling, Commission	(11)	21	170	—
	(72)	95	244	—
	⟨80⟩	98	247	—
	⟨375⟩	—	—	373
See also Calling; Service; Witness				
Catechumens	(171)	207	382	112
	(194)	276	110	49, 66
	(205)	—	146	366
See also Confirmation; Holy Baptism				
Celebration				
See Holy Communion; Worship				
Chaplains	⟨296⟩	—	—	236
Institutional	⟨293⟩	—	—	217, 233
Military	(146)	130	143	—
	295	—	—	218, 234
Prison	294	—	—	217, 234
Children	(129)	127	140	—
Adoption of	(158)	132	145	—
At the birth of	(127)	127	140	—
	(209)	—	146	—
At the death of	(213)	—	147	372
	⟨281⟩	—	—	180
	⟨286⟩	—	—	201
Care of	(128)	127	140	—
In sickness	(211)	—	147	367
Stillborn	(210)	—	147	372
	⟨285⟩	—	—	199
	⟨286⟩	—	—	201
Thanksgiving for recovery from sickness	(212)	—	147	368
Church				
See Community in Christ				
Church Building				
Dedication of	(101)	118	268	308, 324
	⟨324⟩	—	—	305
Disposition of	⟨348⟩	—	—	344
Laying of a cornerstone	⟨322⟩	—	—	299
	⟨323⟩	—	—	301
See also Dedication of Buildings; Dedication of Furnishings				
Church Council	⟨311⟩	—	—	282
Church Musicians	(156)	131	144	—
	⟨317⟩	—	—	288
	⟨337⟩	—	—	318
Church Worker, Professional	⟨309⟩	—	—	274
	⟨310⟩	—	—	274, 279, 364
	⟨376⟩	—	—	373
See also Calling, Church workers; Calling, Teachers; Deaconesses and Deacons; Servants of the Congregation				
Citizenship				
See Society, Citizenship				
Colleges				
See Education				
Comfort and Rest	(181)	266	100	—
	⟨275⟩	—	—	156
For those in affliction or distress	(118)	126	139	370
	(140)	129	142	370
	(196)	277	111	50, 67
	(214)	—	147	367

	Prayer Number	Page Number Pew Edition	Page Number Altar Book	Page Number Agenda
	(228)	—	150	—
	(245)	—	154	—
	(271)	—	—	152
	(272)	—	—	152
For those in bereavement	(139)	129	142	—
	(220)	—	148	371
	(221)	—	149	371
	(278)	—	—	168
	(281)	—	—	180
	(282)	—	—	191
	(357)	—	—	368
	(366)	—	—	371
	(368)	—	—	371
	(369)	—	—	372

See also Community in Christ;
  Consolation; Hope, Christian

Commissioning
See Anniversary, Of a commissioning; Call-
  ing, Teachers; Calling, Commission;
  Teachers, At commissioning

Commitment	(153)	131	144	374
	(174)	232	66	—

See also Faithfulness; Service; Witness

Communion
See Holy Communion

Communion of Saints
See Community in Christ

Community in Christ	(54)	73	222	—
	(71)	94	243	—
	(168)	175, 195	338, 370	—
	(193)	276	110	49, 66
	(200)	286	120	—
	(246)	—	154	—
Excommunication from	(262)	—	—	119
Fellowship with	(161)	144	282	—
	(180)	255	89	—
	(259)	—	—	83
	(284)	—	—	195
	(364)	—	—	370
Mercy for	(61)	81	230	—
Pardon and peace for	(282)	—	—	191
Preservation of	(45)	62	211	—
	(136)	128	141	—
	(160)	132	145	—
	(192)	276	110	49, 65
	(386)	—	—	375
Reinstatement after excommunication	(263)	—	—	119
Righteousness in	(97)	116	265	—

See also Family, the Church as; Officers; Servants of the Congregation

Confession of Sins	(203)	308	383	137

See also Repentance

Confirmation	(171)	207	382	112
	(194)	276	110	49, 66
	(205)	—	146	366
	(353)	—	—	366

Consecration
See Calling, Commission; Dedication of
  Ground; Service; Witness

Consolation	(42)	57	206	—
	(43)	58, 59, 60	207, 208, 209	208, 347, 375
	(369)	—	—	372

	Prayer Number	Page Number		
		Pew Edition	Altar Book	Agenda
See also Comfort and Rest				
Cornerstone, Laying of a	⟨322⟩	—	—	299
	⟨323⟩	—	—	301
Country				
See Society, Nation				
Courage	(145)	130	143	—
	(176)	243, 262	77, 96	—
	(185)	267	101	—
	(246)	—	154	—
Cross				
Of Christ	(91)	107	256	—
	⟨332⟩	—	—	313
Of the Christian	(27)	41	190	—
	(98)	117	266	—
	(113)	125	138	—
See also Dedication of Furnishings, Crucifix or cross; Holy Week; Passion of Christ; Trial				
Danger	(141)	129	142	—
	(173)	221, 242	55, 76	—
	(183)	267	101	—
	(190)	275	109	—
See also Deliverance; Protection, From danger				
Deaconesses and Deacons	(156)	131	144	—
	⟨377⟩	—	—	373
	⟨378⟩	—	—	374
See also Servants of the Congregation; Service				
Deaf				
See Disabled, Deaf				
Death	(220)	—	148	371
	⟨279⟩	—	—	172
	⟨282⟩	—	—	191
	⟨343⟩	—	—	328, 331
	⟨364⟩	—	—	370
	⟨365⟩	—	—	370
For those nearing	(140)	129	142	370
	(219)	—	148	370
	⟨365⟩	—	—	370
Of a child	(213)	—	147	372
	⟨281⟩	—	—	180
	⟨286⟩	—	—	201
Of a parent	⟨368⟩	—	—	371
Of a pastor	(222)	—	149	—
Of a teacher	(223)	—	149	—
Stillbirth	(210)	—	147	372
	⟨285⟩	—	—	199
	⟨286⟩	—	—	201
Sudden	(221)	—	149	371
Suicide	(224)	—	149	372
Thanksgiving for life	⟨278⟩	—	—	168
	⟨283⟩	—	—	193
	⟨367⟩	—	—	371
See also Comfort and Rest, For those in bereavement				
Dedication of Buildings				
Any facility	⟨341⟩	—	—	323
Church	(101)	118	268	308, 324
	⟨324⟩	—	—	305
Dwelling	(141)	129	142	—
	(184)	267	101	—
	⟨344⟩	—	—	335, 336

	Prayer Number	Page Number Pew Edition	Page Number Altar Book	Page Number Agenda
	⟨345⟩	—	—	335, 336
	⟨346⟩	—	—	339
Home for the aged	⟨340⟩	—	—	323
Hospital	⟨339⟩	—	—	322
Parish hall	⟨338⟩	—	—	322
Parsonage or teacherage	⟨344⟩	—	—	335, 336
School	⟨338⟩	—	—	322
Dedication of Furnishings				
Altar	⟨326⟩	—	—	306
Altar linens and paraments	⟨330⟩	—	—	312
Any church ornament	⟨334⟩	—	—	313
	⟨335⟩	—	—	314
Baptismal font	⟨325⟩	—	—	305
Bells	⟨329⟩	—	—	311
Crucifix or cross	⟨332⟩	—	—	313
Organ	⟨336⟩	—	—	317
	⟨337⟩	—	—	318
Pulpit	⟨327⟩	—	—	306
Sacramental vessels	⟨328⟩	—	—	311
Vestments	⟨331⟩	—	—	312
Windows	⟨333⟩	—	—	313
Dedication of Ground	⟨320⟩	—	—	292
	⟨321⟩	—	—	295
Cemetery	⟨342⟩	—	—	328, 329
	⟨343⟩	—	—	328, 331
Deliverance	(1)	10, 139	159, 277	—
	(120)	126	139	—
	⟨245⟩	—	154	—
From fear	(29)	43, 113	192, 262	—
	⟨272⟩	—	—	152
From sin	(4)	14	163	—
	(18)	30	179	—
	(69)	91	240	—
See also Redemption				
Disabled	⟨361⟩	—	—	369
Blind	⟨360⟩	—	—	369
Deaf	⟨359⟩	—	—	369
See also Healing				
Disaster	(228)	—	150	—
See also Weather				
Discipleship	(38)	52	201	—
	(56)	75	224	—
	(57)	77	226	—
	(72)	95	244	—
	(80)	98	247	—
	(84)	100	249	—
	(85)	100	249	—
	(94)	111	260	—
	(97)	116	265	—
	⟨250⟩	—	—	35
See also Commitment; Likeness to Christ; Witness				
Divorce	(149)	130	143	367
Doctrine	(58)	78	227	—
	(76)	96	245	—
	(82)	99	248	—
	(83)	100	249	—
	(107)	124	137	219
Doubt				
See Faith, For those who have lost or doubt the faith				

	Prayer Number	Page Number		
		Pew Edition	Altar Book	Agenda
Dwelling				
Dedication of a	(141)	129	142	—
	(184)	267	101	—
	⟨344⟩	—	—	335, 336
	⟨345⟩	—	—	335, 336
	⟨346⟩	—	—	339
Of Christ in us	(67)	89	238	—
	(199)	278	112	51, 67
Earth, Fruits of				
See Agriculture; Harvest				
Education	⟨374⟩	—	—	373
Christian schools	(150)	131	144	—
Seminaries and Church colleges	(151)	131	144	—
	⟨301⟩	—	—	248
	⟨302⟩	—	—	252
See also Teachers				
Elderly				
See Aged				
Enemies	(98)	117	266	—
	(119)	126	139	—
	(198)	277	111	50, 67
See also Peace				
Engagement				
See Marriage, For those engaged to be married				
Erring, Return of the	(22)	34	183	—
	(116)	125	138	—
	(140)	129	142	370
	(197)	277	111	50, 67
	(239)	—	152	—
	⟨262⟩	—	—	119
See also Community in Christ, Reinstatement after excommunication; Faith				
Eternal Life				
See Life Everlasting				
Eucharist				
See Holy Communion				
Evangelism				
See Service; Witness				
Evangelism Workers	⟨315⟩	—	—	287
Evening	(33)	46	195	—
	(106)	124	137	—
	(174)	232	66	—
	(175)	233	67	—
	(181)	266	100	—
	(182)	267	101	—
	(184)	267	101	—
	(185)	267	101	—
	(186)	267	101	—
	(190)	275	109	—
Excommunication				
See Community in Christ, Excommunication from; Community in Christ, Reinstatement after excommunication; Erring, Return of the				
Faith	(3)	12, 109	161, 258	—
	(29)	43, 113	192, 262	—
	(57)	77	226	—
	(70)	92	241	—
	(77)	97	246	—

	Prayer Number	Page Number		
		Pew Edition	Altar Book	Agenda
	(114)	125	138	—
	(120)	126	139	—
	(176)	243, 262	77, 96	—
	(246)	—	154	—
	⟨282⟩	—	—	191
	⟨354⟩	—	—	367
For those who have lost or doubt the faith	(116)	125	138	—
See also Faithfulness; Fruits of Faith; Profession of Faith				
Faithful Departed, the	(89)	105	254	371
	(139)	129	142	—
	(157)	132	145	—
	⟨280⟩	—	—	180
	⟨342⟩	—	—	328, 329
For families of	(220)	—	148	371
See also Death; Hope, Christian; Life Everlasting				
Faithfulness	(17)	28	177	—
	(44)	61	210	—
	(57)	77	226	—
	(73)	95	244	—
	(79)	97	246	—
	(80)	98	247	—
	(93)	110, 115	259, 264	—
	(171)	207	382	112
	(173)	221, 242	55, 76	—
	⟨257⟩	—	—	82
	⟨279⟩	—	—	172
	⟨280⟩	—	—	180
	⟨288⟩	—	—	207
In marriage	⟨265⟩	—	—	123
	⟨269⟩	—	—	135
	⟨270⟩	—	—	135
Family				
See Home; Marriage; Parents; Society, Home and family				
Family, the Church as	(17)	28	177	—
	(31)	45	194	45, 48, 59
	(159)	132	145	369
	⟨267⟩	—	—	131
	⟨363⟩	—	—	370
See also Community in Christ				
Farming				
See Agriculture; Harvest; Weather				
Fear				
See Deliverance, From fear				
Fellowship				
See Community in Christ, Fellowship with				
Fire, Spiritual	⟨252⟩	—	—	73
Flood, the	⟨255⟩	—	—	82
Forgiveness	(20)	32	181	18
	(25)	38	187	—
	(28)	42	191	—
	(55)	74	223	—
	(59)	79	228	—
	(69)	91	240	—
	(162)	149	297	158
	(190)	275	109	—
	(202)	287	121	—
	(203)	308	383	137
	(238)	—	152	—

	Prayer Number	Page Number		
		Pew Edition	Altar Book	Agenda
	(243)	—	153	—
	⟨262⟩	—	—	119
	⟨277⟩	—	—	163
	⟨282⟩	—	—	191
Freedom	(7)	17	166	—
	⟨257⟩	—	—	82
Fruits of Faith	(30)	44	193	—
	(36)	50	199	—
	(37)	51	200	—
	(47)	65	214	—
	(58)	78	227	—
	(171)	207	382	112
	(246)	—	154	—
	⟨258⟩	—	—	83
	⟨291⟩	—	—	216, 227
	⟨315⟩	—	—	287
See also Fulfillment; Harvest, Spiritual				
Fulfillment	(238)	—	152	—
	⟨255⟩	—	—	82
	⟨261⟩	—	—	83
	⟨382⟩	—	—	374
Gifts of Grace *See* Spirit, Gifts of the				
Glory	(19)	31	180	—
Good News, Gospel	(75)	96	245	—
	(84)	100	249	—
	(102)	119, 130	143, 269	—
See also Scriptures; Word and Sacraments; Word of God				
Good Works	(15)	26	175	—
	(58)	78	227	—
	(65)	86	235	—
	(100)	117	267	—
Goodness of God	(24)	37, 122, 220	54, 186, 272	—
	(69)	91	240	—
	(175)	233	67	—
Gospel *See* Good News, Gospel; Scriptures; Word of God				
Government *See* Society, Government				
Grace	(4)	14	163	—
	(13)	23	172	—
	(16)	27	176	—
	(22)	34	183	—
	(31)	45	194	45, 48, 59
	(56)	75	224	—
	(62)	83	232	—
	(95)	112	261	—
	(112)	125	138	—
	(115)	125	138	—
	⟨275⟩	—	—	156
Growth in	(243)	—	153	—
See also Forgiveness; Mercy				
Ground Breaking *See* Dedication of Ground				
Growth of the Church	⟨298⟩	—	—	242
	⟨300⟩	—	—	245
See also Mission; Witness				

387

	Prayer Number	Page Number Pew Edition	Page Number Altar Book	Page Number Agenda
Guidance	(8)	18, 125, 232	66, 138, 167	342, 347, 375
	(10)	20	169	—
	(21)	33	182	—
	(46)	64	213	—
	(50)	68	217	—
	(53)	71	220	—
	(60)	80	229	—
	(121)	126	139	—
	(136)	128	141	—
	(189)	275	109	—
	(239)	—	152	—
	(244)	—	153	—
	⟨383⟩	—	—	374
	⟨384⟩	—	—	375
See also Faith; Obedience; Trust; Will of God				
Handicapped *See* Disabled				
Harvest	(103)	120	270	—
Spiritual	⟨289⟩	—	—	213
	⟨296⟩	—	—	236
	⟨297⟩	—	—	239
	⟨310⟩	—	—	274, 279, 364
See also Agriculture; Fruits of Faith; Thanksgiving				
Healing	(211)	—	147	367
	(214)	—	147	367
	(215)	—	147	367
	(216)	—	148	367
	(217)	—	148	368
	⟨271⟩	—	—	152
	⟨273⟩	—	—	156
	⟨339⟩	—	—	322
	⟨355⟩	—	—	367
During an epidemic	⟨357⟩	—	—	368
For successful surgery	(216)	—	148	367
For those near death	(219)	—	148	370
For those suffering from addiction	(125)	127	140	368
For those who minister to the sick	(216)	—	148	367
	⟨293⟩	—	—	217, 233
	⟨356⟩	—	—	368
Thanksgiving for health restored	(126)	127	140	369
	(212)	—	147	368
	(218)	—	148	368
Thanksgiving for successful surgery	(217)	—	148	368
See also Comfort and Rest; Disabled; Mental Illness				
Health	(15)	26	175	—
See also Healing				
Heaven *See* Comfort and Rest, For those in bereavement; Life Everlasting				
Heirs of Eternal Life	(11)	21	170	—
	(19)	31	180	—
	(63)	84	233	—
	(168)	175, 195	338, 370	—
	⟨311⟩	—	—	282
	⟨381⟩	—	—	374
Help *See* Comfort and Rest; Deliverance; Guidance				
Holy Baptism	(11)	21	170	—
	(169)	203	378	96, 107

	Prayer Number	Page Number		
		Pew Edition	Altar Book	Agenda
	(170)	203	378	96, 108
	(204)	312	—	—
	(248)	—	273	366
	(249)	—	273	366
	⟨256⟩	—	—	82
	⟨257⟩	—	—	82
	⟨325⟩	—	—	305
	⟨353⟩	—	—	366
Anniversary of	⟨352⟩	—	—	366

See also Faith; Guidance; Resurrection

Holy Communion	(30)	44	193	—
	(162)	149	297	158
	⟨328⟩	—	—	311
After Holy Communion	(133)	128	141	—
	(163)	153, 174, 194	302, 336, 369	70, 160
	(164)	154, 174, 194	302, 336, 369	70
	⟨276⟩	—	—	160
Before Holy Communion	(132)	128	141	—
	(134)	128	141	—
	(167)	171	333	—
For communicants	(206)	—	146	—

See also Worship

Holy Ministry	(109)	124	137	348
	(147)	130	143	—
Ordination to	⟨289⟩	—	—	213
Preparation for	⟨287⟩	—	—	203

See also Pastors; Word and Sacraments

Holy Spirit
See Spirit, Holy Spirit

Holy Trinity	(44)	61	210	—
Holy Week	(27)	41	190	—
	(28)	42	191	—
	(31)	45	194	45, 48, 59
	⟨250⟩	—	—	35

See also Passion of Christ

Home	(141)	129	142	—
	(184)	267	101	—

See also Community in Christ; Dwelling, Dedication of; Marriage; Society, Home and family

Homebound	⟨274⟩	—	—	156
	⟨275⟩	—	—	156
Hope, Christian	(5)	15	164	—
	(6)	16	165	—
	(10)	20	169	—
	(120)	126	139	—
	(165)	156	304	—

See also Faith; Life Everlasting; Resurrection

Hospitals

See Dedication of Buildings, Hospital; Healing

House of God
See Anniversary, Of a Congregation; Community in Christ; Dedication of Buildings, Church; Worship

Human Family
See Parents; Society, Home and family

Human Nature	(9)	19	168	—
	⟨254⟩	—	—	81

	Prayer Number	Page Number		
		Pew Edition	Altar Book	Agenda
Humiliation of Christ	(26)	39	188	—
	(92)	107	256	—
See also Holy Week; Passion of Christ				
Humility	(92)	107	256	—
See also Service; Witness				
Immortality				
See Hope, Christian; Life Everlasting				
Industry				
See Society, Industry				
Indwelling Christ	(67)	89	238	—
	(199)	278	112	51, 67
Inheritance				
See Heirs of Eternal Life				
Installation				
Of a missionary or chaplain	⟨292⟩	—	—	217, 233
	⟨293⟩	—	—	217, 233
	⟨294⟩	—	—	217, 234
	⟨295⟩	—	—	218, 234
	⟨296⟩	—	—	236
Of a pastor	⟨290⟩	—	—	215, 226
Of synodical or District officers	⟨350⟩	—	—	354
	⟨351⟩	—	—	360
See also Officers; Servants of the Congregation				
Intercession, General	(136)	128	141	—
	(160)	132	145	—
	(161)	144	282	—
	(168)	175, 195	338, 370	—
	⟨386⟩	—	—	375
Judgment, the	(6)	16	165	—
	(66)	87	236	—
	(68)	90	239	—
	(115)	125	138	—
Justification				
See Faith; Forgiveness; Redemption				
Labor				
See Society, Labor				
Last Things				
See Hope, Christian; Judgment, the				
Life Everlasting	(5)	15	164	—
	(8)	18, 125, 232	66, 138, 167	342, 347, 375
	(19)	31	180	—
	(34)	47, 49	196, 198	—
	(41)	55	204	—
	(68)	90	239	—
	(71)	94	243	—
	(89)	105	254	371
	(94)	111	260	—
	(97)	116	265	—
	(115)	125	138	—
	(120)	126	139	—
	(182)	267	101	—
	(188)	274	108	46
	⟨252⟩	—	—	73
	⟨279⟩	—	—	172
	⟨280⟩	—	—	180
	⟨284⟩	—	—	195
	⟨343⟩	—	—	328, 331
	⟨364⟩	—	—	370

See also Heirs of Eternal Life;
  Hope, Christian; Resurrection

		Page Number		
	Prayer Number	Pew Edition	Altar Book	Agenda
Light	(5)	15	164	—
	(83)	100	249	—
	(107)	124	137	219
	(140)	129	142	370
	(168)	175, 195	338, 370	—
	(179)	252	86	—
	(183)	267	101	—
	⟨252⟩	—	—	73
	⟨253⟩	—	—	74
	⟨288⟩	—	—	207
Likeness to Christ	(56)	75	224	—
	(113)	125	138	—
	(242)	—	153	—
See also Grace; Newness of Life in Christ				
Loneliness	(159)	132	145	369
	⟨363⟩	—	—	370
See also Aged; Comfort and Rest				
Lord's Supper				
See Holy Communion				
Love	(15)	26	175	—
	(47)	65	214	—
	(49)	67	216	—
	(58)	78	227	—
	(86)	101	250	—
	(100)	117	267	—
Marriage	⟨264⟩	—	—	122
	⟨265⟩	—	—	123
	⟨266⟩	—	—	125
	⟨267⟩	—	—	131
Anniversary of	(155)	131	144	366
	⟨268⟩	—	—	135
	⟨269⟩	—	—	135
	⟨270⟩	—	—	135
For those engaged to be married	(142)	129	142	—
	(207)	—	146	—
	(208)	—	146	—
See also Society, Home and family				
Martyrdom	(79)	97	246	—
Martyrs	(98)	117	266	—
	(99)	117	266	—
Means of Grace				
See Holy Baptism; Holy Communion; Word and Sacraments; Word of God				
Meetings				
Church Council	(8)	18, 125, 232	66, 138, 167	342, 347, 375
	⟨384⟩	—	—	375
Committees	⟨385⟩	—	—	375
Congregational	(43)	58, 59, 60	207, 208, 209	208, 347, 375
	⟨383⟩	—	—	374
Conventions	⟨382⟩	—	—	374
Men's Organizations				
See Servants of the Congregation, Men's organizations				
Mental Illness	⟨358⟩	—	—	368
Mercy	(4)	14	163	—
	(53)	71	220	—
	(54)	73	222	—
	(55)	74	223	—
	(61)	81	230	—

	Prayer Number	Page Number		
		Pew Edition	Altar Book	Agenda
	(63)	84	233	—
	(66)	87	236	—
	(89)	105	254	371
	(188)	274	108	46
	(202)	287	121	—

See also Forgiveness; Grace

Military
See Armed Forces

Ministry
See Holy Ministry

Mission	(102)	119, 130	143, 269	—
	⟨373⟩	—	—	373

See also Missionaries; Service; Witness

Missionaries	⟨292⟩	—	—	217, 233
	⟨296⟩	—	—	236
	⟨373⟩	—	—	373

See also Holy Ministry; Pastors

Morning	(105)	124	137	—
	(173)	221, 242	55, 76	—
	(187)	272	106	—

Mortgage Burning
See Retirement, Of a debt

Mourning
See Comfort and Rest, For those in bereavement

Music
See Church Musicians; Dedication of Furnishings, Organ

Musicians, Church
See Church Musicians

Nation
See Society, Nation

Natural Disaster
See Disaster

Nature
See Agriculture; Harvest

Neighbor	(100)	117	267	—
	(129)	127	140	—

Neighborhood
See Neighbor

New Year	(87)	102	251	—
Newness of Life in Christ	(9)	19	168	—
	(32)	46	195	87
	(34)	47, 49	196, 198	—
	(35)	47	196	—
	(68)	90	239	—
	(76)	96	245	—
	(104)	121, 286	120, 271	—
	(115)	125	138	—
	⟨254⟩	—	—	81
	⟨259⟩	—	—	83
	⟨282⟩	—	—	191

See also Grace; Likeness to Christ; Obedience; Renewal

Obedience	(39)	53	202	344
	(46)	64	213	—

	Prayer Number	Page Number		
		Pew Edition	Altar Book	Agenda
	(47)	65	214	—
	(62)	83	232	—
	(137)	129, 234, 260	68, 94, 142	—
	(172)	220	54	—
	(242)	—	153	—
	⟨274⟩	—	—	156

See also Guidance; Service; Will of God

Offering of Self
See Service; Witness

Officers	(154)	131	144	—
	⟨309⟩	—	—	274
	⟨311⟩	—	—	282
	⟨350⟩	—	—	354
Church school	⟨312⟩	—	—	285
Of congregational auxiliaries	⟨319⟩	—	—	291
Of the Synod or District	⟨350⟩	—	—	354
	⟨351⟩	—	—	360

Ordination
See Anniversary, Of an ordination; Holy Ministry, Ordination to; Pastors, At ordination

Palm Sunday	⟨250⟩	—	—	35

Parents	(128)	127	140	—
	(170)	203	378	96, 108
At the birth of a child	(127)	127	140	—
	⟨209⟩	—	146	—
Of a departed child	(213)	—	147	372
	⟨281⟩	—	—	180
	⟨286⟩	—	—	201
Of a stillborn child	(210)	—	147	372
	⟨285⟩	—	—	199
	⟨286⟩	—	—	201
Of an adopted child	(158)	132	145	—
Those who have departed	⟨368⟩	—	—	371

See also Society, Home and family

Passion of Christ	(25)	38	187	—
	(26)	39	188	—
	(91)	107	256	—
	(188)	274	108	46
	⟨251⟩	—	—	45

See also Holy Week; Humiliation Of Christ

Pastors	(78)	97, 104	246, 253	—
	(81)	98	247	—
	(109)	124	137	348
	(193)	276	110	49, 66
	⟨291⟩	—	—	216, 227
	⟨372⟩	—	—	373
Accepting a new call	⟨298⟩	—	—	242
At installation	⟨290⟩	—	—	215, 226
At ordination	⟨289⟩	—	—	213
	⟨370⟩	—	—	372
At retirement	⟨299⟩	—	—	243
At the death of	(222)	—	149	—
Candidates	⟨287⟩	—	—	203
On an anniversary of ordination	⟨297⟩	—	—	239
	⟨371⟩	—	—	372

See also Calling, Pastors; Chaplains, Holy Ministry; Missionaries

Patience	(26)	39	188	—
	(246)	—	154	—
	⟨276⟩	—	—	160

	Prayer Number	Page Number		
		Pew Edition	Altar Book	Agenda
Peace	(12)	22	171	—
	(50)	68	217	—
	(59)	79	228	—
	(93)	110, 115	259, 264	—
	(137)	129, 234, 260	68, 94, 142	—
	(175)	233	67	—
	(229)	—	150	—
Thanksgiving for restored	(231)	—	151	—
See also Society				
Penitence				
See Confession of Sins; Repentance				
Poor and Neglected	(92)	107	256	—
	(100)	117	267	—
See also Society				
Power				
See Strength				
Praise	(76)	96	245	—
	(110)	125	138	—
	(135)	128	141	—
	(179)	252	86	—
	(180)	255	89	—
	(245)	—	154	—
	(336)	—	—	317
See also Adoration; Thanksgiving; Worship				
Prayer	(12)	22	171	—
	(18)	30	179	—
	(40)	54	203	—
	(180)	255	89	—
	(193)	276	110	49, 66
	(201)	287	121	—
Answer to	(138)	129	142	—
Of the Church	(136)	128	141	—
	(160)	132	145	—
	(161)	144	282	—
	(168)	175, 195	338, 370	—
	(386)	—	—	375
Presence of God	(33)	46	195	—
	(101)	118	268	308, 324
	(141)	129	142	—
	(181)	266	100	—
	(184)	267	101	—
	(324)	—	—	305
	(338)	—	—	322
	(345)	—	—	335, 336
	(348)	—	—	344
	(349)	—	—	347
	(383)	—	—	374
Preservation	(17)	28	177	—
	(21)	33	182	—
	(105)	124	137	—
	(187)	272	106	—
Priesthood of Believers				
See Community in Christ; Service; Witness				
Prison				
See Chaplains, Prison				
Proclamation				
See Profession of Faith; Witness; Word of God				
Profession of Faith	(11)	21	170	—
	(74)	95	244	—

	Prayer Number	Page Number		
		Pew Edition	Altar Book	Agenda
	(79)	97	246	—
	(166)	156, 243, 262	77, 96, 305	349
	(171)	207	382	112
Promises				
Marriage	(207)	—	146	—
	⟨264⟩	—	—	122
	⟨269⟩	—	—	135
	⟨270⟩	—	—	135
Of God	(49)	67	216	—
	(70)	92	241	—
	⟨256⟩	—	—	82
	⟨277⟩	—	—	163
	⟨349⟩	—	—	347
Protection	(54)	73	222	—
	(96)	114	263	—
	(123)	126	139	—
	(142)	129	142	—
	(181)	266	100	—
	⟨386⟩	—	—	375
For children and young persons	(129)	127	140	—
For married couples	⟨267⟩	—	—	131
For the sick	(215)	—	147	367
	⟨272⟩	—	—	152
For travelers	(191)	275	109	349
From danger	(51)	69	218	—
	(141)	129	142	—
	(160)	132	145	—
	(228)	—	150	—
	(243)	—	153	—
From evil	(18)	30	179	—
	(23)	36	185	—
	(201)	287	121	—
	⟨345⟩	—	—	335,336
From sin	(1)	10, 139	159, 277	—
	(21)	33	182	—
	(61)	81	230	—
	(173)	221, 242	55, 76	—
	(187)	272	106	—
From temptation	(14)	25, 287	121, 174	—
	(93)	110, 115	259, 264	—
	(111)	125	138	—
Providence	(21)	33	182	—
	(45)	62	211	—
See also Thanksgiving				
Purity of Heart	(88)	103	252	—
	(90)	107	256	—
	(177)	243, 262	77, 96	—
Recovery from Sickness *See* Healing				
Redemption	(7)	17	166	—
	(25)	38	187	—
	(56)	75	224	—
	(77)	97	246	—
	(167)	171	333	—
Remission of Sins *See* Forgiveness				
Renewal	(178)	248	82	—
	⟨261⟩	—	—	83
	⟨353⟩	—	—	366

See also Community in Christ; Forgiveness; Healing; Newness of Life in Christ

	Prayer Number	Page Number		
		Pew Edition	Altar Book	Agenda
Repentance	(20)	32	181	18
	(22)	34	183	—
	(35)	47	196	—
	(104)	121, 286	120, 271	—
	(180)	255	89	—
	⟨262⟩	—	—	119
	⟨263⟩	—	—	119

See also Confession of Sins; Forgiveness; Grace; Mercy

Rest
See Comfort and Rest

Restoration
See Commitment; Community in Christ; Forgiveness; Healing; Renewal; Strength

	Prayer Number	Page Number		
Resurrection	(26)	39	188	—
	(34)	47, 49	196, 198	—
	(178)	248	82	—
	⟨253⟩	—	—	74
	⟨277⟩	—	—	163
	⟨279⟩	—	—	172
	⟨282⟩	—	—	191
	⟨283⟩	—	—	193
Retirement	⟨362⟩	—	—	369
Of a debt	⟨347⟩	—	—	341
Of a pastor	⟨299⟩	—	—	243
Of a teacher	⟨308⟩	—	—	269
Revelation	(83)	100	249	—
	(107)	124	137	219

Sacraments
See Holy Baptism; Holy Communion; Word and Sacraments

	Prayer Number	Page Number		
Salvation	(3)	12, 109	161, 258	—
	(95)	112	261	—

Sanctification
See Commitment; Guidance; Likeness to Christ; Newness of Life in Christ; Spirit; Trust

Schools
See Education

	Prayer Number	Page Number		
Scriptures	(165)	156	304	—
Second Coming of Christ	(2)	11	160	—

Seminaries
See Education; Teachers

	Prayer Number	Page Number		
Servants of the Congregation	(153)	131	144	374
	⟨303⟩	—	—	252
	⟨309⟩	—	—	274
	⟨351⟩	—	—	360
Acolytes	⟨316⟩	—	—	288
Altar assistants	⟨316⟩	—	—	288
Altar guild	⟨318⟩	—	—	288
Church council	⟨311⟩	—	—	282
Communion assistants	⟨316⟩	—	—	288
Evangelism workers	⟨315⟩	—	—	287
Men's organizations	⟨379⟩	—	—	374
Musicians	⟨317⟩	—	—	288
Readers	⟨316⟩	—	—	288
Teacher-interns	⟨314⟩	—	—	287
Vicars	⟨313⟩	—	—	287
Women's organizations	⟨380⟩	—	—	374

	Prayer Number	Page Number		
		Pew Edition	Altar Book	Agenda
Youth organizations	⟨381⟩	—	—	374
See also Officers; Service				
Service	(3)	12, 109	161, 258	—
	(24)	37, 122, 220	54, 186, 272	—
	(32)	46	195	87
	(50)	68	217	—
	(59)	79	228	—
	(86)	101	250	—
	(104)	121, 286	120, 271	—
	(166)	156, 243, 262	77, 96, 305	349
	(192)	276	110	49, 65
	(200)	286	120	—
	⟨310⟩	—	—	274, 279, 364
	⟨379⟩	—	—	374
Shepherd	(38)	52	201	—
	(117)	126	139	—

Shut-in
See Homebound

Sickness
See Comfort and Rest, For those in affliction or distress; Healing; Mental Illness

Society

	Prayer Number	Pew Edition	Altar Book	Agenda
Citizenship	(122)	126	139	—
Government	(121)	126	139	—
	(122)	126	139	—
	(195)	277	111	50, 66
Home and family	(141)	129	142	—
	(208)	—	146	—
	⟨266⟩	—	—	125
	⟨270⟩	—	—	135
Industry	(144)	130	143	—
Labor	(185)	267	101	—
Nation	(123)	126	139	—
	(244)	—	153	—
Unemployed	(124)	127	140	370
	(232)	—	151	—

Sorrow
See Comfort and Rest, For those in bereavement

Spirit

	Prayer Number	Pew Edition	Altar Book	Agenda
Gifts of the	(13)	23	172	—
	(112)	125	138	—
	⟨311⟩	—	—	282
	⟨312⟩	—	—	285
Holy Spirit	(24)	37, 122, 220	54, 186, 272	—
	(38)	52	201	—
	(42)	57	206	—
	(43)	58, 59, 60	207, 208, 209	208, 347, 375
	(52)	70	219	—
	(60)	80	229	—
	(93)	110, 115	259, 264	—
	(108)	124	137	—
	(114)	125	138	—
	(167)	171	333	—
	(172)	220	54	—
	⟨282⟩	—	—	192
	⟨288⟩	—	—	207
Power of the	(203)	308	383	137

Spread of the Gospel
See Mission; Witness

	Prayer Number	Page Number		
		Pew Edition	Altar Book	Agenda
Strength	(14)	25, 287	121, 174	—
	(16)	27	176	—
Suicide, Burial of	(224)	—	149	372
See also Death				
Teachers	(81)	98	247	—
	(150)	131	144	—
	(303)	—	—	252
	(304)	—	—	257
	(305)	—	—	257, 263
	(306)	—	—	266
	(309)	—	—	274
	(372)	—	—	373
Accepting a new call	(307)	—	—	269
At commissioning	(304)	—	—	257
	(305)	—	—	257, 263
	(375)	—	—	373
At installation	(305)	—	—	257, 263
At retirement	(308)	—	—	269
At seminaries and Church colleges	(301)	—	—	248
	(302)	—	—	252
At the death of	(223)	—	149	—
Candidates	(300)	—	—	245
See also Calling, Teachers; Education				
Thanksgiving	(24)	37, 122, 220	54, 186, 272	—
	(108)	124	137	—
	(110)	125	138	—
	(135)	128	141	—
	(162)	149	297	158
	(244)	—	153	—
	(246)	—	154	—
	(282)	—	—	191
	(284)	—	—	195
	(342)	—	—	328, 329
	(348)	—	—	344
At the retirement of a debt	(347)	—	—	341
For a life that has ended	(220)	—	148	371
	(278)	—	—	168
	(280)	—	—	180
	(283)	—	—	193
	(367)	—	—	371
For health restored	(126)	127	140	369
	(212)	—	147	368
	(218)	—	148	368
For peace	(231)	—	151	—
For rain	(227)	—	150	—
Travelers	(176)	243, 262	77, 96	—
	(191)	275	109	349
Trial	(98)	117	266	—
	(123)	126	139	—
	(201)	287	121	—
	(276)	—	—	160
	(354)	—	—	367
See also Comfort and Rest				
Trust	(87)	102	251	—
	(174)	232	66	—
	(186)	267	101	—
	(250)	—	—	35
	(256)	—	—	82
	(263)	—	—	119
	(276)	—	—	160
	(285)	—	—	199
	(357)	—	—	368

	Prayer Number	Page Number Pew Edition	Page Number Altar Book	Agenda
Unity	(82)	99	248	—
	(117)	126	139	—
	(243)	—	153	—
Unemployed				
See Society, Unemployed				
Vicars				
See Servants of the Congregation, Vicars				
Virgin Mary	(92)	107	256	—
	(95)	112	261	—
War				
After war	(231)	—	151	—
In times of	(229)	—	150	—
	(230)	—	151	—
Water of Life	⟨258⟩	—	—	83
Weather				
In time of scarce rainfall	(225)	—	150	—
Thanksgiving for rain	(227)	—	150	—
Unseasonable	(226)	—	150	—
See also Agriculture; Disaster				
Will of God	(242)	—	153	—
	⟨279⟩	—	—	172
Wisdom	(16)	27	176	—
	(27)	41	190	—
	(43)	58, 59, 60	207, 208, 209	208, 347, 375
	(64)	85	234	—
	(78)	97, 104	246, 253	—
	(166)	156, 243, 262	77, 96, 305	349
Witness	(37)	51	200	—
	(75)	96	245	—
	(99)	117	266	—
	(102)	119, 130	143, 269	—
	(166)	156, 243, 262	77, 96, 305	349
	⟨255⟩	—	—	82
	⟨257⟩	—	—	82
	⟨259⟩	—	—	83
	⟨260⟩	—	—	83
Women's Organizations				
See Servants of the Congregation, Women's organizations				
Word and Sacraments	(33)	46	195	—
	(78)	97, 104	246, 253	—
	(86)	101	250	—
	(101)	118	268	308, 324
	(241)	—	153	—
	(243)	—	153	—
	⟨289⟩	—	—	213
	⟨291⟩	—	—	216, 227
	⟨324⟩	—	—	305
	⟨347⟩	—	—	341
See also Holy Baptism; Holy Communion; Word of God				
Word of God	(73)	95	244	—
	(92)	107	256	—
	(165)	156	304	—
	(166)	156, 243, 262	77, 96, 305	349
	(177)	243, 262	77, 96	—
	(179)	252	86	—
	⟨260⟩	—	—	83
	⟨327⟩	—	—	306
For blessing on	(238)	—	152	—

	Prayer Number	Page Number		
		Pew Edition	Altar Book	Agenda
For profitable use of	(239)	—	152	—
For success of	(240)	—	153	—
See also Word and Sacraments				
Work in God's Kingdom				
See Mission; Service; Witness				
Worship	(2)	11	160	—
	(40)	54	203	—
	(172)	220	54	—
After worship	(131)	128	141	—
	(168)	175, 195	338, 370	—
	(241)	—	153	—
Before worship	(130)	127	140	—
Young Persons	(129)	127	140	—
	⟨381⟩	—	—	374
Youth Organizations				
See Servants of the Congregation, Youth organizations				

INDEX TO PSALMS AND READINGS

Gen. 2:18. 129
Gen. 2:18-24 121
Ex. 33:14. 343
Ex. 33:15, 14 343
Job 19:21-27 181
Job 19:25-26 193
Job 36:15 146
* Ps. 1. 324
Ps. 1:1-3 . . . . 203, 242
Ps. 16. 163–64
Ps. 16:11 149
* Ps. 22. 39–41
Ps. 23. . . . . 149, 164, 169–70, 197–98
Ps. 27:1 149
* Ps. 27:1, 3, 5, 13-14 235
Ps. 30:4-5, 12b 143
Ps. 30:12b 143
Ps. 32:1-5 147
Ps. 34:3; 100:3-5; 84:1b, 4a, 12;
       1:1-3. . . . . 202–3, 242
Ps. 36:7-9 149
Ps. 37:4 . . . . 245, 269
Ps. 38:9, 21-22 146
* Ps. 39. 174–75
* Ps. 40:1, 3-4, 16. 219
Ps. 40:1-3 147
* Ps. 40:9a, 10b, 10c, 1, 3-4, 16 219
* Ps. 46. . . . . 175–76, 294–95
Ps. 46:1, 11 . . . . 245, 269
* Ps. 46:1-3, 7 307
* Ps. 48:1-2 301
Ps. 50:15 147
* Ps. 51. 42–43
Ps. 51:1-4a. 141
Ps. 51:10-12 142
Ps. 78:2-7 . . . . 245, 269
* Ps. 84. 300
* Ps. 84:1; 46. 294–95
* Ps. 84:1-2a. 309, 325–26
Ps. 84:1b, 4a, 12. . . . . 203, 242
* Ps. 87:2; 84 300
Ps. 90. 165, 170–71
* Ps. 90. . . . . 176–77, 330–31
* Ps. 91:1-2 332
* Ps. 91:10; 90 330–31
Ps. 95:1 . . . . 244, 268
* Ps. 96:1 319
Ps. 96:1; 95:1; 78:2-7; 103:1-2;
       46:1, 11; 37:4 . . . . 244–45, 268–69
* Ps. 97:1 236
* Ps. 98:1a, 4. 319
* Ps. 98:5; 150 318
* Ps. 100. . . . . 124, 130
Ps. 100:3-5 . . . . 202, 242
* Ps. 100:4; 1 324
* Ps. 100:5 325
* Ps. 100:5; 100 . . . . 124, 130
Ps. 102:1-2 . . . . 141, 146
Ps. 103:1-2 . . . . 245, 269
Ps. 103:8-12 148
Ps. 118:5, 8-9, 13, 15-17, 19-20. 193

* Ps. 119:46; 46:1-3, 7 307
* Ps. 121. 177–78
* Ps. 121:1-2 295
* Ps. 121:1-3 183
* Ps. 121:5 126
Ps. 121:7-8 . . . . 243, 270
* Ps. 122:1, 4. 308
* Ps. 127:1 296
* Ps. 128:1-2 125
Ps. 130. 171
Ps. 130:1-5 146
* Ps. 135:1b; 97:1 236
* Ps. 135:1b-2 220
* Ps. 139. 178–79
Ps. 139:1-12, 23-24 146
* Ps. 142:7a 332
* Ps. 150. 318
Prov. 3:5-8. 149
Is. 25:6-9 181
Is. 43:1-3a. 156
Is. 61:1-3 181
Lam. 3:22-26. 146
Lam. 3:22-33. 182
Hos. 6:1. 147
Matt. 5:13-16. . . . . 210–11, 231
Matt. 7:24-29. 338
Matt. 9:2-8. 157
Matt. 9:12-13. 148
Matt. 11:28-30. 148
Matt. 19:4-6. . . . . 121, 129
Matt. 20:25-28. . . . . 255, 261, 272, 277
Matt. 28:18-20. . . . . 208–9, 223, 229, 249
Mark 2:1-12. 147–48
Mark 10:13-15. 198
Mark 10:13-16. 189
Mark 16:1-8. . . . . 86–87, 165–66
* Luke 4:18-19; Ps. 27:1, 3, 5, 13-14 235
Luke 10:38-42. 339
Luke 17:10. 224
Luke 19:1-10. 339
John 3:16-21. 166
John 3:17. 147
John 5:24. 172
John 5:24-27. 188
John 6:37-40. 188
John 6:37b. 147
John 10:11-16. 188–89
* John 10:14, 16b. 220
John 10:27-29. . . . . 172, 198
John 11:21-27. 189
John 11:25-26a. 193
John 12:12-19. 35–36
John 12:23-26. 194
John 14:1-6. . . . . 172, 189
John 14:23. 157
John 15:4-5. . . . . 210, 231
John 15:16. 209, 229
John 20:1-18. 166–67
John 20:21-23. . . . . 209, 223, 229, 249
John 21:15-17. . . . . 209, 223, 229, 249
Acts 2:38-39a. 198
* Acts 2:47. 237
Acts 6:2-4. 281

---

* *Set to chant*

Acts 18:7-11 336
Acts 20:28 . . . . 210, 230–31
Rom. 5:8-9 147
Rom. 6:3-5 174
Rom. 6:3-11 84
Rom. 8:15-17 149
Rom. 8:31-39 183
Rom. 12:4-8 . . . . 255, 261, 272, 277, 363
Rom. 14:7-8 193
1 Cor. 1:3-5 174
* 1 Cor. 3:11 302
1 Cor. 4:1-2 . . . . 209, 224, 230
1 Cor. 9:26-27 224
1 Cor. 12:4-7 290
1 Cor. 12:4-9a, 11 359
1 Cor. 15:1-26 183–84
1 Cor. 15:20, 42b-43 . . . . 327, 329
1 Cor. 15:35-57 184–85
1 Cor. 15:42-44, 54-57 200
1 Cor. 15:51-57 . . . . 185, 194
1 Cor. 15:54-57 200
1 Cor. 15:58 224
2 Cor. 1:3-5 157
2 Cor. 3:4-5 . . . . 209, 230
2 Cor. 3:7-8 . . . . 223, 250
2 Cor. 4:5-6 . . . . 223, 250
2 Cor. 5:17-19 148
2 Cor. 5:17-21 . . . . 209, 230
2 Cor. 10:17-18 . . . . 211, 231
Gal. 6:4-5, 9-10 286
Eph. 1:3-7 148
Eph. 4:11-12 . . . . 210, 224, 230
Eph. 5:21-33 121

* Col. 1:18, adapt. 187
Col. 3:12-17 129–30
Col. 3:16-17 . . . . 255, 261, 272–73, 277
1 Thess. 4:13-18 172
1 Tim. 3:1-7 . . . . 210, 230
1 Tim. 4:12b 352, 358
1 Tim. 4:14-16 . . . . 209, 229, 250
1 Tim. 4:16 224
2 Tim. 1:13-14 . . . . 352, 357
2 Tim. 2:1 . . . . 352, 357
* 2 Tim. 2:11b-12a, adapt. 187–88
2 Tim. 2:15 . . . . 352, 357
2 Tim. 2:24-25 223
2 Tim. 3:14 . . . . 352, 357
2 Tim. 3:14-17 . . . . 211, 231
2 Tim. 4:1-5 . . . . 210, 230
2 Tim. 4:2 . . . . 224, 352, 357
Titus 2:11-14 . . . . 352, 357
Heb. 10:35-36 224
Heb. 10:35-38a 150
Heb. 12:1-4 147
Heb. 13:20-21 . . . . 215, 217, 226, 233
James 5:14-16 146
1 Peter 1:3-9 . . . . 150, 185
1 Peter 4:8-11 . . . . 255, 261, 272, 277, 363
1 Peter 5:2-4 . . . . 210, 224, 231
1 Peter 5:6-11 150
1 John 3:1-2 . . . . 150, 185
1 John 4:9-10 148–49
Rev. 7:9-12 167
Rev. 7:9-17 185–86
Rev. 21:2-7 186